THE DRUG
LEGALIZATION
DEBATE

STUDIES IN CRIME, LAW AND JUSTICE

Series Editor: James A. Inciardi,
Division of Criminal Justice, University of Delaware

Studies in Crime, Law and Justice contains original research formulations and new analytic perspectives on continuing important issues of crime and the criminal justice and legal systems. Volumes are research based but are written in nontechnical language to allow for use in courses in criminal justice, criminology, law, social problems, and related subjects.

Studies are both contributions to the research literature and ideal text supplements, and are of interest to academics, professionals, and students.

THE DRUG LEGALIZATION DEBATE

EDITED BY

James A. Inciardi

STUDIES IN CRIME, LAW AND JUSTICE ■ Volume 7

SAGE PUBLICATIONS
The International Professional Publishers
Newbury Park London New Delhi

For information address:

SAGE Publications, Inc.
2455 Teller Road
Newbury Park, California 91320

SAGE Publications Ltd.
6 Bonhill Street
London EC2A 4PU
United Kingdom

SAGE Publications India Pvt. Ltd.
M-32 Market
Greater Kailash I
New Delhi 110 048 India

Printed in the United States of America

Library of Congress Cataloging-in-Publication Data

Main entry under title:

The drug legalization debate / James A. Inciardi, editor
        p.   cm. — (Studies in crime, law, and justice ; v. 7)
    Includes bibliographical references and index.
    ISBN 0-8039-3677-X — ISBN 0-8039-3678-8 (pbk.)
    1. Narcotics, Control of—United States.   2. Narcotic laws—United
States. 3. Decriminalization—United States. I. Inciardi, James
A. II. Series.
HV5825.D7767 1990
363.4'5'0973—dc20   90-41441
                                                                            CIP

FIRST PRINTING, 1991

Sage Production Editor: Astrid Virding

Contents

American Drug Policy and the Legalization Debate

JAMES A. INCIARDI

Public concern over the use and abuse of illegal drugs has been critical throughout the 1980s. Regardless of political affiliation and ideology, socioeconomic status and ethnicity, or geographical and occupational location, most Americans continually rank "drugs" among the major problems facing the nation. During the closing years of the 1980s, furthermore, both politicians and the public at large have been examining American drug policy, pondering its problematic effectiveness, and considering alternatives. New "solutions" have been advocated, ranging from a mandatory death penalty for anyone convicted of selling or trafficking in drugs, to broad legalization of all drugs of abuse.

Within the context of these concerns, assessments, and proposals, it is the intention of this opening commentary to review briefly American drug policy, consider the evidence of its impact and effectiveness, and to present the backdrop for the legalization of drugs debate.

THE AMERICAN DRUG SCENE

The American drug scene evolved within the broader context of the historical relationship between people and the psychoactive organic compounds in their immediate environments. Historians and archaeologists have noted that the use of alcohol is for the most part a human cultural universal. The chewing of coca and other psychoactive plants has existed in many societies for millennia. Marijuana and the opium poppy are indigenous to several regions of the world and have been used as intoxicants and in rituals likely since prehistoric times. The explosion of world trade following the European discovery of America brought local psychoactive plants—from tobacco and marijuana, coca and the opium poppy, and related techniques of distillation, refining, and crossbreeding—to the attention of world consumers. The American drug experience emerged, evolved, and endured within the framework of this worldwide trafficking of what were originally local psychophar-macological agents.[1]

It began with the widespread use of opium in home remedies and over-the-counter patent medicines during the latter part of the eighteenth century, followed by the discovery of morphine, cocaine, heroin, and the hypodermic needle during the ensuing 100-year period. By 1905 there were more than 28,000 pharmaceuticals containing psychoactive drugs readily available throughout the nation, sold in an unrestricted manner by physicians, over-the-counter from apothecaries, grocers, postmasters, and printers, from the tailgates of medicine show wagons as they traveled throughout rural and urban America, and through the mails from newspaper advertisements and catalog sales (Young, 1961: 19-23). Although little data are available as to the number of people dependent on opiates and cocaine during these years, estimates of the addict population at the close of the nineteenth century ranged as high as 3 million (Terry and Pellens, 1928: 1-20; Morgan, 1974). Regardless of the accuracy of the estimates, addiction had become so visible and widespread that the medical community, the media, and the public at large called for government restrictions on the availability of drugs.

With the passage of the Pure Food and Drug Act in 1906, the Harrison Narcotics Act in 1914, and subsequent federal and state legislation, combined with the social and economic upheavals of the Great Depression and World War II, as the United States approached midcentury, drug abuse had significantly receded. During the postwar era of ex-panded world trade, economic growth, and increased urbanization, however, the drug problem grew apace. In the 1950s heroin addiction emerged in the inner cities at epidemic levels, particularly among youth. In the 1960s drug abuse expanded from the cities to suburbia. As part of the social revolution of the decade, adolescents and young adults began to *tune in, turn on,* and *drop out* through a whole new catalog of drugs—marijuana, hashish, and LSD, plus newly synthesized prescription analgesics, stimulants, and sedatives. By the 1970s the psychedelic revolution of the previous decade had run its course, but the heroin epidemic had endured, marijuana consumption continued to increase, cocaine reentered the drug scene after its half-century sojourn in the netherworlds of vice and the *avant garde,* and Quaaludes and PCP became prominent as the new drugs of the moment. And here in the 1980s most of the old drugs have remained prominent, while new entries—designer drugs, ecstasy, and crack—have staked out positions.

FIGHTING THE "WAR ON DRUGS"

Since the passage of the Harrison Act in 1914, the federal approach to drug abuse control has included a variety of avenues for reducing both the supply of, and the demand for, illicit drugs. At first, the supply-and-demand reduction strategies were grounded in the classic deterrence model: Through legislation and criminal penalties, individuals would be discouraged from using drugs; by setting an example of traffickers, the government could force potential dealers to seek out other economic pursuits. In time, other components were added: treatment for the user, education and prevention for the would-be user, and research to determine how best to develop and implement plans for enforcement, treatment, education, and prevention.

By the early 1970s, when it appeared that the war on drugs was winning few, if any, battles, new avenues for supply and demand reduction were added. There were the federal interdiction initiatives: Coast Guard, Customs, and Drug Enforcement Administration operatives were charged with intercepting drug shipments coming to the United States from foreign ports; in the international sector there were attempts to eradicate drug-yielding crops at their source. On the surface, none of these strategies seemed to have much effect, and illicit drug use continued to spread.

The problems were many. Legislation and enforcement alone were not enough, and early education programs of the "scare" variety quickly lost their credibility. For social scientists, clinicians, and others who were watching the drug scene closely, treating drug abuse as a medical problem seemed to be the logical answer. The difficulty there, however, was that, for the most part, a medical model of treatment had been structured around a belief in some curious yet poorly defined "addiction-prone personality"—a deep-rooted personality disorder characteristic of everyone suffering from addiction. However, all drug abusers are *not* the same. The result was high program failure rates, regardless of the method of treatment (Glasscote et al., 1972; Burt et al., 1979; Brown, 1979).

Given the perceived inadequacy of the traditional approaches to drug-abuse control, during the late 1970s federal authorities began drawing plans for a more concerted assault on drugs, both legislative and technological. It began with the RICO (Racketeer-Influenced and Corrupt Organizations) and CCE (Continuing Criminal Enterprise) statutes. What RICO and CCE accomplish is the forfeiture of the fruits of criminal activities (Dombrink and Meeker, 1986). Their intent is to eliminate the rights of traffickers to their personal assets, whether these be cash, bank accounts, real estate, automobiles, jewelry and art, equity in businesses, directorships in companies, or any kind of goods or entitlements that are obtained in or used for a criminal enterprise.

Added to the perceived strength offered by RICO and CCE was a new extradition treaty between the United States and the Republic of Colombia, signed on September 14, 1979, and entered into force on March 4, 1982 (Committee on Foreign Relations, 1981). The treaty was notable in that it added to the list of extraditable crimes a whole variety of offenses related to drug trafficking, aircraft hijacking, obstruction of justice, and bribery. In addition, Article 8 of the treaty was a considerable innovation in international affairs in that it imposed an obligation on the government of Colombia to extradite all persons, including its nationals, when the offense was a punishable act in both countries and was intended to be consummated in the United States (e.g., the export of cocaine and/or marijuana into the United States from Colombia by Colombian citizens).

The new, evolving federal drug strategy considered it crucial to include the U.S. military in its war on drugs, but to do so, something then had to be done about the Posse Comitatus Act, originally passed by the Forty-fifth Congress on June 18, 1878. The act had been a response to post-Civil War reconstruction policies that permitted U.S. marshals in occupied southern states to call upon federal troops to enforce local laws. It had been the goal of southern congressmen to prevent such a practice, and the Posse Comitatus Act accomplished exactly that. It prohibited the army (and eventually other branches of the military) from enforcing federal, state, and local civilian law, and from supplementing the efforts of civilian law-enforcement agencies (U.S. Statutes at Large, 1877-1879). But the Posse Comitatus Act was never a constitutionally mandated statute. In fact, its very wording permitted the assistance of the military if specifically authorized by an act of Congress.[2] As a result, when President Reagan signed the Department of Defense Authorization Act of 1982 into law, it included several amendments to the century-old Posse Comitatus Act. Although military personnel were still prohibited from physically intercepting suspected drug vessels and aircraft, conducting searches and seizures, and making arrests, the entire war chest of U.S. military power did become available to law enforcement—for training, intelligence gathering, and detection. Moreover, members of the U.S. Army, Navy, Air Force, and Marine Corps could operate military equipment for civilian agencies charged with the enforcement of the drug laws (U.S. General Accounting Office, 1987a; Morrison, 1986; Zimmerman, 1982).

Beginning in 1982, the war on drugs had a new look. Put into force was the Bell 209 assault helicopter, more popularly known as the "Cobra." There was none in the military arsenal that was faster, and in its gunship mode it could destroy a tank. There was the Navy's EC-2 and the Air Force's AWACS—"eye-in-the-sky" aircraft equipped with radar disks capable of detecting other aircraft from hundreds of miles away. There were "Fat Albert" and his pals—surveillance balloons 175 feet in length equipped with sophisticated radar and listening devices. Fat Albert not only could pick up communications from Cuba and Soviet satellites, but also could detect traffic in Smugglers' Alley, a wide band of Caribbean sky that is virtually invisible to land-based radar systems. There were NASA satellites to spy on drug operations as far apart as California and Colombia, airborne infrared sensing and imaging equipment that could detect human body heat in the thickest underbrush of Florida's Everglades, plus a host of other high-technology devices. The U.S. Coast Guard also strengthened its equipment and U.S. Customs put Blue Thunder into service, a vessel specifically designed to outrun the high-performance speedboats that drug traffickers use in Florida waters. A 39-foot catamaran with 900 horsepower, Blue Thunder would cut through six-foot seas at speeds better than 60 mph. In all, drug enforcement appeared well-equipped for battle.[3]

The final component added to the drug war armamentarium was "zero-tolerance," a 1988 White House antidrug policy that was never clearly articulated in the national media. It would appear that zero-tolerance is based on a number of premises: (1) that if there were no drug abusers there would be no drug problem, (2) that the market for drugs is created not only by availability, but also by demand, (3) that drug abuse starts with a willful act, (4) that the perception that drug users are powerless to act against the influences of drug availability and peer pressure is an erroneous one, (5) that most illegal drug users can choose to stop their drug-taking behaviors and must be held accountable if they do not, (6) that individual freedom does not include the right to self and societal destruction, and (7) that public tolerance for drug abuse must be reduced to *zero* (*Drug Abuse Report*, April 19, 1988: 6; *Drug Abuse Report*, May 3, 1988: 1-3; U.S. Department of Transportation, 1988).

ASSESSING THE IMPACT OF
AMERICAN DRUG POLICY

By 1988 it had long since been decided by numerous observers that the 74 years of federal prohibition since the passage of the Harrison Act of 1914 were not only a costly and abject failure, but a totally doomed effort as well. It was argued that drug laws and drug enforcement had served mainly to create enormous profits for drug dealers and traffickers, overcrowded jails, police and other government corruption, a distorted foreign policy, predatory street crime carried on by users in search of the funds necessary to purchase black market drugs, and urban areas harassed by street-level drug dealers and terrorized by violent drug gangs (Wisotsky, 1986; Trebach, 1987; Kraar, 1988; McBride et al., 1986; Rosenbaum, 1987; *Newsweek,* March 28, 1988: 20-29; *Miami Herald* "Neighbors," April 24, 1988: 21-25; *New York Times,* March 20, 1988: E9; *Time,* March 7, 1988: 24).

Much of what these observers were remarking about indeed has been the case. To begin with, expenditures for the war on drugs have been considerable. For example, federal disbursements for supply and demand reduction from 1981 through 1988 totaled some $16.5 billion.[4] These figures, furthermore, do not include the many more billions spent by state and local governments on law enforcement and other criminal justice system costs, and on prevention, education, treatment, and research.

On the positive side of the equation, interdiction initiatives resulted in a somewhat impressive set of figures. For example, from 1981 through 1987 some 5.3 million kilograms of marijuana have been seized. And even more importantly, cocaine seizures have increased dramatically, from 2,000 kilograms in 1981 to 36,000 in 1987 (*New York Times,* April 11, 1988: A12).

Yet there is a negative side to the equation as well. Customs, Coast Guard, and Drug Enforcement Administration (DEA) officials have readily admitted that these seizures likely reflect only 10% of the marijuana and cocaine entering the country (U.S. General Accounting Office, 1987b). Furthermore, DEA figures indicate that, despite the seizures and increased expenditures on interdiction, the growing supply of cocaine in the United States has resulted in increased availability and a dramatic decline in price. In 1982 the national wholesale price of a kilogram of cocaine hydrochloride ranged from $47,000 to $70,000. By mid-1988 the national price ranged from $10,000 to $38,000 per kilogram (Renfret, 1988). To further complicate the picture, the purity of cocaine has increased dramatically over this period.

Intimidating as well for the war on drugs has been the fact that in recent years worldwide production of both marijuana and opium has increased (U.S. Department of State, 1988). To this can be added the problem that many countries seem to be unable, or unwilling, to take a stand against major drug traffickers. The extradition of Colombian trafficker Carlos Lehder Rivas to stand trial in the United States was hailed as a courageous act when it occurred in 1987, but the subsequent intimidation of the Colombian justice system by traffickers and the de facto nullification of the extradition treaty between the United States and the Republic of Colombia set back international efforts to curtail drug distribution significantly.[5] And there have been other problems: the continued use of illegal drugs, with many cities seemingly overwhelmed with crack-cocaine; violence in the inner cities and elsewhere, as drug trafficking gangs compete for distribution territories; street crime, committed by users for the sake of supporting their drug habits; and corruption in law enforcement and other branches of government, brought on by the considerable economic opportunities for those involved in drug distribution.

It is within the context of these problems and concerns that the debate over the legalization of drugs emerged in 1988. The articles in this volume address the many sides to the issue as well as comment on a variety of policy alternatives. The papers by Drs. Jonas, Besteman, and Inciardi and McBride are revisions of works that originally appeared in the January 1989 issue of the *American Behavioral Scientist*. Ethan A. Nadelmann's "The Case for Legalization" originally appeared in the Summer 1988 issue of *The Public Interest*. The remainder of the articles were written especially for this book.

NOTES

1. For a history of the drug problem in the United States, see Inciardi (1986: 1-47) and Courtwright (1982). For a review of the archaeological evidence of drug use in antiquity, see Terry and Pellens (1928: 53-60).

2. The Posse Comitatus Act did not, however, prevent the U.S. Coast Guard from intercepting and seizing vessels at sea that were transporting contraband to American ports.

3. For descriptions of the military involvement and the high-technology approaches to drug enforcement, see the *Wall Street Journal*, August 5, 1982: 1, 8; *Newsweek,* August 9, 1982: 14-15; *Motor Boating & Sailing,* September 1982: 46-49, 107-109; *Miami Herald,* January 23, 1983: 11A; *National Law Journal,* February 13, 1984: 1, 27-28; *Time,* May 13, 1985: 27; *New York Times,* June 30, 1985: E4; *Time,* May 30, 1988: 19.

4. Data supplied by the Office of Management and Budget; 1988 costs are estimated.

5. For the most complete account of trafficker intimidation in Colombia, see Castillo (1987). Also, see Eddy et al. (1988).

REFERENCES

Brown, B. S. (Ed.). (1979). *Addicts and aftercare: Community integration of the former drug user.* Beverly Hills, CA: Sage.

Burt, M. R., Pines, S., & Glynn, T. J. (1979). *Drug abuse: Its natural history and the effectiveness of current treatments.* Cambridge: Schenkman.

Castillo, F. (1987). *Los jinetes de la cocaine.* Bogota, Colombia: Editorial Documentos Periodisticos.

Committee on Foreign Relations. (1981, November 20). *Extradition treaty with the Republic of Colombia, Senate report to accompany Treaty Doc. NO. 97-8.*

Courtwright, D. T. (1982). *Dark paradise: Opiate addiction in America before 1940.* Cambridge, MA: Harvard University Press.

Dombrink, J., & Meeker, J. W. (1986, Winter). Beyond "buy and bust"; Nontraditional sanction in federal drug law enforcement. *Contemporary Drug Problems,* pp. 711-740.

Eddy, P., Sabogal, H., & Walden, S. (1988). *The cocaine wars.* New York: W. W. Norton.

Glasscote, R., Sussex, J. N., Jaffe, J. H., Ball, J., & Brill, L. (1972). *The treatment of drug abuse: Programs, problems, prospectus.* Washington, DC: American Psychiatric Association.

Inciardi, J. A. (1986). *The war on drugs: Heroin, cocaine, crime, and public policy.* Palo Alto, CA: Mayfield.

Kraar, L. (1988, June 20). The drug trade. *Fortune,* pp. 27-28.

McBride, D. C., Burgman-Habermehl, C., Alpert, J., & Chitwood, D. D. (1986, June). Drugs and homicide. *Bulletin of the New York Academy of Medicine, 62,* pp. 497-508.

Morgan, H. W. (1974). *Yesterday's addicts: American society and drug abuse.* Norman, OK: University of Oklahoma Press.

Morrison, D. C. (1986, September 6). The Pentagon's drug wars. *National Journal,* pp. 13-19.

Renfret, M. (1988, May 3-4). *Cocaine price, purity, and trafficking trends.* Presented at the National Institute in Drug Abuse Technical Review Meeting on the Epidemiology of Cocaine Use and Abuse, Rockville, MD.

Rosenbaum, R. (1987, February 15). Crack murder: A detective story. *New York Times Magazine,* pp. 24-33, 57, 60.

Terry, C. E., & Pellens, M. (1928). *The opium problem.* New York: Bureau of Social Hygiene.

Trebach, A. S. (1987). *The great drug war.* New York: Macmillan.

U.S. Department of State. (1988). *International narcotics control strategy report.* Washington, DC: Bureau of International Narcotics Matters.

U.S. Department of Transportation. (1988, June 6). Zero tolerance policy on illegal drugs. *Transportation Facts.*

U.S. General Accounting Office. (1987a). *Drug law enforcement: Military assistance for anti-drug agencies.* Washington, DC: General Accounting Office.

U.S. General Accounting Office. (1987b). *Drug smuggling: Large amounts of illegal drugs not seized by federal authorities.* Washington, DC: General Accounting Office.

United States statutes at large (1877-1879) 45th Congress, 20, p. 152.

Wisotsky, S. (1986). *Breaking the impasse in the war on drugs.* Westport, CT: Greenwood.

Young, J. H. (1961). *The toadstool millionaires: A social history of patent medicines in America before federal regulation.* Princeton: Princeton University Press.

Zimmerman, S. (1982, Summer). Posse comitatus. *Drug Enforcement,* pp. 17-22.

1

The Case for Legalization

ETHAN A. NADELMANN

What can be done about the "drug problem"? Despite frequent proc-
lamations of war and dramatic increases in government funding and
resources in recent years, there are many indications that the problem
is not going away and may even be growing worse. During the past
year alone, more than 30 million Americans violated the drug laws on
literally billions of occasions. Drug-treatment programs in many cities
are turning people away for lack of space and funding. In Washington,
D.C., drug-related killings, largely of one drug dealer by another, are
held responsible for a doubling in the homicide rate over the past
year. In New York and elsewhere, courts and prisons are clogged with
a virtually limitless supply of drug-law violators. In large cities and
small towns alike, corruption of policemen and other criminal-justice
officials by drug traffickers is rampant.

President Reagan and the First Lady were not alone in supporting
increasingly repressive and expensive antidrug measures, and in believing that the war against drugs can be won. Indeed, no "war" proclaimed by an American leader during the past 40 years has garnered
such sweeping bipartisan support; on this issue, liberals and conservatives are often indistinguishable. The fiercest disputes are not over
objectives or even broad strategies, but over turf and tactics. Democratic politicians push for the appointment of a "drug czar" to oversee
all drug policy, and blame the Administration for not applying sufficient
pressure and sanctions against the foreign drug-producing countries.
Republicans try to gain the upper hand by daring Democrats to support
more widespread drug testing, increasingly powerful law enforcement
measures, and the death penalty for various drug-related offenses. But
on the more fundamental issues of what this war is about, and what

strategies are most likely to prove successful in the long run, no real debate—much less vocal dissent—can be heard.

If there were a serious public debate on this issue, far more attention would be given to one policy option that has just begun to be seriously considered, but which may well prove more successful than anything currently being implemented or proposed: legalization. Politicians and public officials remain hesitant even to mention the word, except to dismiss it contemptuously as a capitulation to the drug traffickers. Most Americans perceive drug legalization as an invitation to drug-infested anarchy. Even the civil-liberties groups shy away from the issue, limiting their input primarily to the drug-testing debate. The minority communities in the ghetto, for whom repealing the drug laws would promise the greatest benefits, fail to recognize the costs of our drug-prohibition policies. And typical middle-class Americans, who hope only that their children will not succumb to drug abuse, tend to favor any measures that they believe will make illegal drugs less accessible. Yet when one seriously compares the advantages and disadvantages of the legalization strategy with those of current and planned policies, abundant evidence suggests that legalization may well be the optimal strategy for tackling the drug problem.

Interestingly, public support for repealing the drug-prohibition laws has traditionally come primarily from the conservative end of the political spectrum: Milton Friedman, Ernest van den Haag, William F. Buckley, and the editors of the *Economist* have all supported it. Less vocal support comes from many liberals, politicians not among them, who are disturbed by the infringements on individual liberty posed by the drug laws. There is also a significant silent constituency in favor of repeal, found especially among criminal-justice officials, intelligence analysts, military interdictors, and criminal-justice scholars who have spent a considerable amount of time thinking about the problem. More often than not, however, job-security considerations, combined with an awareness that they can do little to change official policies, ensure that their views remain discreet and off the record.

During the spring of 1988, however, legalization suddenly began to be seriously considered as a policy option; the pros and cons of legalization were discussed on the front page of leading newspapers and newsmagazines and were debated on national television programs. Although the argument for legalization was not new, two factors seem to have been primarily responsible for the blitz of media coverage: an intellectual rationale for legalization—the first provided in decades—appeared in my article in the Spring issue of *Foreign Policy* magazine; more importantly, political legitimacy was subsequently bestowed upon the legalization option when Baltimore Mayor Kurt Schmoke, speaking to the National Conference of Mayors, noted the potential benefits of drug legalization and asked that the merits of legalization be debated in congressional hearings.

The idea of legalizing drugs was quickly denounced by most politicians across the political spectrum; nevertheless, the case for legalization appealed to many Americans. The prominent media coverage lent an aura of respectability to arguments that just a month earlier had seemed to be beyond the political pale. Despite the tendency of many journalists to caricature the legalization argument, at long last the issue had been joined. Various politicians, law enforcement officials, health experts, and scholars came out in favor of drug legalization—or at least wanted to debate the matter seriously. On Capitol Hill, three or four congressman seconded the call for a debate. According to some congressional staffers, two dozen additional legislators would have wanted to debate the issue, had the question arisen after rather than before the upcoming elections. Unable to oppose a mere hearing on the issue, Congressman Charles Rangel, chairman of the House Select Committee on Narcotics, declared his willingness to convene his committee in Baltimore to consider the legalization option.

There is, of course, no single legalization strategy. At one extreme is the libertarian vision of virtually no government restraints on the production and sale of drugs or any psychoactive substances, except perhaps around the fringes, such as prohibiting sales to children. At the other extreme is total government control over the production and sale of these goods. In between lies a strategy that may prove more successful than anything yet tried in stemming the problems of drug abuse and drug-related violence, corruption, sickness, and suffering. It is one in which government makes most of the substances that are now banned legally available to competent adults, exercises strong regulatory powers over all large-scale production and sale of drugs, makes drug-treatment programs available to all who need them, and offers honest drug-education programs to children. This strategy, it is worth noting, would also result in a net benefit to public treasuries of at least $10 billion a year, and perhaps much more.

There are three reasons why it is important to think about legalization scenarios, even though most Americans remain hostile to the idea. First, current drug-control policies have failed, are failing, and will continue to fail, in good part because they are fundamentally flawed. Second, many drug-control efforts are not only failing, but also proving highly costly and counter-productive; indeed, many of the drug-related evils that Americans identify as part and parcel of the "drug problem" are in fact caused by our drug-prohibition policies. Third, there is good reason to believe that repealing many of the drug laws would not lead, as many people fear, to a dramatic rise in drug abuse. In this chapter I expand on each of these reasons for considering the legalization option. Government efforts to deal with the drug problem will succeed only if the rhetoric and crusading mentality that now dominate drug policy are replaced by reasoned and logical analysis.

WHY CURRENT DRUG POLICIES FAIL

Most proposals for dealing with the drug problem today reflect a desire to point the finger at those most removed from one's home and area of expertise. New York Mayor Ed Koch, Florida Congressman Larry Smith, and Harlem Congressman Charles Rangel, who recognize government's inability to deal with the drug problem in the cities, are among the most vocal supporters of punishing foreign drug-producing countries and stepping up interdiction efforts. Foreign leaders and U.S. State Department and drug enforcement officials stationed abroad, on the other hand, who understand all too well why it is impossible to crack down successfully on illicit drug production outside the United States, are the most vigorous advocates of domestic enforcement and demand-reduction efforts within the United States. In between, those agencies charged with drug interdiction, from the Coast Guard and U.S. Customs Services to the U.S. military, know that they will never succeed in capturing more than a small percentage of the illicit drugs being smuggled into the United States. Not surprisingly, they point their fingers in both directions. The solution, they promise, lies in greater source-control efforts abroad and greater demand-reduction efforts at home.

Trying to pass the buck is always understandable. But in each of these cases, the officials are half right and half wrong—half right in recognizing that they can do little to affect their end of the drug problem, given the suppositions and constraints of current drug-control strategies; half wrong (if we assume that their finger-pointing is sincere) in expecting that the solution lies elsewhere. It would be wrong, however, to assume that the public posturing of many officials reflects their real views. Many of them privately acknowledge the futility of all current drug-control strategies, and wonder whether radically different options, such as legalization, might not prove more successful in dealing with the drug problem. The political climate pervading this issue is such, however, that merely to ask that alternatives to current policies be considered is to incur a great political risk.

By most accounts, the dramatic increase in drug-enforcement efforts over the past few years has had little effect on the illicit drug market in the United States. The mere existence of drug-prohibition laws, combined with a minimal level of law enforcement resources, is sufficient to maintain the price of illicit drugs at a level significantly higher than it would be if there were no such laws. Drug laws and enforcement also reduce the availability of illicit drugs, most notably in parts of the United States where demand is relatively limited to begin with. Theoretically, increases in drug-enforcement efforts should result in reduced availability, higher prices, and lower purity of illegal drugs. That is, in fact, what has happened to the domestic marijuana market (in at least the first two respects). But in general the illegal drug market has not responded as intended to the substantial increases in federal, state, and local drug-enforcement efforts.

Cocaine has sold for about $100 a gram at the retail level since the beginning of the 1980s. The average purity of that gram, however, has increased from 12% to 60%. Moreover, a growing number of users are turning to "crack," a potent derivative of cocaine that can be smoked; it is widely sold in ghetto neighborhoods now for $5 to $10 per vial. Needless to say, both crack and the 60% pure cocaine pose much greater threats to users than did the relatively benign powder available eight years ago. Similarly, the retail price of heroin has remained relatively constant even as the average purity has risen from 3.9% in 1983 to 6.1% in 1986. Throughout the southwestern part of the United States, a particularly potent form of heroin known as "black tar" has become increasingly prevalent. And in many cities, a powerful synthetic opiate, Dilaudid, is beginning to compete with heroin as the preferred opiate. The growing number of heroin-related hospital emergencies and deaths is directly related to these developments.

All of these trends suggest that drug-enforcement efforts are not succeeding, and may even be backfiring. There are numerous indications, for instance, that a growing number of marijuana dealers in both the producer countries and the United States are switching to cocaine dealing, motivated both by the promise of greater profits and by government drug-enforcement efforts that place a premium on minimizing the bulk of the illicit product (in order to avoid detection). It is possible, of course, that some of these trends would be even more severe in the absence of drug laws and enforcement. At the same time, it is worth observing that the increases in the potency of illegal drugs have coincided with decreases in the potency of legal substances. Motivated in good part by health concerns, cigarette smokers are turning increasingly to lower-tar and nicotine tobacco products, alcohol drinkers from hard liquor to wine and beer, and even coffee drinkers from regular to decaffeinated coffee. This trend may well have less to do with the nature of the substances than with their legal status. It is quite possible, for instance, that the subculture of illicit-drug use creates a bias or incentive in favor of riskier behavior and more powerful psychoactive effects. If this is the case, legalization might well succeed in reversing today's trend toward more potent drugs and more dangerous methods of consumption.

The most "successful" drug-enforcement operations are those that succeed in identifying and destroying an entire drug-trafficking organization. Such operations can send dozens of people to jail and earn the government millions of dollars in asset forfeitures. Yet these operations have virtually no effect on the availability or price of illegal drugs throughout much of the United States. During the past few years, some urban police departments have devoted significant manpower and financial resources to intensive crackdowns on street-level drug dealing in particular neighborhoods. Code-named Operation Pressure Point, Operation Clean Sweep, and so on, these massive police efforts have led to hundreds, even thousands, of arrests of low-level dealers and drug users, and have helped improve the quality of life in the targeted neighborhoods. In most cases, however, drug dealers have adapted relatively easily by moving their operations to nearby neighborhoods. In the final analysis, the principal accomplishment of most domestic drug-enforcement efforts is not to reduce the supply or availability of illegal drugs, or even to raise their price; it is to punish the drug dealers who are apprehended, and cause minor disruptions in established drug markets.

THE FAILURE OF INTERNATIONAL DRUG CONTROL

Many drug-enforcement officials and urban leaders recognize the futility of domestic drug-enforcement efforts and place their hopes in international control efforts. Yet these too are doomed to fail—for numerous reasons. First, marijuana and opium can be grown almost anywhere, and the coca plant, from which cocaine is derived, is increasingly being cultivated successfully in areas that were once considered inhospitable environments. Wherever drug-eradication efforts succeed, other regions and countries are quick to fill the void; for example, Colombian marijuana growers rapidly expanded production following successful eradication efforts in Mexico during the mid-1970s. Today, Mexican growers are rapidly taking advantage of recent Colombian government successes in eradicating marijuana in the Guajira peninsula. Meanwhile, Jamaicans and Central Americans from Panama to Belize, as well as a growing assortment of Asians and Africans, do what they can to sell their own marijuana in American markets. And within the United States, domestic marijuana production is believed to be a multibillion-dollar industry, supplying between 15% and 50% of the American market.

This push-down/pop-up factor also characterizes the international heroin market. At various points during the past two decades, Turkey, Mexico, Southeast Asia (Burma, Thailand, and Laos), and Southwest Asia (Pakistan, Afghanistan, and Iran) have each served as the principal source of heroin imported into the United States. During the early 1970s, Mexican producers rapidly filled the void created by the Turkish government's successful opium-control measures. Although a successful eradication program during the latter part of the 1970s reduced Mexico's share of the U.S. market from a peak of 87% in 1975, it has since retained at least a one-third share in each year. Southwest Asian producers, who had played no role in supplying the American market as late as 1976, were able to supply more than half the American market four years later. Today, increasing evidence indicates that drug traffickers are bringing unprecedented quantities of Southeast Asian heroin into the United States.

So far, the push-down/pop-up factor has played little role in the international cocaine market, for the simple reason that no government has yet pushed down in a significant way. Unlike marijuana- and opium-eradication efforts, in which aerial spraying or herbicides plays a prominent role, coca-eradication efforts are still conducted manually. The long anticipated development and approval of an environmentally safe herbicide to destroy coca plants may introduce an unprecedented push-down factor into the market. But even in the absence of such government pressures, coca growing has expanded rapidly during the past decade within Bolivia and Peru, and has expanded outward into Colombia, Brazil, Ecuador, Venezuela, and elsewhere. Moreover, once eradication efforts do begin, coca growers can be expected to adopt many of the same "guerrilla farming" methods adopted by marijuana and opium growers to camouflage and protect their crops from eradication efforts.

Beyond the push-down/pop-up factor, international source-control efforts face a variety of other obstacles. In many countries, governments with limited resources lack the ability to crack down on drug production in the hinterlands and other poorly policed regions. In some countries, ranging from Colombia and Peru to Burma and Thailand, leftist insurgencies are involved in drug production for either financial or political profit, and may play an important role in hampering government drug-control efforts. With respect to all three of the illicit crops, poor peasants with no comparable opportunities to earn as much money growing legitimate produce are prominently involved in the illicit business. In some cases, the illicit crop is part of a traditional, indigenous culture. Even where it is not, peasants typically perceive little or nothing immoral about taking advantage of the opportunity to grow the illicit crops. Indeed, from their perspective their moral obligation is not to protect the foolish American consumer of their produce, but to provide for their families' welfare. And even among those who do perceive participation in the illicit drug market as somewhat unethical, the temptations held out by the drug traffickers often prove overwhelming.

No illicit drug is as difficult to keep out of the United States as heroin. The absence of geographical limitations on where it can be cultivated is just one minor obstacle. American heroin users consume an estimated six tons of heroin each year. The 60 tons of opium required to produce that heroin represent just 2% to 3% of the estimated 2,000 to 3,000 tons of illicit opium produced during each of the past few years. Even if eradication efforts combined with what often proves to be the opium growers' principal nemesis—bad weather—were to eliminate three-fourths of that production in one year, the U.S. market would still require just 10% of the remaining crop. Since U.S. consumers are able and willing to pay more than any others, the chances are good that they would still obtain their heroin. In any event, the prospects for such a radical reduction in illicit opium production are scanty indeed.

As Peter Reuter has argued, interdiction, like source control, is largely unable to keep illicit drugs out of the United States. Moreover, the past 20 years' experience has demonstrated that even dramatic increases in interdiction and source-control efforts have little or no effect on the price and purity of drugs. The few small successes, such as the destruction of the Turkish-opium "French Connection" in the early 1970s, and the crackdown on Mexican marijuana and heroin in the late 1970s, were exceptions to the rule. The elusive goal of international drug control since then has been to replicate those unusual successes. It is a strategy that is destined to fail, however, as long as millions of Americans continue to demand the illicit substances that foreigners are willing and able to supply.

THE COSTS OF PROHIBITION

The fact that drug-prohibition laws and policies cannot eradicate or even significantly reduce drug abuse is not necessarily a reason to repeal them. They do, after all, succeed in deterring many people from trying drugs, and they clearly reduce the availability and significantly increase the price of illegal drugs. These accomplishments alone might warrant retaining the drug laws, were it not for the fact that these same laws are also responsible for much of what Americans identify as the "drug problem." Here the analogies to alcohol and tobacco are worth noting. There is little question that we could reduce the health costs associated with use and abuse of alcohol and tobacco if we were to criminalize their production, sale, and possession. But no one believes that we could eliminate their use and abuse, that we could created an "alcohol-free" or "tobacco-free" country. Nor do most Americans believe that criminalizing the alcohol and tobacco markets would be a good idea. Their opposition stems largely from two beliefs: that adult Americans have the right to choose what substances they will consume and what risks they will take; and that the costs of trying to coerce so many Americans to abstain from those substances would be enormous. It was the strength of these two beliefs that ultimately led to the repeal of Prohibition, and it is partly due to memories of that experience that criminalizing either alcohol or tobacco has little support today.

Consider the potential consequences of criminalizing the production, sale, and possession of all tobacco products. On the positive side, the number of people smoking tobacco would almost certainly decline, as would the health costs associated with tobacco consumption. Although the "forbidden fruit" syndrome would attract some people to cigarette smoking who would not otherwise have smoked, many more would likely be deterred by the criminal sanction, the moral standing of the law, the higher cost and unreliable quality of the illicit tobacco, and the difficulties involved in acquiring it. Nonsmokers would rarely if ever be bothered by the irritating habits of their fellow citizens. The anti-tobacco laws would discourage some people from ever starting to smoke, and would induce others to quit.

On the negative side, however, millions of Americans, including both tobacco addicts and recreational users, would no doubt defy the law, generating a massive underground market and billions in profits for organized criminals. Although some tobacco farmers would find other work, thousands more would become outlaws and continue to produce their crops covertly. Throughout Latin America, farmers and gangsters would rejoice at the opportunity to earn untold sums of "gringo greenbacks," even as U.S. diplomats pressured foreign governments to cooperate with U.S. laws. Within the United States, government helicopters would spray herbicides on illicit tobacco fields; people would be rewarded by the government for informing on their tobacco-growing, -selling, and -smoking neighbors; urine tests would be employed to identify violators of the antitobacco laws; and a Tobacco Enforcement Administration (the TEA) would employ undercover agents, informants, and wiretaps to uncover tobacco-law violators. Municipal, state, and federal judicial systems would be clogged with tobacco traffickers and "abusers." "Tobacco-related murders" would increase dramatically as criminal organizations competed with one another for turf and markets. Smoking would become an act of youthful rebellion, and no doubt some users would begin to experiment with more concentrated, potent, and dangerous forms of tobacco. Tobacco-related corruption would infect all levels of government, and respect for the law would decline noticeably. Government expenditures on tobacco-law enforcement would climb rapidly into the billions of dollars, even as budget balancers longingly recalled the almost $10 billion per year in tobacco taxes earned by the federal and state governments prior to prohibition. Finally, the State of North Carolina might even secede again from the Union.

This seemingly far-fetched tobacco-prohibition scenario is little more than an extrapolation based on the current situation with respect to marijuana, cocaine, and heroin. In many ways, our predicament resembles what actually happened during Prohibition. Prior to Prohibition, most Americans hoped that alcohol could be effectively banned by passing laws against its production and supply. During the early years of Prohibition, when drinking declined but millions of Americans nonetheless continued to drink, Prohibition's supporters placed their faith in tougher laws and more police and jails. After a few more years, however, increasing numbers of Americans began to realize that laws and the police were unable to eliminate the smugglers, bootleggers, and illicit producers, as long as tens of millions of Americans continued to want to buy alcohol. At the same time, they saw that more laws and police seemed to generate more violence and corruption, more crowded courts and jails, wider disrespect for government and the law, and more power and profits for the gangsters. Repeal of Prohibition came to be seen not as a capitulation to Al Capone and his ilk, but as a means of both putting the bootleggers out of business and eliminating most of the costs associated with the prohibition laws.

Today, Americans are faced with a dilemma similar to that confronted by our forebears 60 years ago. Demand for illicit drugs shows some signs of abating, but no signs of declining significantly. Moreover, there are substantial reasons to doubt that tougher laws and policing have played an important role in reducing consumption. Supply, meanwhile, has not abated at all. Availability of illicit drugs, except for marijuana in some locales, remains high. Prices are dropping, even as potency increases. And the number of drug producers, smugglers, and dealers remains sizable, even as jails and prisons fill to overflowing. As was the case during Prohibition, the principal beneficiaries of current drug policies are the new and old organized-crime gangs. The principal victims, on the other hand, are not the drug dealers, but the tens of millions of Americans who are worse off in one way or another as a consequence of the existence and failure of the drug-prohibition laws.

All public policies create beneficiaries and victims, both intended and unintended. When a public policy results in a disproportionate magnitude of unintended victims, there is good reason to reevaluate the assumptions and design of the policy. In the case of drug-prohibition policies, the intended beneficiaries are those individuals who would become drug abusers but for the existence and enforcement of the drug laws. The intended victims are those who traffic in illicit drugs and suffer the legal consequences. The unintended beneficiaries, conversely, are the drug producers and traffickers who profit handsomely from the illegality of the market, while avoiding arrest by the authorities and the violence perpetrated by other criminals. The unintended victims of drug prohibition policies are rarely recognized as such, however. Viewed narrowly, they are the 30 million Americans who use illegal drugs, thereby risking loss of their jobs, imprisonment, and the damage done to health by ingesting illegally produced drugs; viewed broadly, they are all Americans who pay the substantial costs of our present ill-considered policies, both as taxpayers and as the potential victims of crime. These unintended victims are generally thought to be victimized by the unintended beneficiaries (i.e., the drug dealers), when in fact it is the drug-prohibition policies themselves that are primarily responsible for their plight.

If law-enforcement efforts could succeed in significantly reducing either the supply of illicit drugs or the demand for them, we would probably have little need to seek alternative drug-control policies. But since those efforts have repeatedly failed to make much of a difference and show little indication of working better in the future, at this point we must focus greater attention on their costs. Unlike the demand and supply of illicit drugs, which have remained relatively indifferent to legislative initiatives, the costs of drug-enforcement measures can be affected—quite dramatically—by legislative measures. What tougher criminal sanctions and more police have failed to accomplish, in terms of reducing drug-related violence, corruption, death, and social decay, may well be better accomplished by legislative repeal of the drug laws, and adoption of less punitive but more effective measures to prevent and treat substance abuse.

COSTS TO THE TAXPAYER

Since 1981 federal expenditures on drug enforcement have more than tripled—from less than $1 billion a year to about $3 billion. According to the National Drug Enforcement Policy Board, the annual budgets of the Drug Enforcement Administration (DEA) and the Coast Guard have each risen during the past seven years from about $220 million to roughly $500 million. During the same period, FBI resources devoted to drug enforcement have increased from $8 million a year to more than $100 million; U.S. Marshals resources from $26 million to about $80 million; U.S. Attorney resources from $20 million to about $100 million; State Department resources from $35 million to $100 million; U.S. Customs resources from $180 million to more than $400 million; and Bureau of Prison resources from $77 million to about $300 million. Expenditures on drug control by the military and the intelligence agencies are more difficult to calculate, although by all accounts they have increased by at least the same magnitude, and now total hundreds of millions of dollars per year. Even greater are the expenditures at lower levels of government. In a 1987 study for the U.S. Customs Service by Wharton Econometrics, state and local police were estimated to have devoted 18% of their total investigative resources, or close to $5 billion, to drug-enforcement activities in 1986. This represented a 19% increase over the previous year's expenditures. All told, 1987 expenditures on all aspects of drug enforcement, from drug eradication in foreign countries to imprisonment of drug users and dealers in the United States, totalled at least $10 billion.

Of course, even $10 billion a year pales in comparison with expenditures on military defense. Of greater concern than the actual expenditures, however, has been the diversion of limited resources—including the time and energy of judges, prosecutors, and law-enforcement agents, as well as scarce prison space—from the prosecution and punishment of criminal activities that harm far more innocent victims than do violations of the drug laws. Drug-law violators account for approximately 10% of the roughly 800,000 inmates in state prisons and local jails, and more than one-third of the 44,000 federal prison inmates. These proportions are expected to increase in coming years, even as total prison populations continue to rise dramatically.[1] Among the 40,000 inmates in New York State prisons, drug-law violations surpassed first-degree robbery in 1987 as the number one cause of incarceration, accounting for 20% of the total prison population. The U.S. Sentencing Commission has estimated that, largely as a consequence of the Anti-Drug Abuse Act passed by Congress in 1986, the proportion of federal inmates incarcerated for drug violations will rise from one-third of the 44,000 prisoners sentenced to federal-prison terms today to one-half of the 100,000 to 150,000 federal prisoners anticipated in 15 years. The direct costs of building and maintaining enough prisons to house this growing population are rising at an astronomical rate. The opportunity costs, in terms of alternative social expenditures foregone and other types of criminals not imprisoned, are perhaps even greater.[2]

During each of the last few years, police made about 750,000 arrests for violations of the drug laws. Slightly more than three-quarters of these have not been for manufacturing or dealing drugs, but solely for possession of an illicit drug, typically marijuana. (Those arrested, it is worth noting, represent little more than 2% of the 30 million Americans estimated to have used an illegal drug during the past year.) On the one hand, this has clogged many urban criminal-justice systems: in New York City, drug-law violations last year accounted for more than 40% of all felony indictments—up from 25% in 1985; in Washington, D.C., the figure was more than 50%. On the other hand, it has distracted criminal-justice officials from concentrating greater resources on violent offenses and property crimes. In many cities, law enforcement has become virtually synonymous with drug enforcement.

Drug laws typically have two effects on the market in illicit drugs. The first is to restrict the general availability and accessibility of illicit drugs, especially in locales where underground drug markets are small and isolated from the community. The second is to increase, often significantly, the price of illicit drugs to consumers. Since the costs of producing most illicit drugs are not much different from the costs of alcohol, tobacco, and coffee, most of the price paid for illicit substances is in effect a value-added tax created by their criminalization, which is enforced and supplemented by the law-enforcement establishment, but collected by the drug traffickers. A report by Wharton Econometrics for the President's Commission on Organized Crime identified the sale of illicit drugs as the source of more than half of all organized crime revenues in 1986, with the marijuana and heroin business each providing more than $7 billion, and the cocaine business more than

$13 billion. By contrast, revenues from cigarette bootlegging, which persists principally because of differences among states in their cigarette-tax rates, were estimated at $290 million. If the marijuana, cocaine, and heroin markets were legal, state and federal governments would collect billions of dollars annually in tax revenues. Instead, they expend billions on what amounts to a subsidy of organized crime and unorganized criminals.

DRUGS AND CRIME

The drug/crime connection is one that continues to resist coherent analysis, both because cause and effect are so difficult to distinguish and because the role of the drug-prohibition laws in causing and labeling "drug-related crime" is so often ignored. There are four possible connections between drugs and crime, at least three of which would be much diminished if the drug-prohibition laws were repealed. First, producing, selling, buying, and consuming strictly controlled and banned substances is itself a crime that occurs billions of times each year in the United States alone. In the absence of drug-prohibition laws, these activities would obviously cease to be crimes. Selling drugs to children would, of course, continue to be criminal, and other evasions of government regulation of a legal market would continue to be prosecuted; but by and large the drug/crime connection that now accounts for all of the criminal-justice costs noted above would be severed.

Second, many illicit-drug users commit crimes such as robbery and burglary, as well as drug dealing, prostitution, and numbers running, to earn enough money to purchase the relatively high-priced illicit drugs. Unlike the millions of alcoholics who can support their habits for relatively modest amounts, many cocaine and heroin addicts spend hundreds and even thousands of dollars a week. If the drugs to which they are addicted were significantly cheaper—which would be the case if they were legalized—the number of crimes committed by drug addicts to pay for their habits would, in all likelihood, decline dramatically. Even if a legal-drug policy included the imposition of relatively high consumption taxes in order to discourage consumption, drug prices would probably still be lower than they are today.

The third drug/crime connection is the commission of crimes—violent crimes in particular—by people under the influence of illicit drugs. This connection seems to have the greatest impact upon the popular imagination. Clearly, some drugs do "cause" some people to commit crimes by reducing normal inhibitions, unleashing aggressive and other antisocial tendencies, and lessening the sense of responsibility. Cocaine, particularly in the form of crack, has gained such a reputation in recent years, just as heroin did in the 1960s and 1970s, and marijuana did in the years before that. Crack's reputation for inspiring violent behavior may or may not be more deserved than those of marijuana and heroin; reliable evidence is not yet available. No illicit drug, however, is as widely associated with violent behavior as alcohol. According to Justice Department statistics, 54% of all jail inmates convicted of violent crimes in 1983 reported having used alcohol just prior to committing their offense. The impact of drug legalization on this drug/crime connection is the most difficult to predict. Much would depend on overall rates of drug abuse and changes in the natured of consumption, both of which are impossible to predict. It is worth noting, however, that a shift in consumption from alcohol to marijuana would almost certainly contribute to a decline in violent behavior.

The fourth drug/crime link is the violent, intimidating, and corrupting behavior of the drug traffickers. Illegal markets tend to breed violence—not only because they attract criminally minded individuals, but also because participants in the market have no resort to legal institutions to resolve their disputes. During Prohibition, violent struggles between bootlegging gangs and hijackings of booze-laden trucks and sea vessels were frequent and notorious occurrences. Today's equivalents are the booby traps that surround some marijuana fields, the pirates of the Caribbean looking to rip off drug-laden vessels en route to the shores of the United States, and the machine-gun battles and executions carried out by drug lords—all of which occasionally kill innocent people. Most law enforcement officials agree that the dramatic increases in urban murder rates during the past few years can be explained almost entirely by the rise in drug-dealer killings.

Perhaps the most unfortunate victims of the drug-prohibition policies have been the law-abiding residents of America's ghettos. These policies have largely proven futile in deterring large numbers of ghetto dwellers from becoming drug abusers, but they do account for much of what ghetto residents identify as the drug problem. In many neighborhoods, it often seems to be the aggressive gun-toting drug dealers who upset law-abiding residents far more than the addicts nodding out in doorways. Other residents, however, perceive the drug dealers as heroes and successful role models. In impoverished neighborhoods, they often stand out as symbols of success to children who see no other options. At the same time, the increasingly harsh criminal penalties imposed on adult drug dealers have led to the widespread recruitment of juveniles by drug traffickers. Formerly, children started dealing drugs only after they had been using them for a while; today the sequence is often reversed: many children start using illegal drugs now only after working for older drug dealers. And the juvenile-justice system offers no realistic options for dealing with this growing problem.

The conspicuous failure of law enforcement agencies to deal with this drug/crime connection is probably most responsible for the demoralization of neighborhoods and police departments alike. Intensive police crackdowns in urban neighborhoods do little more than chase the menace a short distance away to infect new areas. By contrast, legalization of the drug market would drive the drug-dealing business off the streets and out of the apartment buildings, and into legal, government-regulated, tax-paying stores. It would also force many of the gun-toting dealers out of business, and would convert others into legitimate business. Some, of course, would turn to other types of criminal activities, just as some of the bootleggers did following Prohibition's repeal. Gone, however, would be the unparalleled financial temptations that lure so many people from all sectors of society into the drug-dealing business.

THE COSTS OF CORRUPTION

All vice-control efforts are particularly susceptible to corruption, but none so much as drug enforcement. When police accept bribes from drug dealers, no victim exists to complain to the authorities. Even when police extort money and drugs from traffickers and dealers, the latter are in no position to report the corrupt officers. What makes drug enforcement especially vulnerable to corruption are the tremendous amounts of money involved in the business. Today, many law enforcement officials believe that police corruption is more pervasive than at any time since Prohibition. In Miami, dozens of law enforcement officials have been charged with accepting bribes, stealing from drug dealers, and even dealing drugs themselves. Throughout many small towns and rural communities in Georgia, where drug smugglers en route from Mexico, the Caribbean, and Latin America drop their loads of cocaine and marijuana, dozens of sheriffs have been implicated in drug-related corruption. In New York, drug-related corruption in one Brooklyn police precinct has generated the city's most far-reaching police-corruption scandal since the 1960s. More than 100 cases of drug-related corruption are now prosecuted each year in state and federal courts. Every one of the federal law enforcement agencies charged with drug-enforcement responsibilities has seen an agent implicated in drug-related corruption.

It is not difficult to explain the growing pervasiveness of drug-related corruption. The financial temptations are enormous relative to other opportunities, legitimate or illegitimate. Little effort is required. Many police officers are demoralized by the scope of the drug traffic, their sense that many citizens are indifferent, and the fact that many sectors of society do not even appreciate their efforts—as well as the fact that many of the drug dealers who are arrested do not remain in prison. Some police also recognize that enforcing the drug laws does not protect victims from predators so much as it regulates an illicit market that cannot be suppressed, but can be kept underground. In every respect, the analogy to Prohibition is apt. Repealing the drug-prohibition laws would dramatically reduce police corruption. By contrast, the measures currently being proposed to deal with the growing problem, including better funded and more aggressive internal investigations, offer relatively little promise.

Among the most difficult costs to evaluate are those that relate to the widespread defiance of the drug-prohibition laws: the effects of labeling as criminals the tens of millions of people who use drugs illicitly, subjecting them to the risks of criminal sanction, and obliging many of these same people to enter into relationships with drug dealers (who may be criminals in many more senses of the word) in order to purchase their drugs; the cynicism that such laws generate toward other laws and the law in general; and the sense of hostility and suspicion that many otherwise law-abiding individuals feel toward law-enforcement officials. It was costs such as these that strongly influenced many of Prohibition's more conservative opponents.

PHYSICAL AND MORAL COSTS

Perhaps the most paradoxical consequence of the drug laws is the tremendous harm they cause to the millions of drug users who have not been deterred from using illicit drugs in the first place. Nothing resembling an underground Food and Drug Administration has arisen to impose quality control on the illegal-drug market and provide users with accurate information on the drugs they consume. Imagine that Americans could not tell whether a bottle of wine contained 6%, 30%, or 90% alcohol, or whether an aspirin tablet contained 5 grams or 500 grams of aspirin. Imagine, too, that no controls existed to prevent winemakers from diluting their product with methanol and other dangerous impurities, and that vineyards and tobacco fields were fertilized with harmful substances by ignorant growers and sprayed with poisonous herbicides by government agents. Fewer people would use such substances, but more of those who did would get sick. Some would die.

The above scenario describes, of course, the current state of the illicit drug market. Many marijuana smokers are worse off for having smoked cannabis that was grown with dangerous fertilizers, sprayed with the herbicide paraquat, or mixed with more dangerous substances. Consumers of heroin and the various synthetic substances sold on the street face even severer consequences, including fatal overdoses and poisonings from unexpectedly potent or impure drug supplies. More often than not, the quality of a drug addict's life depends greatly upon his or her access to reliable supplies. Drug-enforcement operations that succeed in temporarily disrupting supply networks are thus a double-edged sword: they encourage some addicts to seek admission into drug-treatment programs, but they oblige others to seek out new and hence less reliable suppliers; the result is that more, not fewer, drug-related emergencies and deaths occur.

Today, more than 50% of all people with AIDS in New York City, New Jersey, and many other parts of the country, as well as the vast majority of AIDS-infected heterosexuals throughout the country, have contracted the disease directly or indirectly through illegal intravenous drug use. Reports have emerged of drug dealers beginning to provide clean syringes together with their illegal drugs. But even as other governments around the world actively attempt to limit the spread of AIDS by and among drug users by instituting free syringe-exchange programs, state and municipal governments in the United States resist following suit, arguing that to do so would "encourage" or "condone" the use of illegal drugs. Only in January 1988 did New York City approve such a program on a very limited and experimental basis. At the same time, drug-treatment programs remain notoriously under-funded, turning away tens of thousands of addicts seeking help, even as billions of dollars more are spent to arrest, prosecute, and imprison illegal drug sellers and users. In what may represent a sign of shifting priorities, the President's Commission on AIDS, in its March 1988 report, emphasized the importance of making drug-treatment programs available to all in need of them. In all likelihood, however, the criminal-justice agencies will continue to receive the greatest share of drug-control funds.

Most Americans perceive the drug problem as a moral issue and draw a moral distinction between use of the illicit drugs and use of alcohol and tobacco. Yet when one subjects this distinction to reasoned analysis, it quickly disintegrates. The most consistent moral perspective of those who favor drug laws is that of the Mormons and the Puritans, who regard as immoral any intake of substances to alter one's state of consciousness or otherwise cause pleasure: they forbid not only the illicit drugs and alcohol, but also tobacco, caffeine, and even chocolate. The vast majority of Americans are hardly so consistent with respect to the propriety of their pleasures. Yet once one acknowledges that there is nothing immoral about drinking alcohol or smoking tobacco for nonmedicinal purposes, it becomes difficult to condemn the consumption of marijuana, cocaine, and other substances on moral grounds. The "moral" condemnation of some substances and not others proves to be little more than a prejudice in favor of some drugs and against others.

The same false distinction is drawn with respect to those who provide the psychoactive substances to users and abusers alike. If degrees of immorality were measured by the levels of harm caused by one's products, the "traffickers" in tobacco and alcohol would be vilified as the most evil of all substance purveyors. That they are perceived instead as respected members of our community, while providers of the no more dangerous illicit substances are punished with long prison sentences, says much about the prejudices of most Americans with respect to psychoactive substances, but little about the morality or immorality of their activities.

Much the same is true of gun salesmen. Most of the consumers of their products use them safely; a minority, however, end up shooting either themselves or someone else. Can we hold the gun salesman morally culpable for the harm that probably would not have occurred but for his existence? Most people say no, except perhaps where the salesman clearly knew that his product would be used to commit a crime. Yet in the case of those who sell illicit substances to willing customers, the providers are deemed not only legally guilty, but also morally reprehensible. The law does not require any demonstration that the dealer knew of a specific harm to follow; indeed, it does not require any evidence at all of harm having resulted from the sale. Rather, the law is predicated on the assumption that harm will inevitably follow. Despite the patent falsity of that assumption, it persists as the underlying justification for the drug laws.

Although a valid moral distinction cannot be drawn between the licit and the illicit psychoactive substances, one can point to a different kind of moral justification for the drug laws: they arguably reflect a paternalistic obligation to protect those in danger of succumbing to their own weaknesses. If drugs were legally available, most people would either abstain from using them or would use them responsibly and in moderation. A minority without self-restraint, however, would end up harming themselves if the substances were more readily available. Therefore, the majority has a moral obligation to deny itself legal access to certain substances because of the plight of the minority. This obligation is presumably greatest when children are included among the minority.

At least in principle, this argument seems to provide the strongest moral justification for the drug laws. But ultimately the moral quality of laws must be judged not by how those laws are intended to work in principle, but by how they function in practice. When laws intended to serve a moral end inflict great damage on innocent parties, we must rethink our moral position.

Because drug-law violations do not create victims with an interest in notifying the police, drug-enforcement agents rely heavily on undercover operations, electronic surveillance, and information provided by informants. These techniques are indispensable to effective law enforcement, but they are also among the least palatable investigative methods employed by the police. The same is true of drug testing: it may be useful and even necessary for determining liability in accidents, but it also threatens and undermines the right of privacy to which many Americans believe they are entitled. There are good reasons for requiring that such measures be used sparingly.

Equally disturbing are the increasingly vocal calls for people to inform not only on drug dealers but also on neighbors, friends, and even family members who use illicit drugs. The government calls on people not only to "just say no," but also to report those who have not heeded the message. Intolerance of illicit-drug use and users is heralded not only as an indispensable ingredient in the war against drugs, but also as a mark of good citizenship. Certainly every society requires citizens to assist in the enforcement of criminal laws. But societies—particularly democratic and pluralistic ones—also rely strongly on an ethic of tolerance toward those who are different but do no harm to others. Overzealous enforcement of the drug laws risks undermining that ethic and encouraging the creation of a society of informants. This results in an immorality that is far more dangerous in its own way than that associated with the use of illicit drugs.

THE BENEFITS OF LEGALIZATION

Repealing the drug-prohibition laws promises tremendous advantages. Between reduced government expenditures on enforcing drug laws and new tax revenue from legal drug production and sales, public treasuries would enjoy a net benefit of at least $10 billion a year, and possibly much more. The quality of urban life would rise significantly. Homicide rates would decline. So would robbery and burglary rates. Organized criminal groups, particularly the newer ones that have yet to diversify out of drugs, would be dealt a devastating setback. The police, prosecutors, and courts would focus their resources on combating the types of crimes that people cannot walk away from. More ghetto residents would turn their backs on criminal careers and seek out legitimate opportunities instead. And the health and quality of life of many drug users—and even drug abusers—would improve significantly.

All the benefits of legalization would be for naught, however, if millions more Americans were to become drug abusers. Our experience with alcohol and tobacco provides ample warnings. Today, alcohol is consumed by 140 million Americans and tobacco by 50 million. All of the health costs associated with abuse of the illicit drugs pale in comparison with those resulting from tobacco and alcohol abuse. In 1986, for example, alcohol was identified as a contributing factor in 10% of work-related injuries, 40% of suicide attempts, and about 40% of the approximately 46,000 annual traffic deaths in 1983. An estimated 18 million Americans are reported to be either alcoholics or alcohol abusers. The total cost of alcohol abuse to American society is estimated at more than $100 billion annually. Alcohol has been identified as the direct cause of 80,000 to 100,000 deaths annually, and as a contributing factor in an additional 100,000 deaths. The health costs of tobacco use are of similar magnitude. In the United States alone, an estimated 320,000 people die prematurely each year as a consequence of their consumption of tobacco. By comparison, the National Council on Alcoholism reported that only 3,562 people were known to have died in 1985 from use of all illegal drugs combined. Even if we assume that thousands more deaths were related in one way or another to illicit drug abuse but not reported as such, we are still left with the conclusion that all of the health costs of marijuana, cocaine, and heroin combined amount to only a small fraction of those caused by tobacco and alcohol.

Most Americans are just beginning to recognize the extensive costs of alcohol and tobacco abuse. At the same time, they seem to believe that there is something fundamentally different about alcohol and tobacco that supports the legal distinction between those two substances, on the one hand, and the illicit ones, on the other. The most common distinction is based on the assumption that the illicit drugs are more dangerous than the licit ones. Cocaine, heroin, the various hallucinogens, and (to a lesser extent) marijuana are widely perceived as, in the words of the President's Commission on Organized Crime, "inherently destructive to mind and body." They are also believed to be more addictive and more likely to cause dangerous and violent behavior than alcohol and tobacco. All use of illicit drugs is therefore thought to be abusive; in other words, the distinction between use and abuse of psychoactive substances that most people recognize with respect to alcohol is not acknowledged with respect to the illicit substances.

Most Americans make the fallacious assumption that the government would not criminalize certain psychoactive substances if they were not in fact dangerous. They then jump to the conclusion that any use of those substances is a form of abuse. The government, in its effort to discourage people from using illicit drugs, has encouraged and perpetuated these misconceptions—not only in its rhetoric but also in its purportedly educational materials. Only by reading between the lines can one discern the fact that the vast majority of Americans who have used illicit drugs have done so in moderation, that relatively few have suffered negative short-term consequences, and that few are likely to suffer long-term harm.

The evidence is most persuasive with respect to marijuana. U.S. drug-enforcement and health agencies do not even report figures on marijuana-related deaths, apparently because so few occur. Although there are good health reasons for children, pregnant women, and some others not to smoke marijuana, there still appears to be little evidence that occasional marijuana consumption does much harm. Certainly, it is not healthy to inhale marijuana smoke into one's lungs; indeed, the National Institute on Drug Abuse (NIDA) has declared that "marijuana smoke contains more cancer-causing agents than is found in tobacco smoke." On the other hand, the number of joints smoked by all but a very small percentage of marijuana smokers is a tiny fraction of the 20 cigarettes a day smoked by the average cigarette smoker; indeed, the average may be closer to one or two joints a week than one or two a day. Note that NIDA defines a "heavy" marijuana smoker as one who consumes at least two joints "daily." A heavy tobacco smoker, by contrast, smokes about 40 cigarettes a day.

Nor is marijuana strongly identified as a dependence-causing substance. A 1982 survey of marijuana use by young adults (18 to 25 years old) found that 64% had tried marijuana at least once, that 42% had used it at least 10 times, and that 27% had smoked in the last month. It also found that 21% had passed through a period during which they smoked "daily" (defined as 20 or more days per month), but that only one-third of those currently smoked "daily" and only one-fifth (about 4% of all young adults) could be described as heavy daily users (averaging two or more joints per day). This suggests that daily marijuana use is typically a phase through which people pass, after which their use becomes more moderate.

Marijuana has also been attacked as the "gateway drug" that leads people to the use of even more dangerous illegal drugs. It is true that people who have smoked marijuana are more likely that people who have not to try, use, and abuse other illicit substances. It is also true that people who have smoked tobacco or drunk alcohol are more likely than those who have not to experiment with illicit drugs and to become substance abusers. The reasons are obvious enough. Familiarity with smoking cigarettes, for instance, removes one of the major barriers to smoking marijuana, which is the experience of inhaling smoke into one's lungs. Similarly, familiarity with altering one's state of consciousness by consuming psychoactive substances such as alcohol or marijuana decreases the fear and increases the curiosity regarding other substances and "highs." But the evidence also indicates that there is nothing inevitable about the process. The great majority of people who have smoked marijuana do not become substance abusers of either legal or illegal substances. At the same time, it is certainly true that many of those who do become substance abusers after using marijuana would have become abusers even if they had never smoked a joint in their life.

DEALING WITH DRUGS' DANGERS

The dangers associated with cocaine, heroin, the hallucinogens, and other illicit substances are greater than those posed by marijuana, but not nearly so great as many people seem to think. Consider the case of cocaine. In 1986 NIDA reported that more than 20 million Americans had tried cocaine, that 12.2 million had consumed it at least once during 1985, and that nearly 5.8 million had used it within the past month. Among those between the ages of 18 and 25, 8.2 million had tried cocaine, 5.3 million had used it within the past year, 2.5 million had used it within the past month, and 250,000 had used it weekly. Extrapolation might suggest that a quarter of a million young Americans are potential problem users. But one could also conclude that only 3% of those between the ages of 18 and 25 who had ever tried the drug fell into that category, and that only 10% of those who had used cocaine monthly were at risk. (The NIDA survey did not, it should be noted, include people residing in military or student dormitories, prison inmates, or the homeless.)

All of this is not to deny that cocaine is a potentially dangerous drug, especially when it is injected, smoked in the form of crack, or consumed in tandem with other powerful substances. Clearly, tens of thousands of Americans have suffered severely from their abuse of cocaine, and a tiny fraction have died. But there is also overwhelming evidence that most users of cocaine do not get into trouble with the drug. So much of the media attention has focused on the small percentage of cocaine users who become addicted that the popular perception of how most people use cocaine has become badly distorted. In one survey of high school seniors' drug use, the researchers questioned recent cocaine users, asking whether they had ever tried to stop using cocaine and found that they couldn't. Only 3.8% responded affirmatively, in contrast to the almost 7% of marijuana smokers who said they had tried to stop and found they couldn't, and the 18% of cigarette smokers who answered similarly. Although a similar survey of adult users would probably reveal a higher proportion of cocaine addicts, evidence such as this suggests that only a small percentage of people who use cocaine end up having a problem with it. In this respect, most people differ from monkeys, who have demonstrated in experiments that they will starve themselves to death if provided with unlimited cocaine.

With respect to the hallucinogens such as LSD and psilocybic mushrooms, their potential for addiction is virtually nil. The dangers arise primarily from using them irresponsibly on individual occasions. Although many of those who have used one or another of the hallucinogens have experienced "bad trips," others have reported positive experiences, and very few have suffered any long-term harm.

Perhaps no drugs are regarded with as much horror as the opiates, and in particular heroin, which is a concentrated form of morphine. As with most drugs, heroin can be eaten, snorted, smoked, or injected. Most Americans, unfortunately, prefer injection. There is no question that heroin is potentially highly addictive, perhaps as addictive as nicotine. But despite the popular association of heroin use with the most down-and-out inhabitants of urban ghettos, heroin causes relatively little physical harm to the human body. Consumed on an occasional or regular basis under sanitary conditions, its worst side effect, apart from addiction itself, is constipation. That is one reason why many doctors in early twentieth-century America saw opiate addiction as preferable to alcoholism, and prescribed the former as treatment for the latter when abstinence did not seem a realistic option.

It is important to think about the illicit drugs in the same way we think about alcohol and tobacco. Like tobacco, many of the illicit substances are highly addictive, but can be consumed on a regular basis for decades without any demonstrable harm. Like alcohol, most of the substances can be, and are, used by most consumers in moderation, with little in the way of harmful effects; but like alcohol, they also lend themselves to abuse by a minority of users who become addicted or otherwise harm themselves or others as a consequence. And as is the case with both the legal substances, the psychoactive effects of the various illegal drugs vary greatly from one person to another. To be sure, the pharmacology of the substance is important, as is its purity and the manner in which it is consumed. But much also depends upon not only the physiology and psychology of the consumers, but also their expectations regarding the drug, their social milieu, and the broader cultural environment—what Harvard University psychiatrist Norman Zinberg has called the "set and setting" of the drug. It is factors such as these that might change dramatically, albeit in indeterminate ways, were the illicit drugs made legally available.

CAN LEGALIZATION WORK?

It is thus impossible to predict whether legalization would lead to much greater levels of drug abuse, and exact costs comparable to those of alcohol and tobacco abuse. The lessons that can be drawn from other societies are mixed. China's experience with the British opium pushers of the nineteenth century, when millions became addicted to the drug, offers one worst-case scenario. The devastation of many native American tribes by alcohol presents another. On the other hand, the legal availability of opium and cannabis in many Asian societies did not result in large addict populations until recently. Indeed, in many countries U.S.-inspired opium bans imposed during the past few decades have paradoxically contributed to dramatic increases in heroin consumption among Asian youth. Within the United States, the decriminalization of marijuana by about a dozen states during the 1970s did not lead to increases in marijuana consumption. In the Netherlands, which went even further in decriminalizing cannabis during the 1970s, consumption has actually declined significantly. The policy has succeeded, as the government intended, in making drug use boring. Finally, late nineteenth-century America was a society in which there were almost no drug laws or even drug regulations—but levels of drug use then were about what they are today. Drug abuse was considered a serious problem, but the criminal-justice system was not regarded as part of the solution.

There are, however, reasons to believe that none of the currently illicit substances would become as popular as alcohol or tobacco, even if they were legalized. Alcohol has long been the principal intoxicant in most societies, including many in which other substances have been legally available. Presumably, its diverse properties account for its popularity—it quenches thirst, goes well with food, and promotes appetite as well as sociability. The popularity of tobacco probably stems not just from its powerful addictive qualities, but from the fact that its psychoactive effects are sufficiently subtle that cigarettes can be integrated with most other human activities. The illicit substances do not share these qualities to the same extent, nor is it likely that they would acquire them if they were legalized. Moreover, none of the illicit substances can compete with alcohol's special place in American culture and history.

An additional advantage of the illicit drugs is that none of them appears to be as insidious as either alcohol or tobacco. Consumed in their more benign forms, few of the illicit substances are as damaging to the human body over the long term as alcohol and tobacco, and none is as strongly linked with violent behavior as alcohol. On the other hand, much of the damage caused today by illegal drugs stems from their consumption in particularly dangerous ways. There is good reason to doubt that many Americans would inject cocaine or heroin into their veins even if given the chance to do so legally. And just as the dramatic growth in the heroin-consuming population during the 1960s leveled off for reasons apparently having little to do with law enforcement, so we can expect a leveling-off—which may already have begun—in the number of people smoking crack. The logic of legalization thus depends upon two assumptions: that most illegal drugs are not so dangerous as is commonly believed, and that the drugs and methods of consumption that are most risky are unlikely to prove appealing to many people, precisely because they are so obviously dangerous.

Perhaps the most reassuring reason for believing that repeal of the drug-prohibition laws will not lead to tremendous increases in drug-abuse levels is the fact that we have learned something from our past experiences with alcohol and tobacco abuse. We now know, for instance, that consumption taxes are an effective method of limiting consumption rates. We also know that restrictions and bans on advertising, as well as a campaign of negative advertising, can make a difference. The same is true of other government measures, including restrictions on time and place of sale, prohibition of consumption in public places, packaging requirements, mandated adjustments in insurance policies, crackdowns on driving while under the influence, and laws holding bartenders and hosts responsible for the drinking of customers and guests. There is even some evidence that government-sponsored education programs about the dangers of cigarette smoking have deterred many children from beginning to smoke.

Clearly it is possible to avoid repeating the mistakes of the past in designing an effective plan for legalization. We know more about the illegal drugs now than we knew about alcohol when Prohibition was repealed, or about tobacco when the anti-tobacco laws were repealed by many states in the early years of this century. Moreover, we can and must avoid having effective drug-control policies undermined by powerful lobbies like those that now protect the interests of alcohol and tobacco producers. We are also in a far better position than we were 60 years ago to prevent organized criminals from finding and creating new opportunities when their most lucrative source of income dries up.

It is important to stress what legalization is not. It is not a capitulation to the drug dealers—but rather a means to put them out of business. It is not an endorsement of drug use—but rather a recognition of the rights of adult Americans to make their own choices free of the fear of criminal sanctions. It is not a repudiation of the "just say no" approach—but rather an appeal to government to provide assistance and positive inducements, not criminal penalties and more repressive measures, in support of that approach. It is not even a call for the elimination of the criminal-justice system from drug regulation—but rather a proposal for the redirection of its efforts and attention.

There is no question that legalization is a risky policy, since it may lead to an increase in the number of people who abuse drugs. But that is a risk—not a certainty. At the same time, current drug-control policies are failing, and new proposals promise only to be more costly and more repressive. We know that repealing the drug-prohibition laws would eliminate or greatly reduce many of the ills that people commonly identify as part and parcel of the "drug problem." Yet legalization is repeatedly and vociferously dismissed, without any attempt to evaluate it openly and objectively. The past 20 years have demonstrated that a drug policy shaped by exaggerated rhetoric designed to arouse fear has only led to our current disaster. Unless we are willing to honestly evaluate our options, including various legalization strategies, we will run a still greater risk: we may never find the best solution for our drug problems.

NOTES

1. The total number of state and federal prison inmates in 1975 was under 250,000; in 1980 it was 350,000; and in 1987 it was 575,000. The projected total for the year 2000 is one million.

2. It should be emphasized that the numbers cited do not include the many inmates sentenced for "drug-related" crimes such as acts of violence committed by drug dealers, typically one against another, and robberies committed to earn the money needed to pay for illegal drugs.

2

The Case Against *Legalization*

JAMES A. INCIARDI
DUANE C. McBRIDE

Ever since the passage of the Harrison Act in 1914, American drug policy has had its critics (see Lindesmith, 1965; King, 1972; Musto, 1973). The basis of the negative assessments has been the restrictive laws designed to control the possession and distribution of narcotics and other "dangerous drugs," the mechanisms of drug law enforcement and the apparent lack of success in reducing both the *supply of* and the *demand for* illicit drugs.

During 1988 concerns over the perceived failure of American drug policy spirited a national debate over whether contemporary drug control approaches ought to be abandoned, and replaced with the decriminalization, if not the outright legalization, of most or all illicit drugs. Most vocal in supporting legalization have been Ernest van den Haag (1985), professor of jurisprudence and public policy at Fordham University; Ethan A. Nadelmann (1987, 1988a, 1988b) of the Woodrow Wilson School of Public and International Affairs at Princeton University; free-market economist Milton Friedman (Friedman and Friedman, 1984); Gary S. Becker (1987), professor of economics and sociology at the University of Chicago; and freelance writer Harry Schwartz (1987).

The arguments posed by the supporters of legalization seem all too logical. *First,* they argue, the drug laws have created evils far worse than the drugs themselves—corruption, violence, street crime, and disrespect for the law. *Second,* legislation passed to control drugs has failed to reduce demand. *Third,* you cannot have illegal that which a significant segment of the population in any society is committed to doing. You simply cannot arrest, prosecute, and punish such large numbers of people, particularly in a democracy. And specifically in this behalf, in a liberal democracy, the government must not interfere with personal behavior if liberty is to be maintained. And *fourth,* they add, if marijuana, cocaine, heroin, and other drugs were legalized, a number of very positive things would happen:

(1) drug prices would fall
(2) users could obtain their drugs at low, government-regulated prices and would no longer be financially forced to engage in prostitution and street crime to support their habits
(3) the fact that the levels of drug-related crime would significantly decline would result in less crowded courts, jails, and prisons, and would free law enforcement personnel to focus their energies on the "real criminals" in society
(4) drug production, distribution, and sale would be removed from the criminal arena; no longer would it be within the province of organized crime, and therefore, such criminal syndicates as the Medellín Cartel and the Jamaican posses would be decapitalized, and the violence associated with drug distribution rivalries would be eliminated
(5) government corruption and intimidation by traffickers as well as drug-based foreign policies would be effectively reduced, if not eliminated entirely
(6) the often draconian measures undertaken by police to enforce the drug laws would be curtailed, thus restoring to the American public many of its hard-won civil liberties

To these contentions can be added the argument that legalization in any form or structure would have only a minimal impact on current drug-use levels. Apparently, there is the assumption that given the existing levels of access to most illegal drugs, current levels of use closely match demand. Thus there would be no additional health, safety, behavioral, and/or other problems accompanying legalization. And, finally, a few protagonists of legalization make one concluding point. Through government regulation of drugs, the billions of dollars spent annually on drug enforcement could be better utilized. Moreover, by taxing government-regulated drugs, revenues would be collected that could be used for preventing drug abuse and treating those harmed by drugs.

The argument for legalization seems to boil down to the basic belief that America's prohibitions against marijuana, cocaine, heroin, and other drugs impose far too large a cost in terms of tax dollars, crime, and infringements on civil rights and individual liberties. And while the overall argument may be well intended and appear quite logical, it is highly questionable in its historical, sociocultural, and empirical underpinnings and demonstrably naive in its understanding of the negative consequences of a legalized drug market.

Within the context of these opening remarks, what follows is an analysis of the content of legalization proposals combined with a discussion of the more likely consequences of such a drastic alteration in drug policy.

THE INCOMPLETE CONTENT OF
DRUG LEGALIZATION PROPOSALS

At the outset, current legalization proposals are not proposals at all! Although legalizing drugs has been debated ever since the passage of the Harrison Act in 1914, never has an advocate of the position structured a logical and concrete proposal. Any attempt to legalize drugs would be extremely complex, but proponents seem to proceed from a simplistic "shoot-from-the hip" position without first developing any sophisticated proposals. Even in 1988, amid the clamor of legalization, there was still no specific proposal on the table. And in this regard, there are many questions that would need to be addressed, including:

(1) What drugs should be legalized? Marijuana? Heroin? Cocaine? And if cocaine is designated for legalization, should proposals include such coca products as crack and other forms of freebase cocaine? Should the list include *basuco* (coca paste), that potent and highly toxic processing derivative of the coca leaf? There are other drugs to be considered as well. Which hallucinogenic drugs should be legalized? LSD? Peyote? Mescaline? What about Quaaludes? Should they be returned to the legal market? And let's not forget *ecstasy* and the various designer drugs. In short, which drugs should be legalized, according to what criteria, and who should determine the criteria?

(2) Assuming that some rationally determined state of drugs could be designated for legalization, what potency levels should be permitted? Like 80, 100, and 151 proof rum, should marijuana with 5%, 10%, and 14% THC (delta-9-tetrahydrocannabinol) content be permitted? Should legalized heroin be restricted to Burmese No. 3 grade, or should Mexican "black tar" and the mythical "China White" be added to the ledger?

(3) As with alcohol, should there be age limits as to who *can* and *cannot* use drugs? Should only those old enough to drive be permitted to buy and use drugs? And which drugs? Should it be that 16-year-olds can buy pot and Quaaludes, but have to wait until age 18 for cocaine and crack, and age 21 for heroin?

(4) Should certain drugs be limited to only those already dependent on them? In other words, should heroin sales be restricted to heroin addicts and cocaine sales limited to cocaine addicts? And if this approach is deemed viable, what do we say to the heroin addicts who want to buy

cocaine? In other words, do we legalize heroin and cocaine sales but forbid speedballing? And then, what about drug experimenters? Should they be permitted access to the legal drug market? And, assuming that these issues can be decided, *in what amounts* can users—regardless of their drugs of choice—purchase heroin, cocaine, marijuana, Quaaludes, and other chemical substances?

(5) Where should the drugs be sold? Over-the-counter in drug and grocery stores, as is the case with many pharmaceuticals? Through mail-order houses? In special vending machines strategically located in public restrooms, hotel lobbies, and train and bus stations? In tax-supported "drug shacks," as Representative Charles Rangel (*Drug Abuse Report*, May 17, 1988: 7) satirically asked? Should some, or all, of the newly legalized drugs be available only on a prescription basis? And if this be the case, should a visit to a physician be necessary to get a prescription? And for how many tabs, lines, lids, bags, rocks, joints, or whatever should prescriptions be written? How often should these prescriptions be refillable?

(6) Where should the raw material for the drugs originate? Would cultivation be restricted to U.S. land, or would foreign sources be permitted? Coca from Bolivia and Peru, or from all of South America and Java, as well? Marijuana from Colombia and Jamaica? Opium from Mexico, Laos, Thailand, or from the "Golden Crescent" countries of Iran, Afganistan, and Pakistan? Should trade restrictions of any type be imposed—by drug, amount, potency, purity, or by country? Should legalization policies permit the introduction of currently little-known drugs of abuse into the United States from foreign ports, such as *qat* from Yemen, *bekaro* from Pakistan, and *manbog* from the Southeast Asian countries?[1]

(7) If drugs are to be legalized, should the drug market be a totally free one, with private industry establishing the prices, as well as levels of purity and potency? What kinds of advertising should be permitted? Should advertisements for some drugs be allowed, but not others? Should Timothy Leary and Manuel Noriega be permitted to endorse certain drugs or brands of drugs as part of advertising programs?

(8) If drugs are to be legalized, what types of restrictions on their use should be structured? Should transportation workers, nuclear plant employees, or other categories of workers be forbidden to use them at all times, or just while they are on duty?

(9) As is the case with alcohol, will certain establishments be permitted to serve drugs (and which drugs) to their customers? And similarly, as is the case with cigarettes, should there be separate drug-using and non-drug-using sections in restaurants, or planes and trains, and in the workplace? As with coffee and cigarette breaks, should users be permitted pot and coke breaks as part of their union contracts or employer policies?

(10) For any restrictions placed on sales, potency levels, distribution, prices, quantity, and advertising in a legalized drug market, what government bureaucracy should be charged with the enforcement of the legalization statutes? The Federal Bureau of Investigation (FBI)? The Drug Enforcement Administration (DEA)? The Food and Drug Administration (FDA)? The Bureau of Alcohol, Tobacco, and Firearms (ATF)? State and local law enforcement agencies? Or should some new federal bureaucracy be created for the purpose? Going further, what kinds of penalties ought to be established for violation of the legalization restrictions?

There are likely many more questions. In short, the whole idea of even articulating a legalization policy is complex. Not only have legalization proponents failed to answer the questions, they have yet to even pose them. Moreover, anyone attempting to structure a serious proposal highlighting the beneficial expectations of a legalization policy would find little support for his or her arguments in either published research data or clinical experience. By contrast, there are numerous legitimate arguments against the legalization of drugs, all of which have considerable empirical, historical, pharmacological, and/or clinical support.

SOME PUBLIC HEALTH AND BEHAVIORAL CONSEQUENCES OF DRUG USE

Considerable evidence exists to suggest that the legalization of drugs would create behavioral and public health problems to a degree that would far outweigh the current consequences of the drug prohibition. There are some excellent reasons why marijuana, cocaine, heroin, and other drugs are now controlled, and why they ought to remain so. What follows is a brief look at a few of these drugs.

Marijuana. There is considerable misinformation about marijuana. To the millions of adolescents and young adults who were introduced to the drug during the social revolution of the 1960s and early 1970s, marijuana was a harmless herb of ecstasy. As the "new social drug" and a "natural organic product," it was deemed to be far less harmful than either alcohol or tobacco (see Smith, 1970; Grinspoon, 1971; Sloman, 1979). More recent research suggests, however, that marijuana smoking is a practice that combines the hazardous features of both tobacco and alcohol with a number of pitfalls of its own. Moreover, there are many disturbing questions about marijuana's effect on the vital systems of the body, on the brain and mind, on immunity and resistance, and on sex and reproduction (Jones and Lovinger, 1985).

One of the more serious difficulties with marijuana use relates to lung damage. The most recent findings in this behalf should put to rest the rather tiresome argument by marijuana devotees that smoking just a few "joints" daily is less harmful than regularly smoking several times as many cigarettes. Researchers at the University of California at Los Angeles reported early in 1988 that the respiratory burden in smoke particulates and absorption of carbon monoxide from smoking just one marijuana joint is some four times greater than from smoking a single tobacco cigarette (MacDonald, 1988). Specifically, it was found that one "toke" of marijuana delivers three times more tar to the mouth and lungs than one puff of a filter-tipped cigarette; that marijuana deposits four times more tar in the throat and lungs and increases carbon monoxide levels in the blood fourfold to fivefold.

There seem to be three distinct sets of facts about marijuana its apologists tend to downplay, if not totally ignore—about its chemical structure, its "persistence-of-residue" effect, and its changing potency.

First, the *cannabis sativa* plant from which marijuana comes is a complex chemical factory. Marijuana, which is made up of the dried leaves and flowering tops of the plant, contains 426 known chemicals, which are transformed into 2,000 chemicals when burned during the smoking process. Seventy of these chemicals are *cannabinoids,* substances that are found nowhere else in nature. Since they are fat-soluble, they are immediately deposited in those body tissues that have a high fat content—the brain, lungs, liver, and reproductive organs.

Second, the fact that THC (delta-9-tetrahydrocannabinol), the active ingredient and most potent psychoactive chemical in marijuana, is soluble in fat but not in water has a significant implication. The human body has a water-based waste disposal system—blood, urine, sweat, and feces. A chemical such as THC that does not dissolve in water becomes trapped, principally in the brain, lungs, liver, and reproductive organs. This is the "persistence-of-residue" effect. One puff of smoke from a marijuana cigarette delivers a significant amount of THC, half of which remains for several weeks. As such, if a person is smoking marijuana more than once a month, the residue levels of THC are not only retained but also building up—in the brain, lungs, liver, and reproductive organs.

Third, the potency of marijuana has risen dramatically over the years. During the 1960s the THC content of marijuana was only two-tenths of one percent. By the 1980s the potency of imported marijuana was up to 5%, representing a 25-fold increase. Moreover, California *sinsemilla,* a seedless, domestic variety of marijuana, has a THC potency of 14%. In fact, so potent is sinsemilla that it has become the "pot of choice" both inside and outside the United States. On the streets of Bogota, Colombia, sinsemilla is traded for cocaine on an equal weight basis (*Street Pharmacologist,* May/June 1988: 5).

Fourth, and finally, aside from the health consequences of marijuana use, recent research on the behavioral aspects of the drug suggests that it severely affects the social perceptions of heavy users. Findings from the Center for Psychological Studies in New York City, for example, indicated that adults who smoked marijuana daily believed the drug helped them to function better—improving their self-awareness and relationships with others (Hendin et al., 1987). In reality, however, marijuana had served to be a "buffer," so to speak, enabling users to tolerate problems rather than face them and make changes that might increase the quality of their social functioning and satisfaction with life. The study found that the research subjects used marijuana to avoid dealing with their difficulties, and the avoidance inevitably made their problems worse—on the job, at home, and in family and sexual relationships.

This research documented what clinicians had been saying for years. Personal growth evolves from learning to cope with stress, anxiety, frustration, and the many other difficulties that life presents, both small and large. Marijuana use (and the use of other drugs as well, including alcohol), particularly among adolescents and young adults, interferes with this process, and the result is a drug-induced arrested development (see DuPont, 1984).

Cocaine. Lured by the Lorelei of orgasmic pleasure, millions of Americans use cocaine each year—a snort in each nostril and the user is up and away for 20 minutes or so. Alert, witty, and with it, the user has no hangover, no lung cancer, and no holes in the arms or burned-out cells in the brain. The cocaine high is an immediate, intensively vivid, and sensation-enhancing experience. Moreover, it has the reputation for being a spectacular aphrodisiac: It is believed to create sexual desire, to heighten it, to increase sexual endurance, and to cure frigidity and impotence.

Given all these positives, it is no wonder that cocaine has become an "all-American drug" and a multibillion-dollar-a-year industry. It permeates all levels of society, from Park Avenue to the ghetto: Lawyers and executives use cocaine; baby boomers and yuppies use cocaine; college students and high school drop-outs use cocaine; police officers, prosecutors, and prisoners use cocaine; politicians use cocaine; housewives and pensioners use cocaine; Democrats, Republicans, Independents, and Socialists use cocaine; barmaids and stockbrokers and children and athletes use cocaine; even some priests and members of Congress use cocaine.

Yet the pleasure and feelings of power that cocaine engenders make its use a rather unwise recreational pursuit. In very small and occasional doses it is no more harmful than equally moderate doses of alcohol, but there is a side to cocaine that can be very destructive. That euphoric lift, with its feelings of pleasure, confidence, and being on top of things, that comes from but a few brief snorts is short-lived and invariably followed by a letdown. More specifically, when the elation and grandiose feelings begin to wane, a corresponding deep depression is often felt, which is in such marked contrast to users' previous states that they are strongly motivated to repeat the dose and restore the euphoria. This leads to chronic, compulsive use. And when chronic users try to stop using cocaine, they are typically plunged into a severe depression from which only more cocaine can arouse them. Most clinicians estimate that approximately 10% of those who begin to use cocaine "recreationally" will go on to serious, heavy, chronic, compulsive use (Grabowski, 1984; Kozel and Adams, 1985; Erickson et al., 1987; Spitz et al., 1987). To this can be added what is known as the "cocaine psychosis" (Weiss and Mirin, 1987: 50-53). As dose and duration of cocaine use increase, the development of cocaine-related psychopathology is not uncommon. Cocaine psychosis is generally preceded by a transitional period characterized by increased suspiciousness, compulsive behavior, fault finding, and eventually paranoia. When the psychotic state is reached, individuals may experience visual and/or auditory hallucinations, with persecutory voices commonly heard. Many believe that they are being followed by police, or that family, friends, and others are plotting against them. Moreover, everyday events tend to be misinterpreted in ways that support delusional beliefs. When coupled with the irritability and hyperactivity that the stimulant nature of cocaine tends to generate in almost all of its users, the cocaine-induced paranoia may lead to violent behavior as a means of "self-defense" against imagined persecutors.

Not to be forgotten are the physiological consequences of cocaine use. Since the drug is an extremely potent central nervous system stimulant, its physical effects include increased temperature, heart rate, and blood pressure. In addition to the many thousands of cocaine-related hospital emergency visits that occur each year, there has been a steady increase in the annual number of cocaine-induced deaths in the United States, from only 53 in 1976 to almost 1,000 a decade later. And while these numbers may seem infinitesimal when compared with the magnitude of alcohol- and tobacco-related deaths, it should be remembered that at present only a small segment of the American population uses cocaine.

Crack. Given the considerable media attention that crack has received since the summer of 1986, it would appear that only a minimal description of the drug is warranted here. Briefly, *crack*-cocaine is likely best described as a "fast-food" variety of cocaine. It is a pebble-sized crystalline form of cocaine base, and has become extremely popular because it is inexpensive and easy to produce. Moreover, since crack is smoked rather than snorted, it is more rapidly absorbed than cocaine—reportedly crossing the blood-brain barrier within six seconds (Inciardi, 1987a)—creating an almost instantaneous high.

Crack's low price (as little as $3 per rock in some locales) has made it an attractive drug of abuse for those with limited funds, particularly adolescents. Its rapid absorption initiates a faster onset of dependence than is typical with cocaine, resulting in higher rates of addiction, binge use, and psychoses. The consequences include higher levels of cocaine-related violence and all the same manifestations of personal, familial, and occupational neglect that are associated with other forms of drug dependence.[2]

Heroin. A derivative of morphine, heroin is a highly addictive narcotic, and the drug historically most associated with both addiction and street crime. Although heroin overdose is not uncommon, unlike alcohol, cocaine, tobacco, and many prescription drugs, the direct physiological damage caused by heroin use tends to be minimal. And it is for this reason that the protagonists of drug legalization include heroin in their arguments. By making heroin readily available to users, they argue, many problems could be sharply reduced if not totally eliminated, including the crime associated with supporting a heroin habit; the overdoses resulting from problematic levels of heroin purity and potency; the HIV (human immunodeficiency virus) and hepatitis infections brought about by needle-sharing; and the personal, social, and occupational dislocations resulting from the drug-induced criminal life-style.[3]

The belief that the legalization of heroin would eliminate crime, overdose, infections, and life dislocations is for the most part delusional, for it is likely that the heroin use life-style would change little for most American addicts, regardless of the legal status of the drug. And there is ample evidence to support this argument—in the biographies and autobiographies of narcotics addicts (Anonymous, 1903; Burroughs, 1953; Street, 1953; Hirsch, 1968; Fisher, 1972; Rettig et al., 1977), in the clinical and ethnographic assessments of heroin addiction (Fiddle, 1967; Gould et al., 1974; Rosenbaum, 1981), and in the treatment literature (Nyswander, 1956; Smith and Gay, 1971; Peele, 1985; Platt, 1986). And to this can be added the many thousands of conversations conducted by the authors with heroin users during the past two decades.

The point is this: Heroin is a highly addicting drug. For the addict, it becomes life consuming: It becomes mother, father, spouse, lover, counselor, confidant, and confessor. Because heroin is a short-acting drug, with its effects lasting at best four to six hours, it must be taken regularly and repeatedly. Because there is a more rapid onset when taken intravenously, most heroin users inject the drug. Because heroin has a depressant effect, a portion of the user's day is spent in a semistupefied state. Collectively, these attributes result in a user more concerned with drug-taking than health, family, work, or anything else.

As a final note to this section, and perhaps most importantly, recently completed research by professors Michael D. Newcomb and Peter M. Bentler (1988) of the University of California at Los Angeles has documented the long-term behavioral effects of drug use on teenagers. Beginning in 1976 a total of 654 Los Angeles County youths were tracked for a period of eight years. Most of these youths were only occasional users of drugs, using drugs and alcohol moderately at social gatherings, whereas upwards of 10% were frequent, committed users. The impact of drugs on these frequent users was considerable. In teenagers, drug use tended to intensify the typical adolescent problems with family and school. In addition, drugs contributed to such psychological difficulties as loneliness, bizarre and disorganized thinking, and suicidal thoughts. Moreover, frequent drug users left school earlier, started jobs earlier, and formed families earlier, and as such, they moved into adult roles with the maturity levels of adolescents. The consequences of this pattern included rapid family break-ups, job instability, serious crime, and ineffective personal relationships. In short, frequent drug use prevented the acquisition of the coping mechanisms that are part of maturing; it blocked teenagers' learning of interpersonal skills and general emotional development.

DRUGS, STREET CRIME, AND
THE ENSLAVEMENT THEORY OF ADDICTION

For the better part of the current century there has been a concerted belief in what has become known as the "enslavement theory of addiction"—the conviction that because of the high prices of heroin and cocaine on the drug black market, users are forced to commit crimes in order to support their drug habits (Inciardi, 1986: 145-173). In this regard, supporters of drug legalization argue that if the criminal penalties attached to heroin and cocaine possession and sale were removed, three things would occur: The black market would disappear, the prices of heroin and cocaine would decline significantly, and users would no longer have to engage in street crime in order to support their desired levels of drug intake. Yet there has never been any solid empirical evidence to support the contentions of this enslavement theory.

From the 1920s through the close of the 1960s, hundreds of studies of the relationship between crime and addiction were conducted.[4] Invariably, when one analysis would support enslavement theory, the next would affirm the view that addicts were criminals first, and that their drug use was but one more manifestation of their deviant lifestyles. In retrospect, the difficulty lay in the way the studies had been conducted, with biases and deficiencies in research designs that rendered their findings to be of little value.

Research since the middle of the 1970s with active drug users in the streets of New York, Miami, Baltimore, and elsewhere, on the other hand, has demonstrated that enslavement theory has little basis in reality, and that the contentions of the legalization proponents in this behalf are mistaken (Stephens and McBride, 1976; McBride and McCoy, 1982; Johnson et al., 1985; Nurco et al., 1985; Inciardi, 1986: 115-143). All of these studies of the criminal careers of heroin and other drug users have convincingly documented that while drug use tends to intensify and perpetuate criminal behavior, it usually does not initiate criminal careers. In fact, the evidence suggests that among the majority of street drug users who are involved in crime, their criminal careers were well established prior to the onset of either narcotics or cocaine use.

SOME COST/BENEFIT CONSIDERATIONS OF LEGALIZATION

An explicit, or at least considerably implicit, assumption of the legalization argument is that the purported benefits of legalization (reduced crime, corruption, criminal justice system costs, and increased tax revenues) will far outweigh any costs that may ensue (increased drug use and its consequences, if any). In particular, any increases in the use of the legalized substances will be insignificant, and thus there will be only minimal increases in the costs of health care and public safety. Given this, it would appear that the prolegalization lobby believes that since marijuana, cocaine, crack, heroin, and other illegal drugs are so widely available, to a significant extent there is market demand saturation. While hard evidence of the validity of this assumption is anything but apparent, there are a variety of historical and empirical data that seriously contradict its basic contention.

At the outset, it should be noted that national and local surveys clearly indicate that young people perceive fairly open access to most illegal substances. Consider, first, some findings from one of the more recent surveys of America's high school seniors, conducted each year by the Institute of Social Research at the University of Michigan. Among those surveyed in 1986, for example, just over 50% reported that access to cocaine was easy, with 85% suggesting the same for marijuana, and 22% reporting the same ease of access to heroin (Bachman et al., 1987). By contrast, less than one-third of the nation's high school seniors reported that it was probably impossible to obtain any of these drugs. In addition, similar perceptions of easy access to drugs have been found even among small-town and rural mid-American high school students (McBride et al., 1988). As such, the assumption of ease of access appears to have a reasonable basis in empirical data.

The more important question revolves around the assumption that legalization will have minimal impact on use, that most or all those who would use drugs are now doing so. Such an assumption appears to ignore one of the most powerful aspects of American tradition: the ability of an entrepreneurial market system to create, expand, and maintain high levels of demand.

As noted previously, specific legalization proposals do not exist at present. As such, there has never been any serious discussion of how the issues of advertising and marketing might be handled. However, if the treatment of such *legal* drugs as alcohol and tobacco are used as models of regulatory control, then it is reasonable to assume an application of free speech rights to legalized drugs. And this indeed would be logical; for after all, the drugs would be *legal* products. And similarly, it would not seem unreasonable to assume that the American market economy would become strongly involved in expanding and maintaining demand for the legalized substances. The successes of tobacco and alcohol advertising programs are eminently conspicuous. The linking of smoking with women's rights has been masterful. The linking of alcohol with the pursuit of happiness after work, in recreational activities, and in romantic liaisons has been so effective that during 1987 alone, Americans spent some $71.9 billion on beer, wine, and distilled spirits (*Drug Abuse Update*, June 1988: 5).

In an America where drugs are legal, how far will advertisers go? Will they show students, executives, and truck drivers—overworked and faced with tight schedules and deadlines—reaching for a line of cocaine instead of a cup of coffee? Will cocaine be touted as the mark of success in an achievement-oriented society? Will heroin be portrayed as the real way to relax after a harried day? Will the new "Marlboro man" be smoking marijuana or crack instead of tobacco? These are not fanciful speculations, for there are many controlled substances that are regularly advertised, even if only in the medical media. Regardless, the focus of advertising is to market a product by creating and maintaining demand.

The issue, then, of whether the market is saturated fails to recognize the ability of a free-enterprise system to expand demand. And there are epidemiological data that confirm that there is considerable room for increasing the demand for drugs. Estimates projected from the National Institute on Drug Abuse's (1986: 5) most recent household survey of drug abuse suggest that only 10% of the population ages 12 years and older are "current users" (use during the past month) of marijuana and only 3% are current users of cocaine. The survey also demonstrated, however, that the majority of adolescents and young adults are current users of the major available legal drug—alcohol—and that in all, there are no less than 60.3 million current users of cigarettes and more than 113 million users of alcohol. To assume that the legalization of drugs would maintain the current, relatively low levels of drug use when there are high rates of both alcohol and tobacco use seems rather naive. Moreover, it considerably underestimates the advertising industry's ability to create a context of use that appears integral to a meaningful, successful, liberated life.

Another point should be added here. It was noted above that there is the general "perception" that drugs are readily available. Yet perceptions are one thing. There are times when the real world is something very different. This may indeed be the case regarding cocaine. While some 50% of the students surveyed in 1986 believed that access to cocaine was easy, for example, data from the household surveys conducted by the National Institute on Drug Abuse (NIDA) provide some interesting insights. As indicated in Table 2.1, for example, *most people in the general population have never had a chance to use cocaine.* Moreover, this proportion has remained fairly stable over the seven-year period of the three NIDA surveys. What this suggests is that cocaine is not really all that available within the general population, but that if it were, usage rates would likely be much higher.

Table 2.1
Trends in Percentage of Respondents Reporting Chance to Use Cocaine
(U.S. household population, age 12 years and older)

	1979	1982	1985
No chance to use cocaine	81.1	75.5	79.4
Chance but did not use	10.1	12.6	8.8
Chance and did use cocaine	8.8	11.8	11.8

SOURCE: Rouse (1988).

If the assumption of a minimal increase in drug use as the result of legalization is not valid and there indeed occurs a significant escalation in use, then the presumed cost/benefit ratio is dramatically affected. Already the estimated health care and lost productivity costs of alcohol use alone approach $90 billion annually (*Time,* May 30, 1988: 14). How much greater will these be if the use of other toxic substances increases, particularly cocaine?

LEGALIZATION AND THE
DRUGS/VIOLENCE CONNECTION

There seem to be three models of drug-related violence—the psychopharmacologic, the economically compulsive, and the systemic (Goldstein, 1986). The *psychopharmacological model of violence* suggests that some individuals, as the result of short-term or long-term ingestion of specific substances, may become excitable, irrational, and exhibit violent behavior. The paranoia and aggression associated with the cocaine psychosis fit into the psychopharmacological model, as does most alcohol-related violence.

The *economically compulsive model of violence* holds that some drug users engage in economically oriented violent crime to support drug use. This model is illustrated in the many studies of drug use and criminal behavior that have demonstrated that while drug sales, property crimes, and prostitution are the primary economic offenses committed by users, armed robberies and muggings do indeed occur. The *systemic model of violence* maintains that violent crime is intrinsic to the very involvement with illicit substances. As such, systemic violence refers to the traditionally aggressive patterns of interaction within systems of illegal drug trafficking and distribution.

s the systemic violence associated with trafficking in crack in the
cities that has brought the most attention to drug-related violence
ecent years. Moreover, it is concerns with this same violence that
used the recent interest on the possibility of legalizing drugs.[5] And
is certainly logical to assume that if heroin, cocaine, and marijuana
were *legal* substances, systemic drug-related violence would indeed
decline significantly. But, too, there are some very troubling considerations. *First,* to achieve the desired declines in systemic violence, it
would require that crack be legalized as well. For after all, it is in
the crack distribution system that much of the drug-related violence is
occurring. *Second,* it is already clear that there is considerable psychopharmacologic violence associated with the cocaine psychosis.
Moreover, research has demonstrated that there is far more psychopharmacologic violence connected with heroin use than is generally
believed (Goldstein, 1979: 126; McBride, 1981; Inciardi, 1986: 135).
Given that drug use would certainly increase with legalization, in all
likelihood *any declines in systemic violence would be accompanied by
corresponding increases in psychopharmacologic violence.* The United
States already pays a high price for alcohol-related violence, a phenomenon well documented by recent research (Collins, 1981). Why
compound the problem with the legalization of additional violence-
producing substances?

LEGALIZATION IN THE LIGHT OF
CURRENT DRUG USE TRENDS

It would appear that agitation for such a drastic policy change as
would be involved in the legalization of drugs is in great part an outgrowth of frustration. "After having spent billions of dollars on interdiction, education, prevention, treatment, and research," many ask, "what
do we have to show for it?" *What indeed do we have to show for it?*

To many, the response being offered here might seem a bit odd, but
it would appear that, to a measurable extent, America is beginning to
show some very positive gains in its war on drugs, at least in the middle
class. Consider the data. *First,* there is the National Institute on Drug
Abuse's annual survey of high school seniors, conducted each year by
the University of Michigan.[6] As indicated in Figure 2.1, for example,
marijuana use has been on a steady decline since its peak usage levels
at the close of the 1970s.

Whereas 60.4% of high school seniors in 1979 had used marijuana
at least once in their lives, by 1988 that figure had dropped to 47.2%.

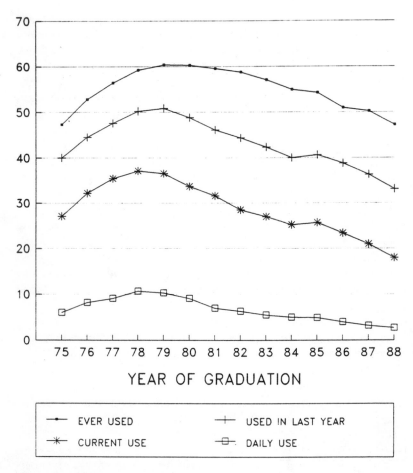

Figure 2.1. Trends in Marijuana Use

Even sharper declines are apparent with regard to use in the past year and current use (any use in the past 30 days). Perhaps the most significant drop has been in the daily use of marijuana, from a high of 10.7% in 1978 to 2.7% in 1988. Preliminary data from the 1989 survey indicated that lifetime use of marijuana had dropped to 43.7%, and current use from 18% in 1988 to 16.6% by 1989 (*Substance Abuse Report,* March 1, 1990: 1).

Second, the results of the 1987 survey also reflected the first significant drop in the use of cocaine after a decade of rising trends in use. As indicated in Figure 2.2, the survey found a decrease of about

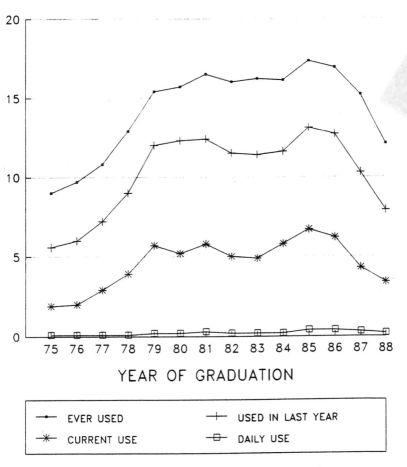

Figure 2.2. Trends in Cocaine Use

one-third—from 6.2% in 1986 to 4.3% in 1987—in the proportion of
seniors who they said were current users of cocaine, and a decline of
about one-fifth, from 12.7% to 10.3%, in seniors who had used the drug
at least once in the past year. The proportion of seniors who had "ever
used" and who used "daily" also declined. These downward trends
continued in the 1988 survey. In 1988 only 7.9% of the seniors reported
cocaine use in the last year, and only 3.4% reported current use.
Preliminary data from the 1989 survey indicated that, as in the case of
marijuana, cocaine use continued to drop, with only 2.8% reporting

current use and 10.3% reporting lifetime use (*Substance Abuse Report,* March 1, 1990: 1).

Third, while there are limited crack use data in these surveys, the 1987-1989 surveys suggest that crack use is not at all widespread in the American high school population. In 1987, for example, 5.4% of high school seniors reported having ever used crack. In 1989, this had declined to 4.7%. With respect to the use of crack in the last 30 days, less than 2% of high school seniors reported involvement (*New York Times,* February 14, 1990, p. A16).

Fourth, focusing on a different population, since 1980 the University of Michigan survey team has been collecting data on drug use among college students. As indicated in Table 2.2, the proportion of college students reporting "any use during the past year" declined since 1986 and overall. Marijuana use has been on a steady decline in this population since 1980, and cocaine use experienced a major drop in 1987 and again in 1988. Moreover, the use of most other drugs declined when comparing 1980 with 1988.

Fifth, there are other data indicative of declining drug use in the general population. NIDA's National Household Surveys on Drug Abuse tend to confirm the findings of the high school surveys. In addition, there are the worldwide surveys of American military personnel (Burt and Biegel, 1980; Bray et al., 1983; Bray et al., 1986). In 1980, 27% of all military personnel reported using an illicit drug during the past 12 months, but this dropped to 19% in the 1982 survey and to 9% by 1985.

In short, drug using behavior in the general population is changing. Just as importantly, research documents decreasing peer support for most drug use. As indicated in Table 2.3, in 1978, 43.5% of the nation's high school seniors disapproved of occasional marijuana use; by 1988 this had increased to more than 74%. Drugs such as LSD, barbiturates, and heroin had smaller but consistent increases in disapproval ratings. These data vividly demonstrate not only that peer group support can change, but also that it has—quite markedly.

LEGALIZATION AND UNDERCLASS POPULATION CONTROL

As the protagonists of legalization might wish to point out, the high school senior data and the national household survey data reflect stable populations. These data do not include dropouts, transients, the

Table 2.2
Trends in Drug Use During the Past Year Among American College Students

| | *Percentage Who Used in the Last 12 Months* | | | | | | | | |
	1980	*1982*	*1982*	*1983*	*1984*	*1985*	*1986*	*1987*	*1988*
Marijuana	51.2	51.3	44.7	45.2	40.7	41.7	40.9	37.0	34.6
Cocaine	16.9	15.9	17.2	17.2	16.4	17.3	17.1	13.7	10.0
LSD	6.1	4.6	6.3	4.2	3.7	2.2	3.9	4.0	3.6
Heroin	0.4	0.2	0.1	0.0	0.1	0.2	0.1	0.2	0.2
Other opiates	5.1	4.4	3.8	3.8	3.8	2.4	4.0	3.1	3.1
Barbiturates	2.9	2.8	3.2	2.2	1.9	1.3	2.1	1.2	1.1
Methaqualone	7.2	6.5	6.6	3.1	2.5	1.4	1.2	0.8	0.5
Tranquilizers	6.9	4.8	4.7	4.6	3.5	3.5	4.4	3.8	3.1

NOTE: For other opiates, barbiturates, methaqualone, and tranquilizers, only use that was not under a physician's orders is included here.

homeless, members of deviant subcultures living "on the street," so to speak, prison inmates, and other groups of people not readily accessible through standard survey techniques, and that it is reasonable to assume that drug use, and crack use in particular, is higher among high school dropouts in urban areas than in other segments of the population. In fact, for decades, research has been documenting that illegal drug use tends to be concentrated in America's inner cities (Faris and Dunham, 1925; Dai, 1937; Illinois Institute for Juvenile Research, 1953; Schmid, 1960; Chein et al., 1964; Inciardi, 1974; McBride and McCoy, 1981). But this is hardly a reason to legalize drugs. On the contrary, it is perhaps the primary justification for rejecting *all* legalization proposals.

A timeless feature of cities has been concentrated poverty. Concentrations of poverty appear in all metropolitan areas and are greatest in inner cities. Moreover, poverty in American cities tends to be more concentrated among the members of minority groups than among whites. As such, minority group membership and living in the ghetto tend to go hand-in-hand across the American urban landscape. Numerous explanations for this situation have been offered: that cities tend to attract the poor, many of whom cannot or will not help themselves and, therefore, create and sustain the conditions of their own degradation (Banfield, 1974); that in great part many of the poor adapt to their impoverished conditions by creating a set of attitudes and behaviors that tend to perpetuate poverty—the so-called "culture of poverty" thesis (Lewis, 1961); that the cause of poverty is not with the poor but with the systematic limitation of opportunity imposed by the wider society (Ryan, 1971); that attempts by the urban poor to improve their

Table 2.3
Trends in Proportions of High School Seniors Disapproving of Drug Use (percentages disapproving)

	Class of 1978	Class of 1979	Class of 1980	Class of 1981	Class of 1982	Class of 1983	Class of 1984	Class of 1985	Class of 1986	Class of 1987	Class of 1988
Q: Do you disapprove of people (who are 18 or older) doing each of the following?											
try marijuana once or twice	33.4	34.2	39.0	40.0	45.5	46.3	49.3	51.4	54.6	56.5	60.8
smoke marijuana occasionally	43.5	45.3	49.7	52.6	59.1	60.7	63.5	65.8	69.0	71.6	74.0
smoke marijuana regularly	67.5	69.2	74.6	77.4	80.6	82.5	84.7	85.5	86.6	89.2	89.3
try LSD once or twice	85.4	86.6	87.3	86.4	88.8	89.1	88.9	89.5	89.2	91.6	89.8
take LSD regularly	96.4	96.9	96.7	96.8	96.7	97.0	96.8	97.0	96.6	97.8	96.4
try cocaine once or twice	77.0	74.7	76.3	74.6	76.6	77.0	79.7	79.3	80.2	87.3	89.1
take cocaine regularly	91.9	90.8	91.1	90.7	91.5	93.2	94.5	93.8	94.3	96.7	96.4
try heroin once or twice	92.0	93.4	93.5	93.5	94.6	94.3	94.0	94.0	93.3	96.2	95.0
take heroin occasionally	96.4	96.8	96.7	97.2	96.9	96.9	97.1	96.8	96.6	97.9	96.9
take heroin regularly	97.8	97.9	97.6	97.8	97.5	97.7	98.0	97.6	97.6	98.1	97.2
try amphetamines once or twice	74.8	75.1	75.4	71.1	72.6	72.3	72.8	74.9	76.5	80.7	82.5
take amphetamines regularly	93.5	94.4	93.0	91.7	92.0	92.6	93.6	93.3	93.5	95.4	94.2
try barbiturates once or twice	82.4	84.0	83.9	82.4	84.4	83.1	84.1	84.9	86.8	89.6	89.4
take barbiturates regularly	94.3	95.2	95.4	94.2	94.4	95.1	95.1	95.5	94.9	96.4	95.3
try one or two drinks of an alcoholic beverage (beer, wine, liquor)	15.6	15.8	16.0	17.2	18.2	18.4	17.4	20.3	20.9	21.4	22.6
take one or two drinks nearly every day	67.7	68.3	69.0	69.1	69.9	68.9	72.9	70.9	72.8	74.2	75.0
take four of five drinks nearly every day	90.2	91.7	90.8	91.8	90.9	90.0	91.0	92.0	91.4	92.2	92.8
have five or more drinks once or twice each weekend	56.2	56.7	55.6	55.5	58.8	56.6	59.6	60.4	62.4	62.0	65.3

economic power are hindered by "ghetto colonialization"—the owner-ship of ghetto businesses by persons from outside the ghetto (Blauner, 1969; Aldrich, 1973); and that the wider society encourages the persistence of poverty because it has positive functions, providing (a) an underclass to do the "dirty work" of society, (b) a pool of low-wage laborers, (c) a place where less qualified members of the professions can practice, (d) a population that can be exploited by businesses and served by social agencies, and (e) a reference point to justify the norms and behavior patterns of the wider society (Gans, 1972). And there are other reasons for urban poverty and its persistence that have been put forth. Whatever the reasons, it seems to be generally agreed that part of the problem lies in the wider society—that the American social structure has economically disenfranchised significant portions of its urban inner cities.

Urban ghettos are not particularly pleasant places in which to live. There are vice, crime, and littered streets. There is the desolation of people separated culturally, socially, and politically from the mainstream. There are the disadvantages of a tangle of economic, family, and other problems—delinquency, teenage pregnancy, unemployment, child neglect, poor housing, substandard schools, inadequate health care, and limited opportunities. There are many modes of adaptation to ghetto life (see McCord et al., 1969). A common one is drug use, perhaps the main cause of the higher drug use rates in inner cities. And it is for this reason that the legalization of drugs would be a nightmare.

The social fabric of the ghetto is already tattered, and drugs are further shredding what is left of the fragile ghetto family. A great number of inner city families are headed by women, and for reasons that are not all that clear, women seem to be more disposed to become dependent on crack than men. In New York City since 1986, this led to a 225% increase in child neglect and abuse cases involving drugs, and a dramatic rise in the number of infants abandoned in city hospitals and those born addicted or with syphilis, as well as a surge in children beaten or killed by drug-addicted parents (*New York Times,* June 23, 1988: A1).

Within this context, the legalization of drugs would be an elitist and racist policy supporting the neocolonialist views of underclass population control. In a large sense, since legalization would increase the levels of drug dependence in the ghetto, it represents a program of social management and control that would serve to legitimate the chemical destruction of an urban generation and culture.

LEGALIZATION AND PUBLIC OPINION

A "democracy," in the most literal sense, is government by the people as a whole, rather than by any section, class, or interest group within it. And because America is a democracy, the legalization of drugs would be an inappropriate policy to implement at the present time. It may be introduced, tendered, and presented, and it may be pondered, debated, argued, and contested. But alas, in the final analysis, it must be put to pasture because the American people simply do not want it. Even the legalization or decriminalization of marijuana has only minimal support within the general population. Consider the data.

(1) In Gallup surveys conducted from 1969 through 1985, people were asked: "Do you think the use of marijuana should be made legal, or not?" The responses were as follows (*Gallup Poll,* June 20, 1985):

Legalization of Marijuana

Year of Survey	Favor	Oppose	No Opinion
1985	23%	73%	4%
1980	25%	70%	5%
1979	25%	70%	5%
1977	28%	66%	6%
1973	16%	78%	6%
1972	15%	81%	4%
1969	12%	84%	4%

(2) Surveys of college freshmen conducted each year by the American Council on Education (*San Diego Union,* April 10, 1988: C5) have found that the overwhelming majority of students are opposed to the legalization of marijuana. For example:

Proportion of College Students Opposed to the Legalization of Marijuana

Class of:	Percentage
1976	53.4
1977	51.8
1978	53.3
1979	52.8
1980	51.1
1981	47.1
1982	50.5
1983	53.9
1984	60.7
1985	66.0

Proportion of College Students Opposed
to the Legalization of Marijuana

Class of:	*Percentage*
1986	70.6
1987	74.3
1988	77.1
1989	78.2
1990	78.7
1991	80.7

(3) In an *ABC News* poll conducted in 1986,[7] respondents were asked about the legalization of several drugs. The responses were as follows:

	Favor	Oppose	No Opinion
• Do you favor or oppose legalizing the possession of small amounts of marijuana for personal use? - - - -	24%	75%	1%
• Do you favor or oppose legalizing the possession of small amounts of cocaine for personal use? - - - - - -	5%	94%	< .5%
• Do you feel that all drugs should be made legal? - - - - - - - - - - - -	4%	96%	—

(4) In a *Parents Magazine* poll conducted in 1987,[8] an even broader spectrum of questions about legalization was asked. For example:

	Yes	No	Not Sure
• Do you think prescription drugs such as Valium or amphetamines should be legally available to any adult who wants them? - - - - - - -	29%	65%	6%
• Do you think marijuana should be legally available to any adult who wants it? - - - - - - - - - - - - - - - - -	14%	81%	5%
• Do you think cocaine or crack should be legally available to any adult who wants it? - - - - - - - - -	2%	97%	1%
• Do you think other illegal drugs, such as heroin, should be legally available to any adult who wants them? - - - - - - - - - - - - - - - - - -	2%	96%	2%

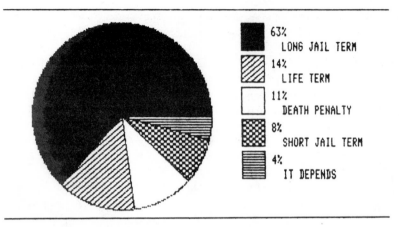

Figure 2.3. *Washington Post* Poll Responses to the Question: "Do you think that people convicted of selling cocaine should be given the death penalty, life imprisonment, a long jail term, or a short jail term?"

Most recently, the findings of a *Washington Post* (June 26, 1988: C1, C4) poll of 1,012 randomly selected adults interviewed during the period June 15-19, 1988, demonstrated that even at a time when drug-related violence was receiving the most, and highly negative, media attention, the legalization option was overwhelmingly rejected. Specifically, some 90% of those surveyed indicated opposition to legalizing drugs. Furthermore, as indicated in Figure 2.3, most supported the harsh punishment of anyone convicted of selling cocaine.

LEGALIZATION AND JOHN STUART MILL'S LIBERTY PRINCIPLES

Perhaps a useful philosophical framework for analyzing the issue of the legalization of drugs is contained in John Stuart Mill's noted essay *On Liberty*, first published in 1859. Mill, an eighteenth-century philosopher and economist, played a significant role in defining both British and American concepts of individual liberty and the proper limitation of government intrusion into individual behavioral choice (Mill, 1863, 1921).

Mill's utilitarian ideals might argue that drugs should be legalized if the benefits in doing so would outweigh the harms caused by drug use. The liberty principle implies that government has no right to interfere with adult behaviors that do not harm others. Government may educate, it may inform, and it may even cajole, he argued, but its laws must not restrict individual choice, even if the actions in question may be harmful to the individual involved. Whether implicitly or explicitly, all arguments for the legalization of drugs draw upon these principles.

In considering this framework, it should be remembered that from Mill's perspective, government can legitimately interfere with adult behavioral choice *only if* there is ample evidence of *actual* (not potential) harm to others. Even then, he added, interference must be restricted to individuals actually *doing* the harm, and not extend to those having the *potential* for doing harm. Or as Mill (1921) put it: "I deem it perfectly legitimate that a person, who had once been convicted of any act of violence to others under the influence of drink, should be placed under a special legal restriction personal to himself."

What, then, might be done with Mill's principles of utilitarianism and liberty in their implications of the legalization of drugs? Both principles underlie American beliefs in the common good and individual liberty. From the utilitarian perspective it could be argued that drugs should be legal if the benefits outweighed the costs. The perceived *benefits* of legalization include the redirection of law enforcement to "real" crime, reductions in levels of drug-related violence, street crime, and corruption, increased tax revenues, and the protection of civil liberties. The costs include the probability of increased drug use and its consequent social, physiological, psychological, and private safety costs.

Although the benefits of legalization are only *potential,* the costs are readily apparent in existing levels of illegal drug use. American society already pays a rather high tariff as a result of the public health, safety, and violence problems associated with drug use—both legal and illicit. This would necessarily increase when levels of drug consumption increase through legalization. Furthermore, and quite simply, there is no reason to believe that the real costs of legalization would outweigh the potential benefits for the public good. Existing data do not support the utilitarian benefit of legalization.

The issues raised by Mill's principle of liberty are more complex. As noted earlier, integral here is the argument that government has no right to protect citizens from their own harmful choices. To do so represents a denial of basic civil rights. Interference is justified only when behavioral choice actually—not potentially—harms others, since all human action may unintentionally harm others. In addition, Mill suggests that the government may individualize laws. That is, when certain people are found to have harmed others as the result of drug use, *then* and only then may they be denied any further use. This aspect of

Mill's perspective is apparent in the parole and probation conditions in many jurisdictions that prohibit alcohol use by persons convicted of alcohol-related violent crimes (Inciardi, 1987b: 633, 657).

Within this context, Mill's principle of liberty fails to support the legalization of drugs. The weight of evidence would seem to argue that the harm to others is *actual,* not potential. For example:

(1) *Crime.* The research discussed earlier in this essay demonstrates that there are significant psychopharmacological and behavioral relationships between cocaine use and violent behavior. These relationships transcend the situational context emerging from cocaine's illegality. The weight of evidence is that violence to others is a *general* consequence of chronic cocaine use.

(2) *Public health and safety costs.* Marijuana, cocaine, crack, and other illegal drugs have demonstrably major health consequences in and of themselves. Additional health consequences are associated with specific modes of ingestion, particularly with the use of unsterile needles, injection sites, and addict life-styles. Any policy change that increases consumption would also increase the health costs of public safety problems associated with drug use on the highway and in the workplace. Currently, American society pays a considerable health and safety price for current levels of chemical consumption. To be the victims of impaired drivers and transportation workers, or of inflated insurance and health care costs as the result of drug consumption, constitutes *actual,* rather than potential harm.

(3) *Practical considerations.* One might well argue that these contentions are mere possibilities of harm rather than inevitable, integral results of drug consumption. As such, drugs should be legal for all except those who have already caused actual harm through drug-taking. Such a view is of only idealistic merit, however, for the enforcement of individual consumption bans would present an application nightmare in densely populated and highly mobile postindustrial societies. In all likelihood, enforcement would result in exactly the violations of liberty with which Mill was most concerned.

(4) *The denial of freedom.* To a very great extent, arguments for the legalization of drugs emerge from concerns over the widespread use of drugs in the ghetto. Yet to legalize drugs and thereby make them more available would likely result in a further chemicalization of America's inner cities. As such, rather than extending legitimate economic opportunity and quality education and housing—the basic tools for the exercising of liberty—to inner city residents, the legalization of drugs would actually reduce opportunity and choice.

(5) *The will of the people.* The unfettered pursuit of chemically based happiness has never been viewed by the courts as a constitutional right. Furthermore, knowledge and experience have led the American public

to conclude that adding to the pharmacopoeia of already legal substances would not benefit society. Survey after survey shows an increasing lack of support for legalization.

DISCUSSION

As the drug legalization debate lingers on, two positions have become relatively clear. In one corner is William J. Bennett, director of the Office of National Drug Control Policy. Bennett's position in the debate is unequivocal—legalization is simply and utterly immoral, a policy option that guarantees addiction, degradation, injury, and death to millions of Americans. It would appear that both the political establishment and the majority of the general population support Bennett's view. In the opposite corner is a small group of intellectuals—academicians, civil libertarians, and free-market economists—arguing that the social costs of the war on drugs (crime, violence, and the erosion of civil liberties) are far too great in a skirmish that is being lost.

At the close of 1989 and during the months following, the debate took on a second component—a fray between public policy and academic freedom. In a speech delivered at Harvard University, Bennett challenged intellectuals to "get with the program, or at the very least, get with the game" (46 *Criminal Law Reporter* 1262 [1989]). Frustrated by the belief that most intellectuals were opposed to the effort to control illegal drugs, he urged that academicians reject the notion of legalizing drugs. He complained that the prolegalization rhetoric was a distraction from the important drug policy issues and initiatives. Not surprisingly, voices in the academic community responded, claiming that Bennett's suggestion as to what people should and should not believe was an infringement on academic freedom, and even "Stalinist" (*Chronicle of Higher Education,* January 3, 1990: A1, A18). In this respect, and aside from pros and cons of legalizing drugs, there are a few things that need to be said in defense of academics, and in defense of Bennett as well.

Two of Bennett's allegations were that most intellectuals have been against the war on drugs, and that the academic community has had little to contribute to American drug policy. Both of these points are overgeneralizations. The prolegalization group is a small but vocal minority that does not necessarily represent academia. And quite curiously, none of the "legalizers" come from the ranks of the many hundreds of social and behavioral scientists conducting drug-abuse research in colleges and universities across the nation. No one in this latter group who has access to the drug problem on a first-hand basis appears to support the legalization thesis. Many feel that legalizing drugs is far too absurd and unworkable an idea to waste precious time, energy, and resources quarreling about.

In defense of Bennett, the legalization arguments are phenomenally existential in character. They reflect a remarkable surety of belief in the elixir of legalization—that the removal of the criminal penalties attached to the possession, sale, and distribution of heroin, marijuana, cocaine, crack, and other mind-altering substances would be an effective solution to the violence, corruption, street crime, international terrorism, foreign policy dilemmas, and even tax revenue deficits attributed to the current legal controls. These wonderful claims, this marvelous existential leap, all in the absence of empirical data and sound logic, can restore one's faith in the gullibility of the ivory tower—or one of its chambers, at any rate.

Going further, the logic used by the legalizers is often both simplistic and sophist. They pose the argument, for example, that rates of injury and death from illegal drugs are relatively low when compared with those of alcohol and tobacco use, or of ladder and bicycle accidents. The "logical" deduction offered is that heroin and cocaine aren't really all that bad, and hence should be legalized. What is summarily ignored is that the death rates from alcohol and tobacco use are high because these substances are readily available and widely used, and that the death rates from heroin and cocaine use are low because these drugs are not readily available and not widely used. And indeed, illegal drugs are *not* widely used!

Another feature of the legalizers' circular thinking involves their portrayal of the drug-enforcement establishment as an ineffective, inefficient, power hungry, and sometimes corrupt bureaucracy attempting to enforce impossible laws. Yet this cynical disdain for drug enforcement is replaced with a naive faith in the effectiveness of government regulation. "Don't criminalize drugs," they argue, "legalize and regulate them." While the specifics of regulation have yet to emerge, all of the legalization proposals actually involve *increased* regulation. Yet with alcohol and tobacco, it is quite clear that regulation does not work very well. Using the alcohol analogy, the legalizers seem to be suggesting that American society's best defense against the use of cocaine and crack by youths is to distributed the drugs to those 21 years and older, but only after carefully explaining to them that they must not share their government-sanctioned and -supplied drugs with adolescents. The point is that there is a real naiveté to the belief that drug *laws* are unenforceable but drug *regulations* are not.

Shifting to an alternative segment of the debate, many drug legalization proponents seem to believe that the willingness of political conservatives and free-market economists to support their arguments somehow provides them with at least the appearance of broad-based social and even moral support. Yet the fact that a few free-market economists support legalization should be seen for the purely material, or at least intellectual, self-interest that it is. Nineteenth-century capitalists were willing to fight a war in China to keep opiates legal. From a free-market economic perspective, producing, distributing, and expanding the market for a product that is immediately consumed and readily addictive would appear to be a fantasy come true.

Under the free-market arrangement, would there be the so-called "market segmentation" practices that the alcohol and tobacco industries use for targeting their products toward blacks and other minorities in America's inner cities? Even if this were prohibited, since research has documented that illegal drug use is concentrated in the inner city, in all likelihood drug use would expand dramatically in socioeconomically marginal communities under a free-market system.

Shifting the perspective again, much is made of the wonderful Dutch model. The legalizers point to the humanity of the Dutch in making drugs available, and how this has reduced the crime problem. Again, this is wholeheartedly accepted without any focused analysis of what is going on across the Atlantic. The legalizers tend to ignore the many newspaper reports from Amsterdam describing the demonstrations by local residents who object to their society becoming an international refuge and flophouse for hard-drug users. They object to being disenfranchised from their public parks and buildings, and from their streets and neighborhoods (for example, see, Madrid *Cambio*, January 1, 1990: 140-143). And, too, the legalizers continually disregard the fact that, like American addicts, Dutch addicts also commit crimes.

And speaking of crime, the prolegalization rhetoric argues for moving from a criminal justice model to a public health model of drug control. But there are two very good reasons for retaining the criminal justice model. *First* of all, urine-surveillance studies have repeatedly documented that the majority of offenders in urban jails across the nation have illegal drugs in their systems at the time of arrest (Wish, 1990). *Second*, an even greater number of studies have demonstrated that addicts who are coerced into treatment through the criminal justice system do better than voluntary patients (see, Leukefeld and Tims, 1988). It would appear that the key factor most related to success in treatment is length of stay in treatment, and those coerced into treatment stay longer than those who are not.

As a final point here, in untangling the logic of the legalization thesis, a more focused look should be directed toward those who make up the prolegalization lobby. In all likelihood their arguments are born of frustration—frustration with the lack of immediate major successes in the prevention and control of drug use. Part of the problem is reflected in the old saying about a little bit of knowledge being dangerous. As academics, economists, and civil libertarians from *outside* of the drug field, their experience has yet to expose them to the full dynamics of addiction, drug craving, and drug-taking and drug-seeking behaviors. It should be noticed as well that those who have spent their lives and careers in the trenches, researching the drug problem, treating the drug problem, or otherwise coping with the drug problem, feel that legalization would initiate a public health problem of unrestrained proportions.

The other part of the problem is cultural. This is a society that seeks and expects immediate and effective solutions. But drug abuse is an intractable problem that simply will not yield to good intentions and cultural success desires.

POSTSCRIPT

If not legalization in the light of a problematic "war" on drugs, what then?

It is eminently sensible to strengthen the supply-side programs aimed at keeping heroin, cocaine, marijuana, and other illegal drugs out of the country. However, the emphasis of federal policy has been a bit lopsided. Between 1981 and the passage of the Anti-Drug Abuse Act of 1986, federal funding for drug treatment was cut by 40% (Inciardi, 1988). The results included sharp reductions in the available number of treatment slots, overcrowded treatment centers, and the turning away of tens of thousands of drug abusers seeking help. Then, of the $1.7 billion authorized by the 1986 legislation, almost 80% was earmarked for enforcement efforts. Moreover, much of the $363 million Congress targeted for state education and treatment programs became bogged down by the red tape of an entrenched bureaucratic process.

The difficulty lies in the fact that allocating resources for warring on drugs is always more of a political rather than a commonsense process. Arrests and seizures are easy to count, making for attractive press releases and useful political fodder. And in recent years the figures were indeed dramatic. Reporting on the number of persons in treatment is far less impressive to a constituency. But the tragedy of it all is that the waiting time for treatment entry in some cities is up to a year.

In the final analysis, drug abuse is a complicated and intractable problem that cannot be solved with quick-fix approaches tended to by politically appointed boards. Deploying more patrol boats in the Caribbean or diverting additional high-technology military hardware will not guarantee an end to or even a slowing of the war. Intercepting drugs at the borders or cutting off illegal drugs at their sources are praiseworthy goals, but they are likely impossible ones. And pressuring source countries into compliance with U.S. objectives is also an elusive task, even when there is willingness.

Thus, if total elimination of the supply of drugs is impossible, then more attention must be focused on the demand side of the equation. For after all, without drug users there would be no drug problem. The weapons here are treatment and education, initiatives that seem to be both working and failing—working for some but failing for others.

On the treatment side, many drug users seeking help are unable to find it, for, as noted earlier, treatment resources fail to match the demand. This problem is easily solved by a financial restructuring of the war on drugs. For the many thousands of users in need of help but unwilling to enter treatment programs, compulsory treatment may be in order.

On the education side, it is already clear that American youths are beginning to turn away from drugs. Moreover, surveys by the University of Michigan's Institute for Social Research suggest that this trend will continue. But all of these positive indicators relate only to mainstream American teenagers. Crack-cocaine is now tragically abundant in inner-city neighborhoods throughout the country. The antidrug messages from government, schools, parent groups, sports figures, and the entertainment media are either not reaching, or have little meaning to, ghetto youth. Like the situation with treatment, the bottom line involves a restructuring of ideas, resources, and goals.

NOTES

1. *Qat* (also known as khat, chat, jimma, and mirra) is the evergreen shrub *Catha edulis,* the leaves and buds of which are either chewed or brewed into a beverage. Qat engenders stimulant effects similar to, but milder than, those of the amphetamines, and psychic dependence has been known to develop. *Bekaro*, the seeds of the Tula tree (*Pterygota alata*), is well known in many parts of India and Pakistan as an effective opiate substitute. *Mambog,* a thick syrup made from the tropical Asian shrub *Mitragyna*

speciosa, is a hallucinogenic drug with stimulant effects similar to cocaine. (See Emboden, 1979; Weir, 1985.)

2. For example, see *New York Times,* March 7, 1987: 29, 32; *New York Times,* June 23, 1988: A1, B4.

3. This point of view is most thoroughly articulated in Trebach (1982).

4. For bibliographies and analyses of the literature on drugs and crime, see Austin and Lettieri (1976) and Greenberg and Adler (1974).

5. See, Wilmington (Delaware) *News-Journal,* April 3, 1988: E2; *Drug Abuse Report,* April 6, 1988: 7-8; *USA Today,* May 18, 1988: 10A; *Time,* May 20, 1988: 12-19; *Newsweek,* May 30, 1988: 36-38; *New York Times,* June 2, 1988: A26; *Fortune,* June 20, 1988: 39-41.

6. These surveys have been conducted since 1976, and the data reported here have been drawn from three sources: Johnston et al. (1986), Bachman et al. (1987), and a University of Michigan News and Information Services release (January 12, 1988).

7. National telephone survey of 2,326 persons ages 16 and over, August 14-26, 1986. Data provided by Roper Center, Storrs, Connecticut, June 15, 1988.

8. National telephone survey of 1,003 adults conducted for *Parents Magazine* by Kane, Parsons & Associates, May 2-20, 1987. Data provided by Roper Center, June 26, 1988.

REFERENCES

Aldrich, H. E. (1973, May). Employment opportunities for blacks in the black ghetto: The role of white-owned business. *American Journal of Sociology, 78:* 1403-1425.

Anonymous (1903). *Twenty years in hell, or the life, experience, trials, and tribulations of a morphine fiend.* Kansas City, MO: Author's Edition.

Austin, G. A., & Lettieri, D. J. (1976). *Drugs and crime: The relationship of drug use and concomitant criminal behavior.* Rockville, MD: National Institute on Drug Abuse.

Bachman, J. G., Johnston, L. D., & O'Malley, P. M. (1987). *Monitoring the future: Questionnaire responses from the nation's high school seniors.* Ann Arbor: University of Michigan, Institute for Social Research.

Banfield, E. C. (1974). *The unheavenly city revisited.* Boston: Little, Brown.

Becker, G. S. (1987, August 17). Should drug use be legalized? *Business Week:* 22.

Blauner, R. (1969, Spring). Internal colonization and ghetto revolt. *Social Problems:* 393-408.

Bray, R. M., Guess, L. L., Mason, R. E., Hubbard, R. L., Smith, D. G., Marsden, M. E., & Rachel, J. V. (1983). *Highlights of the 1982 worldwide survey of alcohol and nonmedical drug use among military personnel.* Research Triangle, NC: Research Triangle Institute.

Bray, R. M., Guess, L. L., Mason, R. E., Hubbard, R. L., Smith, D. G., Marsden, M. E., & Rachel, J. V. (1986). *Highlights of the 1985 worldwide survey of alcohol and nonmedical drug use among military personnel.* Research Triangle, NC: Research Triangle Institute.

Burroughs, W. (1953). *Junkie.* New York: Ace.

Burt, M. R., & Biegel, M. M. (1980). *Worldwide survey of nonmedical drug use and alcohol use among military personnel: 1980.* Bethesda, MD: Burt Associates.

Chein, I., Gerard, D. L., Lee, R. S., & Rosenfeld, E. (1964). *The road to H: Narcotics, delinquency, and social policy.* New York: Basic Books.

Collins, J. J. (Ed.). (1981). *Drinking and crime: Perspectives on the relationships between alcohol consumption and criminal behavior.* New York: Guilford.

Dai, B. (1937). *Opium addiction in Chicago.* Shanghai: Commercial.

DuPont, R. L. (1984). *Getting tough on gateway drugs.* Washington, DC: American Psychiatric Press.

Emboden, W. (1979). *Narcotic plants.* New York: Macmillan.

Erickson, P., Adlaf, E. M., Murray, G. F., & Smart, R. G. (1987). *The steel drug: Cocaine in perspective.* Lexington, MA: Lexington Books.

Faris, R. E. L., & Dunham, H. W. (1925). *Mental disorders in urban areas.* Chicago: University of Chicago Press.

Fiddle, S. (1967). *Portraits from a shooting gallery.* New York: Harper & Row.

Fisher, F. (1972). *The lonely trip back.* New York: Bantam.

Friedman, M., & Friedman, R. (1984). *Tyranny of the status quo.* San Diego: Harcourt Brace Jovanovich.

Gans, H. J. (1972, September). The positive functions of poverty. *American Journal of Sociology, 78:* 275-289.

Goldstein, P. J. (1979). *Prostitution and drugs.* Lexington, MA: Lexington Books.

Goldstein, P. J. (1986, June). Homicide related to drug traffic. *Bulletin of the New York Academy of Medicine, 62:* 509-516.

Gould, L., Walker, A. L., Crane, L. E., & Litz, C. W. (1974). *Connections: Notes from the heroin world.* New Haven: Yale University Press.

Grabowski, J. (Ed.). (1984). *Cocaine: Pharmacology, effects, and treatment of abuse.* Rockville, MD: National Institute on Drug Abuse.

Greenberg, S. W., & Adler, F. (1974). Crime and addiction: An empirical analysis of the literature, 1920-1973. *Contemporary Drug Problems, 3:* 221-270.

Grinspoon, L. (1971). *Marijuana reconsidered.* Cambridge: Harvard University Press.

Hendin, H., Haas, A. P., Singer, P., Ellner, M., & Ullman, R. (1987). *Living high: Daily marijuana use among adults.* New York: Human Sciences Press.

Hirsch, P. (1968). *Hooked.* New York: Pyramid.

Illinois Institute for Juvenile Research and the Chicago Area Project. (1953). *Report of the Chicago narcotics survey.* Unpublished manuscript.

Inciardi, J. A. (1974). The vilification of euphoria: Some perspectives on an elusive issue. *Addictive Diseases: An International Journal, 1:* 241-267.

Inciardi, J. A. (1979, July). Heroin use and street crime. *Crime and Delinquency:* 335-346.

Inciardi, J. A. (1986). *The war on drugs: Heroin, cocaine, crime, and public policy.* Palo Alto, CA: Mayfield.

Inciardi, J. A. (1987a, Fall). Beyond cocaine: Basuco, crack, and other coca products. *Contemporary Drug Problems, 14:* 461-492.

Inciardi, J. A. (1987b). *Criminal justice.* San Diego: Harcourt Brace Jovanovich.

Inciardi, J. A. (1988, February). Revitalizing the war on drugs. *The World & I, 3:* 132-139.

Johnston, B. D., Goldstein, P. J., Preble, E., Schmeidler, J., Lipton, D. S., Spunt, B., & Miller, T. (1985). *Taking care of business: The economics of crime by heroin users.* Lexington, MA: Lexington Books.

Johnson, L. D., O'Malley, P. M., & Bachman, J. G. (1986). *Drug use among American high school students, college students, and other young adults, national trends through 1985.* Rockville, MD: National Institute on Drug Abuse.

Jones, H. C., & Lovinger, P. W. (1985). *The marijuana question.* New York: Dodd, Mead.

King, R. (1972). *The drug hang-up: America's fifty-year folly.* New York: W. W. Norton.

Kozel, N. J., & Adams, E. H. (Eds.). (1985). *Cocaine use in America: Epidemiologic and clinical perspectives.* Rockville, MD: National Institute on Drug Abuse.

Leukefeld, C. G., & Tims, F. M. (Eds.). (1988). *Compulsory treatment of drug abuse: Research and clinical practice*. Rockville, MD: National Institute on Drug Abuse.

Lewis, O. (1961). *The children of sanchez*. New York: Random House.

Lindesmith, A. R. (1965). *The addict and the law*. Bloomington: Indiana University Press.

MacDonald, D. I. (1988, June 17). Marijuana smoking worse for the lungs. *Journal of the American Medical Association, 259:* 3384.

McBride, D. C. (1981). Drugs and violence. In J. A. Inciardi (Ed.) *The drugs-crime connection* (pp. 105-123). Beverly Hills, CA: Sage.

McBride, D. C., & McCoy, C. B. (1981, August). Crime and drug-using behavior: An areal analysis. *Criminology: An Interdisciplinary Journal, 19:* 281-302.

McBride, D. C., & McCoy, C. B. (1982, Spring). Crime and drugs: The issues and the literature. *Journal of Drug Issues:* 137-152.

McBride, D. C., Mutch, P., & Julian, A. (1988). *Substance use and abuse prevalence survey of high school students in south western Michigan: A report to the state of Michigan Human Resources Commission*. Berrien Springs, MI: Andrews University.

McCord, W., Howard, J., Friedberg, B., & Harwood, E. (Eds.). (1969). *Life styles in the black ghetto*. New York: W. W. Norton.

Mill, J. S. (1863). Utilitarianism. *Frazer's Magazine*. London: Parker, Son & Bourn.

Mill, J. S. (1921). *On liberty*. Boston: Atlantic Monthly Press.

Musto, D. F. (1973). *The American disease: Origins of narcotic control*. New Haven: Yale University Press.

Nadelmann, E. A. (1987, June 2-3). *The real international drug problem*. Presented at the Defense Academic Research Support Conference, "International Drugs: Threat and Response," National Defense College, Defense Intelligence Analysis Center, Washington, DC.

Nadelmann, E. A. (1988a, Spring). U.S. drug policy: A bad export. *Foreign Policy, 70:* 83-108.

Nadelmann, E. A. (1988b, Summer). The case for legalization. *Public Interest, 92:* 3-31.

National Institute on Drug Abuse. (1986, October 26). Overview of the 1985 household survey on drug abuse. *NIDA Capsules:* 5.

Newcomb, M. D., & Bentler, P. M. (1988). *Consequences of adolescent drug use: Impact on the lives of young adults*. Newbury Park, CA: Sage.

Nurco, D. N., Ball, J. C., Shaffer, J. W., & Hanlon, T. F. (1985). The criminality of narcotic addicts. *Journal of Nervous and Mental Disease, 173:* 94-102.

Nyswander, M. (1956). *The drug addict as patient*. New York: Grune & Stratton.

Peele, S. (1985). *The meaning of addiction*. Lexington, MA: Lexington Books.

Platt, J. J. (1986). *Heroin addiction*. Malabar, FL: Robert E. Keieger.

Rettig, R. P., Torres, M. J., & Garrett, G. R. (1977). *Manny: A criminal addict's story*. Boston: Houghton Mifflin.

Rosenbaum, M. (1981). *Women on heroin*. New Brunswick, NJ: Rutgers University Press.

Ryan, W. (1971). *Blaming the victim*. New York: Vintage.

Schmid, C. F. (1960, October). Urban crime areas: Part II. *American Sociology Review:* 655-678.

Schwartz, H. (1987, October 12). We can't win the war, let's made drugs legal. *USA Today:* 12A.

Sloman, L. (1979). *Reefer madness: The history of marijuana in America*. Indianapolis: Bobbs-Merrill.

Smith, D. E. (Ed.). (1970). *The new social drug: Cultural, medical, and legal perspectives on marijuana*. Englewood Cliffs, NJ: Prentice-Hall.

Smith, D. E., & Gay, G. R. (Eds.). (1971). *It's so good, don't even try it once.* Englewood Cliffs, NJ: Prentice-Hall.

Spitz, H. I., & Rosecan, J. S. (1987). *Cocaine abuse: New directions in treatment and research.* New York: Brunner/Mazel.

Stephens, R. C., & McBride, D. C. (1976). Becoming a street addict. *Human Organization, 35:* 87-93.

Street, L. (1953). *I was a drug addict.* New York: Random House.

Trebach, A. S. (1982). *The heroin solution.* New Haven: Yale University Press.

van den Haag, E. (1985, August 8). Legalize those drugs we can't control. *New York Times:* 22.

Weir, S. (1985). *Quat in Yemen: Consumption and social change.* London: British Museum Publications.

Weiss, R. D., & Mirin, S. M. (1987). *Cocaine.* Washington, DC: American Psychiatric Press.

Wish, E. D. (1990). U.S. drug policy in the 1990's: Insights from new data from arrestees. *International Journal of the Addictions.*

3

A Model Legalization Proposal

RICHARD B. KAREL

INTRODUCTION

During an April 1988 meeting of the U.S. Conference of Mayors, Baltimore Mayor Kurt L. Schmoke called for a national debate on the issue of drug legalization. Since that time, the debate has grown in fury, generating much heat, and occasionally some light.

Although many of the critiques of legalization have been couched in highly emotional terms, one valid critique that withstands scrutiny has been that legalization proposals have lacked concrete and specific recommendations. The following chapter is in response to this criticism. It does not attempt to deal with a variety of social and ethical issues, in the belief that such issues are worthy of separate consideration and could not be adequately discussed in a paper of such pragmatic orientation. Because the subject of marijuana legalization is not dealt with below, it is worth mentioning that any move toward decriminalization, legalization, and regulation of the currently illicit narcotics will certainly be foreshadowed by a shift in that direction regarding marijuana. Unlike the other substances discussed below, I believe that marijuana could be regulated in a fashion similar to alcohol. As will become clear, this is not necessarily the model I embrace regarding regulation of other drugs.

Coca, Cocaine, and Crack

It is crucial to distinguish between coca, cocaine, and crack. The differences in toxicity and abuse potential of these different but related substances are extremely significant. Coca, in the form of leaves or simple extracts of leaves, has far more in common with coffee than it does with granular cocaine (Bedford et al., 1982). There is a long history of use of coca and coca-containing beverages without concurrent social problems. It is fair to say that the habit-forming potential of coca is similar to that of coffee and tea (Brecher, 1972). Even daily use of what we would consider extraordinarily large quantities of leaves by South American Indians is not correlated with social dysfunction or ill health (Von Glascoe et al., 1977).

Drug researchers have drawn sharp distinctions between the effects of crack, cocaine, and coca (Kolata, 1988). The euphoria induced by crack, and by intranasal use of cocaine, they explain, stems from the abnormal stimulation of a pleasure center in the base of the brain. The sense of euphoria, however, depends not only on blood levels of cocaine, but on the rate at which blood levels rise. Hence, the faster the increase, the greater the euphoria. Dr. Herbert Kleber of Yale, an expert in the field, and currently Deputy Director of the Office of National Drug Control Policy, observed that the slow absorption of cocaine as occurs through the Indian habit of leaf-chewing would create high blood levels but no euphoria. "It would have an effect like caffeine," Kleber said (Kolata, 1989).

It would not be unreasonable to allow simple coca tea to be sold as tea is now sold in a supermarket. The effects and risks are comparable. Extracts containing more than a designated amount of leaves might be regulated like alcoholic beverages. It would also make sense to allow limited cultivation of coca for personal use.

In addition to the original Coca Cola, the rather colorful history of coca records use of a beverage called Vin Mariani's Coca Wine. It contained two ounces of fresh coca leaves to a pint of Bordeaux (Gomez et al., 1984, p. 59). Testimonials for the wine were recorded from then-President of the United States William McKinley, patriotic composer John Phillip Sousa, inventor Thomas Alva Edison, and Pope Leo XIII (Gomez et al., 1984).[1] Despite the widespread use of coca-containing beverages, there is little evidence that social or medical problems ensued (Brecher, 1972).

The jump from coca to cocaine, and from cocaine to crack is a difference in kind, not merely in potency. Although crack appears to be far more addicting and dangerous than granular cocaine, the latter is highly addicting to a small but significant number of cocaine users. Accordingly, legal regulations must reflect the medical and social problems associated with use. Crack seems to pose unreasonable risks, and therefore, at this juncture, appears an unlikely candidate for even carefully controlled legalization. If, after legalization of coca and granular cocaine, a substantial black market in crack persists, with all the attendant ills, than it will be time to look at providing orderly access to smokable cocaine. Initially, however, it is worthwhile to see what occurs following legalization of the other forms of the drug without significantly altering the legal status of crack.

The question arises, then, of what to do with crack addicts who prefer smoking to any other route of administration. There is no easy answer. While researchers feel that addiction to the crack form of cocaine is the hardest to kick, some have recently expressed optimism that it can be treated if environmental factors are given emphasis (Kolata, 1989). It may be plausible to provide a less dangerous form of cocaine to the crack addict. The availability of other forms of cocaine, and other legal drugs, would act to minimize a black market in crack even if that form of the drug remained illegal. It would not eliminate the medical complications of habitual crack use, if it persisted, but would be likely to eliminate the violence associated with an illicit and highly profitable cocaine market. There are no panaceas, only hard choices.

Cocaine, although problematic, has a lower addiction potential than crack (Kolata, 1988). Making granular cocaine available in unrestricted quantities to the general public as a recreational drug may be unnecessary and unwise. It could, however, be made available to the public in the form of a chewing gum similar to that now used to treat nicotine addiction. The nicotine gum has proved effective in assisting more smokers to quit, although a certain percentage become addicted to the gum (Drug Abuse Research, 1987). A cocaine gum is a reasonable option. Some years back Dr. Andrew Weil of Harvard suggested consideration of a coca chewing gum (Weil, 1977).

In order to minimize the excessive use of the gum, and in order to send a signal that restraint must be exercised, a restricted distribution system would be employed for this form of the drug. The gum would be available in packages of 20, each piece containing a small amount— perhaps 10 to 20 milligrams—of pharmaceutical cocaine (Siegel, 1989, pp. 178-179, 300-301). It would be almost impossible to overdose from this form of the drug, and intake would be limited by the physical limitations inherent in mastication. To further regulate use, however, an automatic teller machine (ATM) bank card, would be used, limiting purchase to one package every 48 to 72 hours. If a purchase was attempted more frequently, the card would indicate that not enough time had elapsed, and sale withheld. Undoubtedly, people would sometimes circumvent the system by having friends purchase gum for them. This would certainly be better than forcing users to become involved with a criminal subculture, however.

This system might be used to permit distribution of granular cocaine in one-gram quantities. Initially, however, it would be worthwhile to see if a slightly more restrictive approach to the granular form of the substance, as described below, would be effective in both eliminating the black market and curtailing the entry of new users into the marketplace.

In either case, a pharmacist would do the actual dispensing. The card would simply be an electronic time log. Further compliance with the system could be ensured by requiring presentation of corroborating photo identification at time of purchase. The system would only monitor most recent purchase, and not invade privacy by keeping a long-term log.

The treatment of the addicted user, either of crack or granular cocaine, presents other problems. Addicts could be supplied with the cocaine gum under a clinical distribution system separate from regular pharmacies, or through prescription. Physicians operating through the clinical distribution system would be permitted to use other approaches as they deemed fit. This could include prescription of other forms of cocaine or treatment with other drugs, such as antidepressants (Gawin and Kleber, 1984).

Legal sanctions would not be used to force abstinence upon addicts, except in cases where they have committed crimes that render them subject to special restrictions. Protestations to the contrary (see Inciardi and McBride, 1989, pp. 282-283), this follows Mill's principle of individual liberty, i.e., that government may educate and inform the citizen, but must not restrict individual choice, even if the behavior in question might prove harmful to the individual. Government, wrote Mill, may only interfere with adult behavior if there is strong evidence of actual, not potential, harm to others, and even then such interference must be limited to those actually doing the harm and should not be so broad as to include those who might render harm. It would be acceptable, for example, to impose special legal restraints on an habitual drunkard who had behaved violently or irresponsibly while under the influence of alcohol (Mill, 1921). In fact, such restraints are currently used with the otherwise legal drug alcohol, whereby probationers and other individuals may be prohibited from consuming alcohol as a condition of probation or parole. The notion of mandatory treatment for mere drug use would, in general, become an anachronism. Exceptions, noted below, would include mandatory treatment for possession of still prohibited narcotics or forms of narcotics.

Administration of cocaine to addicts through a clinical system would undermine any remaining black market and keep the addict in touch with an environment where his addiction was treated as a medical problem and not a crime. By keeping the distribution network within a medical framework, it would place a check on the social legitimization of cocaine. An analogy might be drawn with the current distribution of methadone. Placed within a medical framework, this has not resulted in a general social-recreational legitimization of either that drug or other, related narcotics, such as heroin (Brecher, 1972).

Clearly, approaches to treatment of addicts presenting themselves to the clinical distribution centers would have to evolve as experience was gained. Treatment of cocaine and other stimulant addiction is a complex and challenging sociomedical problem. Stricter legal sanctions do little to address the treatment issue, and have been counterproductive in reducing the availability of cocaine (NNICC, 1989). Those behaving in a violent or antisocial manner under the influence of cocaine or any substance would be subject to appropriate legal sanctions. Such behavior, and any underlying psychological problems, would, in a postlegalization world, be dealt with on its own merit.

The criteria, then, for the regulation of cocaine, are both medical and economic. Resources saved on incarceration and arrest procedures would be applied to setting up and administering distribution and treatment facilities. The economic incentive for a black market would be minimized by a system such as that described.

Based on the available evidence, provision of coca and cocaine gum would not create serious social and medical problems. Use of the substances in this form, particularly the milder coca, might be beneficial to many people in the same way that various forms of caffeine are now. The manner in which the substances would be taxed, and how revenues might be allocated, will be discussed in a later section.

Opium and Opiates

In addressing the problem of opiate use and addiction, a number of criteria are pertinent. These are related to medical effects and the form in which an opiate is consumed.

In the hysteria over illicit drug use, a remarkable medical fact about opiates—all opiates, including heroin—has been overlooked. This is that opiate use and even addiction, isolated from problems caused by illegality and improper use of hypodermic needles, is medically quite innocuous. The primary medical problem attributable to long-term opiate addiction is chronic constipation (Brecher, 1972; Ray, 1972). Even this effect can be mitigated through intelligent measures. Once the medically innocuous nature of opiates is understood, it becomes clear that the most serious problems now associated with their use are caused by the circumstances surrounding their illegality (Brecher, 1972; Nadelmann, 1988).

Although legislators and others debating the issue of drug use and abuse in America may find it remarkable, it was a widespread practice in the United States in the late nineteenth and early twentieth centuries for physicians to prescribe opiates as a substitute for alcohol use by alcoholics. The medical reasoning was and remains quite sound. It has been well documented in a study published in 1969 on narcotics addicts in Kentucky (O'Donnell, 1969). The medical reasoning was that opiate addiction would arrest the cellular degeneration associated with alcoholism. The social rationale was that opiate addicts generally made far better citizens than alcoholics, being far less likely to engage in violent or antisocial behavior (Brecher, 1972; Siegel, 1986).

Before further explicating my regulatory suggestions, it is worthwhile to briefly discuss how U.S. drug policy has led to progressively more dangerous forms of opiate use.

There is no debate that opium and its derivatives are addicting. There is widespread evidence that such addiction is not incompatible with a productive existence, although the conventional wisdom denies the probability. In fact, the attempt to uniformly proscribe all opiate use, prohibiting opium equally with heroin, has led to the common form of opiate use we see today—intravenous heroin. In the illicit drug market, there is a premium on simplifying the smuggling process by increasing potency and thereby reducing bulk (Boaz, 1988).

In the Consumers Union book *Licit and Illicit Drugs,* there is an illustrative discussion of the effect of banning opium smoking in the United States between 1875 and 1914. Opium smoking is something of a misnomer, since the traditional method actually involves inhalation of vapor. There is no inhalation of tars and other carcinogens, such as occurs with the smoking of tobacco or marijuana. In addition, the naturally occurring drug opium contains a relatively small amount of morphine and other psychoactive agents. The development of tolerance and addiction through opium smoking takes far longer than with other forms of opiate use. Intake is also far easier to stabilize, and far less likely to lead to acute overdose (Brecher, 1972).

The effective banning of opium smoking was successful in causing people to adopt more hazardous forms of opiate use. Generally, the smokers first used legally available morphine, and, when later legislation made morphine unavailable, switched to heroin. Today, heroin is the universally available street opiate (Brecher, 1972). More recently, the pattern has been repeated in countries such as Iran and Pakistan, where pressure to limit the availability of opium has resulted in an explosion of heroin use, which was previously far less prevalent (White, 1985).

Opium is addictive, and there is legitimate social interest in discouraging addiction of any kind. In view of the far more innocuous nature of opium as compared to alcohol, heroin, and other frequently used sedative and narcotic drugs, however, it would make sense to make a smokable and edible form of opium available through use of the ATM card system suggested above for cocaine chewing gum. This would convey societal concern and encourage restraint. It would not appear advisable to make opium widely available in the form of laudanum, as that preparation traditionally contained a substantial amount of alcohol in which the substance was dissolved. As with marijuana and coca, cultivation of the opium poppy for personal use would be permitted, as would limited purchase of the opium-containing poppy heads (known as "poppy straw") through the ATM card system.

As with granular cocaine, the application of the ATM card system for distribution of the more potent opiates, including heroin, would be considered only if the more restrictive clinical/prescription system resulted in the perpetuation of an unacceptably large black market. The initial approach would be more conservative, limiting dispensing of the more potent opiates to the clinical/prescription system.

The heroin addict should be provided with heroin, methadone, or other narcotics, and encouraged, but not forced, to abstain. Clearly sterile syringes and pharmaceutically pure and measured drugs would have a salutary effect on most addicts. The use of a clinical distribution and treatment system, such as that discussed for cocaine users, would be implemented. The psychological problems inherent in cocaine addiction are not symptomatic of opiate addiction. A legal opiate-addict population would not be subject to the medical and psychological problems that make dealing with compulsive stimulant users so problematic.

In all cases, publicly available drugs would be taxed and revenues turned to administer and expand drug treatment and distribution centers and drug education programs. In those cases where there is interest in the legitimate medical and psychological applications of specific drugs, tax revenues could be applied to research on those applications. Some examples might be further investigation of the use of cannabis in reducing chemotherapeutically induced nausea, or examination of the applications of psychedelics in psychotherapeutic and creative situations.

Provision of drugs to addicts would be based on ability to pay—an addict would never have to steal or sell drugs to pay for an addiction that is a medical-psychological problem.

PCP

PCP is a drug that appears to have great potential for abuse with serious antisocial consequences. Reports of violence precipitated by use of the drug, particularly in combination with alcohol and other drugs, suggest that PCP is a substance that may, in some individuals, be impossible to use safely even on an occasional basis. Anecdotal evidence, which may not be entirely reliable, indicates that use can precipitate psychosis, bizarre behavior, and, as noted, violence. PCP seems to be the illicit drug version of our worst nightmares. It would remain illegal for human use, although the outlawing of the drug as a veterinary anesthetic might be reevaluated.

A lesson is suggested from the epidemic of PCP (and crack) use in some urban areas. It is that uniform proscription of both extremely dangerous and much less dangerous psychoactive drugs may lead to disregard of legitimate warnings about drug use, and muddle the distinction between more and less harmful illicit drugs and more and less harmful modes of consumption. When marijuana is equated with PCP, the unfortunate end result appears to be a tendency to disregard the very real distinctions in the potential dangers of the two substances.

It is probable that some black market in PCP or pharmacologically similar substances will remain. With law enforcement resources freed from the pursuit of many other categories of drug offenders, however, it would be possible to focus on enforcement of PCP (and crack) prohibition. In addition, the economic incentive for a PCP black market would be greatly reduced if users knew they could obtain other potent substances cheaply and legally.

Psychedelics

The term psychedelics is used in reference to certain drugs that profoundly alter perception without causing tranquilization. It does not include PCP or pharmacologically similar substances. In an earlier paper, I used the term "hallucinogens," but altered this after it was pointed out that this term is often loosely used to group substances such as PCP with pharmacologically dissimilar substances such as LSD.

Psychedelics, including the naturally occurring plant drugs such a psilocybin and peyote, as well as synthetics such as LSD and MDMA (ecstasy), would be regulated quite differently from all other drug categories (Riedlinger, 1986).

Because these drugs have positive potential when properly used, but are dangerous to a very small percentage of psychologically unstable individuals, the legal provision of such drugs would be conditioned on demonstration of knowledge as to their effects (Krippner, 1985; Kurland, 1985; Yensen, 1985; Wolfson, 1986). This could involve completion of a written examination, screening test, and interview. Cultivation of psilocybin, peyote cacti, or other psychedelic plants for personal use would be permitted.

This category of drugs is not currently a source of much social discord in the United States or elsewhere. It is unfortunate, however, that sweeping prohibitions on legal use have driven such drugs underground and gainsaid their use by individuals willing to undergo appropriate preparation.

What is worse, of course, is that the user of purported psychedelics may be exposed to dangerous chemicals either deliberately or accidentally substituted for another drug. There is considerable evidence that this occurs repeatedly in the street sale of supposed psilocybin (Furst, 1986).

Prior to the LSD hysteria of the late 1960s and early 1970s research with great potential on the applications of that drug was being conducted by a large number of individuals. It is a tragedy of drug policy that the irresponsible behavior of a few prominent individuals led to the curtailment of potentially valuable medical and psychological research.

Prescription Drugs

The authority of physicians to prescribe drugs as they see fit would be restored. This does not mean that clear-cut instances of excessive prescribing to unknown patients would be tolerated. It does mean, however, that a physician would be able to prescribe various psychoactive drugs based on his judgment and the needs of his patients. This would necessitate a doctor-patient relationship. While it is not desirable to have physicians prescribing to patients they do not know, it is equally undesirable to have drug enforcement authorities setting up arbitrary restrictions, which preclude medical personnel from prescribing drugs to patients on a regular basis within the context of a medical relationship, simply because it might constitute maintenance of addiction.

The elimination of maintenance prescribing was the final result of judicial interpretations of the Harrison Narcotics Act, which many contend was originally conceived as a regulatory and tax measure, rather than a prohibitive fiat (Musto, 1987).

Repeal or reinterpretation of the Harrison Act would allow physicians to once again treat alcoholism through opiate substitution and to undercut the growth of a black market in other kinds of prescription drugs. It would do away with the necessity for subterfuge on the part of both physician and patient, and put the patient into a context where he could openly discuss with his physician the effects of specific drugs and how negative consequences of use might be mitigated.

Availability

In discussing regulation and distribution of narcotics, the implicit assumption was that these substances be made legal only for adults with the restrictions noted. The definition of adult might vary from state to state and for different substances. Previously, before the federal government pushed the states to make 21 the mandatory drinking age nationwide by threatening to withhold highway funds to those not in compliance, the District of Columbia made 18 the legal age for beer and wine and 21 the legal age for hard liquor. Drugs would not be made available to children. Age limitations could be either 18 or 21, depending on both the specific substance and the judgment of the individual states.

One of the most important reasons to consider legalization is the effect it would have in eliminating the association between drugs and an underground, criminal subculture. Currently, youngsters who seek out illicit drugs are often exposed to people who are criminals in other ways than just their possession or sale of prohibited substances. Critics of legalization are probably correct in assuming that it would be impossible to keep drugs, whether legal or illegal, completely out of the hands of children. The elimination of the profit motive, however, would reduce the incentive to deliberately employ children in the drug trade or otherwise entice them into contact with drugs.

Opponents of legalization have argued that prohibition works to the extent that it reduces accessibility, and that legalization, by increasing accessibility, would ipso facto lead to increased use. At least as regards marijuana, however, there is serious cause to question this reasoning. Recent survey data indicate that although 85% or more of high school seniors reported that marijuana has remained readily available in the past decade, daily use in 1988 had declined to the lowest level in more than a decade. Hence, availability does not appear to have been a significant factor in declining use (Reuter, 1987; National High School Senior Survey, 1989).

Most psychotropic drugs, then, would be made available to anyone who wants them, with certain restrictions, as noted above. Addicts would be handled somewhat differently, and the widespread availability of treatment slots, funded by newly available drug revenues, would replace the long waiting lines that now characterize our rather feeble efforts to assist those crying out for help. The answer as to whom drugs would be made available, like any carefully considered response to a complex problem, is complex.

Production

One of the benefits of legalization would be the opportunity to legitimize commerce in the raw materials and drug products of the current drug-producing countries, whether in South America, Southeast Asia, or elsewhere. With the exception of the United States, which is a major producer of high-quality marijuana, most of the countries currently involved in illicit drug production are poor. While the people of these countries have experienced substantial benefits from the illicit international drug market, the influx of narco-dollars has resulted in severe economic distortion, undermining of governmental authority, and an inability to rationally implement economic reforms.

Because a legally produced product would be subject to strict standards of purity and cleanliness, there would be some advantages to purchasing raw materials, such as coca and opium from foreign sources, while producing refined products in the United States. In fact, this is precisely what occurs now with the small legal production of medical cocaine and opiates in the United States and European countries. Another advantage of domestic production would be the provision of employment at various skill levels here. The establishment of cannabis, opium, and coca as domestic cash crops might eliminate the need for costly farm subsidies, while providing employment for farmers, unskilled laborers, pharmacists, chemists, and retailers. Conversely, the lower cost of labor in the major producing countries might dictate a heavy reliance on imports.

The latter would provide major economic benefits to the South American and other producing countries. There would be little incentive to continue illicit cocaine production since it would no longer be an irrationally valuable commodity. Similar effects would occur in relationship to the international opium market. This would virtually eliminate the corruption and violence now associated with the highly profitable black market. One is hard-pressed to recall an instance where the highly profitable commerce in coffee resulted in violence or corruption.

The United States currently produces a tremendous amount of high-quality marijuana, and, according to the DEA, will probably be the largest producer of that substance by the 1990s (Kupfer, 1988). Therefore, the crop would be both a domestic boon to American farmers and a cash export crop that could redress, to some extent, our international trade imbalance.

Distribution

The question as to precisely where and how drugs would be made available is not insignificant. Although a partial answer was provided earlier, further elaboration may be useful.

The response must be framed in terms of both providing drugs to the public and dealing with the specific problems of addicts or heavy users.

As noted, the government would act as a regulator, not a provider of drugs. There is no reason that legitimate pharmaceutical companies should be denied the opportunity to make a reasonable profit from drugs. In the case of coca tea and beverages, other marketing entities beside pharmaceutical houses would undoubtedly be involved. Marijuana would be sold as a regulated commodity, combining some of the regulatory constraints now applied to the marketing and distribution of both tobacco and alcohol, as well as additional restrictions on advertising. Experience indicates that the market would find a reasonable price level once the costs of illegality were not a factor.

Cocaine chewing gum, and smoking and edible opium, would be available through existing pharmaceutical outlets. It would be relatively easy for such outlets to acquire the equipment to monitor the ATM card system described earlier.

Provision of other forms of cocaine or opiates to addicts or heavy users would occur through combination clinic/distribution centers similar to current methadone centers and also through authorized individual physicians. The current methadone clinics could actually be incorporated into the new system in modified form.

Physicians could apply for a special narcotics-distribution license, which would be provided subject to certain criteria. These criteria would include establishing a regular physician-client relationship with all patients receiving narcotics and a pledge to periodically review the patients' patterns of drug use and suggest health options. While care must be taken that this oversight authority does not become a means of circumventing legalization, as many suggest happened with the Harrison Narcotics Act of 1914 (Musto, 1987), it would serve as a check on physicians becoming prescription writers without actively monitoring the health of their patients. Oversight authority might reside in a radically revamped and legally constrained DEA.

Coca-containing beverages and coca tea would be treated as foodstuffs unless the preparation contained an extract exceeding a designated percentage of coca. Simple coca tea and low-concentration beverages would be distributed as are coffee, tea, and colas now. The more potent beverages, including coca wine, would be distributed through liquor stores or other places selling alcohol, and regulated similarly. The determination as to what percentage coca extract would fall under alcohol-type regulation could be determined by toxicologists as the final step prior to legalization.

Cannabis, whether as marijuana or hashish, could be distributed through tobacconists or similar shops devoted exclusively to cannabis distribution. Sale of cannabis through liquor outlets would not be permitted in order to encourage a distinction between the two. While this may appear trivial to some, both the danger of additive effects from combining cannabis and alcohol, and the fact that cannabis used alone is considerably less dangerous than alcohol used alone, mandate maintaining a separation.

Due to the unique nature of the psychedelics and the necessity for the screening and testing process described above, it would make sense to establish dispensaries in which a user might also remain to ingest the substance if he so desired. Whether this would be cost-effective would have to be examined. The idea is for a comfortable but prosaic setting in which those unfamiliar with the psychological effects of a given drug would have access to knowledgeable, trained facilitators. The dispensaries would also serve as the screening and testing centers for those wishing to legally obtain psychedelics.

Regulation of Purity and Content

The question of how and by whom psychoactive drugs, both in plant form and other forms, would be regulated for purity and content is an important issue. It makes sense to examine existing mechanisms with an eye to adapting them to regulation of the psychoactive drug market.

Currently, the U.S. Department of Agriculture (USDA) and the Bureau of Alcohol, Tobacco and Firearms (BATF) share responsibility for regulating aspects of the commerce in alcohol and tobacco.

These existing regulatory bodies could be employed for quality control of a new legally regulated drug market. USDA, for example, could be responsible for grading marijuana for quality, presence of adulterants, and pesticide residues. BATF could function, as it does now for tobacco, to see that merchants comply with interstate commerce and tax regulations applicable to the cannabis trade. The question of tar and THC content in marijuana (and hashish), if modeled on the tobacco industry, would not be problematic.

Whether cannabis would be made available in convenient, prepackaged cigarettes, which, symbolically, might be unwise, or merely retailed the way pipe tobacco is now, could be decided upon legalization. In either case, however, the retailer would be required by law to display tar and THC content on the container from which the substance was dispensed. Currently, the Federal Trade Commission (FTC), which deals with all aspects of advertising, has a voluntary agreement with tobacco manufacturers regarding display of tar and nicotine content on cigarette packages and advertisements. No cannabis product would be offered through a vending machine, even on the premises of a licensed dispensary.

Regulation of plant psychedelics, such as psilocybin mushrooms, could also be handled by the USDA. In the case of some of these naturally occurring substances, the problem of spoilage would be a factor. USDA, however, has extensive experience dealing with perishables such as milk. It would seem unnecessary to create another bureaucracy strictly for regulating the quality of naturally occurring psychoactive agents.

Regulation of raw coca and opium would also be handled by the USDA; although once the coca went into the marketplace, it would be regulated, like coffee or tea, by the Food and Drug Administration (FDA) as a foodstuff. As noted previously, more concentrated coca extract would be regulated like alcohol, in which case purity and content would fall under the jurisdiction of BATF.

Prescription drugs would be regulated as they are today, by the FDA. No changes would be necessary.

Objections to this scenario have been raised in regard to the difficulty of having the FDA involved for substances that could prove carcinogenic. This objection may not be applicable, however, since the smokable plant substances would fall under USDA regulation. As evidence regarding the specific health effects of different drugs accumulates, this could be incorporated into a warning label on the various products as occurs now with tobacco. Efforts to employ such labels on alcoholic beverages recently came to fruition.

Use of Tax Revenues

As noted above, a large part of tax revenues from drugs available to the public would be channeled toward drug distribution and treatment centers for addicts. The system would be self-financing, with revenues being used to cover administrative overhead. Addicts would be provided drugs based on their ability to pay. They would never be forced to resort to crime to support a habit.

The creation of innovative training programs, the provision of therapy, and the harnessing of manpower, from among those undergoing clinical treatment, to rebuild and renovate housing in economically depressed areas would be integral parts of the legalization program. The determination of a fair rate of taxation would rely on Grinspoon's concept of a harmfulness tax (Grinspoon, 1988), as well as historical experience with alcohol, tobacco, coffee, and tea. It is crucial, however, to keep the rate low enough so as not to create strong incentives for a black market. Taxes must be economically viable.

Advertising and Public Consumption

Advertising, other than basic telephone business listings, and point-of-sale information-only bulletins for cannabis, tobacco, and alcohol, would be prohibited. Opiates, cocaine in any form other than coca, and the entire panoply of drugs, including psychedelics, would be handled much as Class Five or "ledger narcotics" are now, i.e., the consumer would have to learn, through the appropriate governmental authority, or, more likely, word-of-mouth, where the substances are dispensed and could then inquire by telephone or at the location. As discussed above, coca and coca-containing beverages, except when combined with alcohol or containing a high concentration of coca extract, could be marketed and advertised like coffee and tea.

Public consumption should generally be prohibited, and violation of this prohibition should be punishable by a fine similar to a parking ticket. Intravenous drug use and use of crack or PCP in public would be punishable by overnight incarceration similar to that sometimes employed for public drunkenness.

Legalization as a Public Safety Issue

The question as to whether drug use, even if legal, should be proscribed for employees in certain occupations is one of the most difficult and challenging issues in the debate on regulatory reform. Marijuana is of particular interest here, since traces may sometimes be identified for weeks following use. The difficulty is determining the meaning of such residuals.

There is one study suggesting that use of marijuana may cause impairment in piloting ability for up to 24 hours following use. Although there has not been replication of the study, the findings deserve scrutiny because they indicated some degree of impairment even when the pilots no longer perceived themselves as impaired (Yesavage et al., 1985).

The study has been criticized for inadequate methodology in structuring of controls. The implications of this criticism are significant and suggest that caution must be exercised in making far-ranging policy decisions prior to accumulation of ample, replicable data (Morgan, 1987).[2] It is clear that the mere existence of traces of cannabinoids in the body days or weeks after use does not indicate impairment. It is important that individuals entrusted with the public safety be unimpaired. This need must be balanced against the constitutional protection provided by the Fourth Amendment. All drug testing is intrusive, and the most effective testing related to current impairment, through blood sampling, is most intrusive.

Also problematic is the fallibility of even sophisticated testing techniques (Bearman, 1988). While there is no resolution to the constitutional issue raised by testing, and while there is currently no way to correlate traces of cannabinoids with impairment, there is a partial solution to the problem.

In lieu of random drug testing among public safety officials and operators of common carriers, random psychomotor testing could be performed. This would directly measure the variables involved in safe operation of vehicles and equipment. Where there appears to be impairment, blood samples might then be taken. This would avoid interference in private behavior unless it had a direct impact upon on-the-job performance.

Another technological device, the interlock, could be applied to operators of common carriers. One possible version entails an electrically wired panel of lights that flash in sequence. Before the ignition will operate, the lights must be punched back in the same sequence by the prospective driver within a limited interval. The sequence would be randomly varied. If the driver took too long or punched the incorrect sequence, the vehicle would not start. Indeed, suggestions are being heard that such devices might be employed for first-time DWI (driving while intoxicated) offenders to prevent them from operating their vehicles in the future if impaired. While circumvention of systems could not be totally avoided, the implementation of laws making it a felony to tamper with an interlock, or for individuals to operate an interlock for an impaired person, would serve as a deterrent to such tampering and circumvention of intent. Unlike laws generally prohibiting use of drugs or alcohol, such a clearly public-safety-oriented law would stand a very good chance of eliciting cooperation, even from those individuals who feel that drug or alcohol use in nonhazardous circumstances is a private decision.

In the case of common carriers, it would represent an extremely modest additional expenditure to employ a safety technician responsible for monitoring interlocks to see that they were in working order and had not been tampered with. The advantage of a combination of random psychomotor testing and interlocks would be that all forms of impairment, including those caused by illness and neurological or psychiatric abnormalities, would be detected. In addition, the possibility of sophisticated drug or alcohol abusers circumventing accurate drug testing, which has already occurred, would become a non-issue. The public safety would be better addressed by this system, and the question of Fourth Amendment violations would be avoided. It would not be appropriate to subject educators, financial managers, and others not directly linked to public safety to this regimen.

It is also important to remember that some forms of substance-use do not cause impairment. The use of amphetamines to temporarily enhance alertness has been a common practice in the U.S. military and that of other nations. No one, for example, believes that a pilot is a menace following his morning cup of coffee. The use of coca tea or beverages would have to be viewed in the same light.

Medical Assessments of the Legalization Option

There is no unanimity of opinion among so-called medical and drug experts. It is not difficult to find individuals on both sides of the issues, and there are individuals in a variety of medical and health-related professions who now favor some form of drug legalization.

In the current climate it is difficult for anyone, physician or otherwise, to suggest that any drug use might be beneficial. It is relevant to recall, however, that although alcohol is one of the most damaging drugs of abuse (O'Driscoll, 1988) by any standard (tobacco causes more deaths, but less social tragedy), there are studies indicating that moderate consumption of alcoholic beverages may be beneficial (Law, 1980; Werth, 1980; Kagan et al., 1981; Marmot et al., 1981). There are probably physicians who feel that the same thing is true for moderate consumption of some other substances. There are certainly mental health professionals who feel that the use of psychedelics and related drugs has potential benefits under the right circumstances (Brecher, 1972; Krippner, 1985; Kurland, 1985; Yensen, 1985; Wolfson, 1986).

Open communication with the family physician is a good idea, and would be far more likely to occur if the paranoia induced by drug prohibition was removed. It is probable that many physicians would suggest abstinence as the ideal. It is also probable that, in an atmosphere of open communication, medical professionals would not hesitate to advise their patients on how to minimize the health risks involved in drug use. Former U.S. Surgeon General C. Everett Koop promoted the use of condoms while asserting that the unattainable ideal for safe sexual behavior was abstinence or monogamy. Due to drug prohibition, such a realistic, health-oriented approach is currently impossible with drugs.

Impact on Rates of Use and Addiction

In postulating what might happen to rates of use, addiction, and accidental drug-related deaths if drugs were legalized under the regimen explicated here, it is important to look to history both here and abroad for possible answers. Reformed drug policy in the Netherlands has resulted in decreased use of marijuana, despite its de facto legalization. Heroin use there has also declined (Ruter, 1988). Use of other opiates and cocaine has risen, although crack use is virtually nonexistent, and medical and social indices of drug use have stabilized. The Dutch system is not similar to my proposals, however, and does not provide for as much regulation or direct generation of revenues through taxation as do the proposals elaborated herein. The Dutch do tax the income produced from the sale of cannabis.

Another clue to the effects of legalization is available by looking at nineteenth-century America prior to widespread drug prohibition. In brief, all the historical evidence indicates that despite widespread and fully legal supplies of marijuana, cocaine, and opiate preparations, there were relatively few social problems associated with their use. There were medical problems and overdose deaths, but even these were minimized by the existence of orderly and pharmaceutically pure supplies of these substances. In many cases, such problems as did exist were caused by misleading labeling of patent medicines and immoderate medical use of drugs. People were often unaware of what drugs various patent medicines and remedies contained, and became addicted unwittingly. The patent medicine problem was remedied by passage of the Pure Food and Drug Act of 1906, but drug prohibition and its

concomitant social problems did not begin until 1914, with passage of
the Harrison Narcotics Act (Brecher, 1972).

An extremely important study, which is rarely cited in the current
debate, was published in December 1967 in the *American Journal of
Public Health*. Titled "Epidemiology of Cirrhosis of the Liver: National
Mortality Data," it provides compelling evidence that, while the United
States was experiencing a combination of public health benefits and
social discord under Prohibition, the British were able to gain all of the
public health benefits without recourse to prohibition (Terris, 1967).
Not only did the British exceed the Americans in reduction of cirrhosis
of the liver linked to alcohol consumption, they also succeeded in
keeping the rate at a relatively low plateau. This contrasts sharply with
the American experience, where alcohol consumption rose toward pre-
Prohibition levels in the years following repeal, bringing with it a
corresponding increase in cirrhosis.

This study is crucial in responding to legitimate concerns about the
impact of liberalized narcotics laws on public health. The argument now
heard in many quarters is that the tremendous health costs of legal
alcohol provide grounds for dreading the effects of legalizing other
drugs. Nowhere do opponents stop to consider how effective the British
combination of taxation, rationing, and restricted hours were in reducing alcohol abuse without creating black markets and social disruption.
Surely those who invoke the public health success of Prohibition must,
in fairness, examine data that indicate there is an alternative to the polar
extremes of complete prohibition or laissez faire legalization.

Another recently released study also provides grounds for optimism.
The study, released in June 1988, is titled "Liver Cirrhosis Mortality in
the United States, 1971-1985" (NIAA, 1988). It indicates that across
virtually every age group (with the exception of over-75, where factors
other than alcohol use may significantly contribute to cirrhosis), cirrhosis of the liver peaked between 1973 and 1975. Per capita consumption
of hard liquor peaked at about the same time, and beer consumption a
little later. While the reason for this encouraging development is not
certain, a combination of education and the emphasis on health may
have been important factors. It suggests that our culture is able to
develop a responsible relationship with legally available psychoactive
substances over time.

Depending on the assumptions used, it would be possible to paint
either a grim or rosy postlegalization scenario. It is important to remember that the mere fact of drug use is not necessarily an evil, and an
increase in use would not necessarily be a hallmark of failure. The best
analogy would be that use of alcohol could remain stable or increase,

but we would consider it progress if alcoholism and alcohol-related traffic and other fatalities declined.

Tolerance

Tolerance has a ceiling and is not unlimited, as some have implied (Rangel, 1988). It is true, however, that a small percentage of addicts may use enormous doses of drugs. It is the failure of stabilize drug habits that causes problems with tolerance; but there is no reason to think that in an orderly system such problems could not be minimized. The history of America in the nineteenth century indicates that many addicts not faced with an illegal life-style were able to stabilize thier addiction and be productive members of society. In fact, a surprising number of eminent individuals were addicts; and there is evidence that addicted physicians were (and are) generally able to function effectively (Brecher, 1972).

The problems of tolerance and the interfacing of the addict or heavy user and the medical community has been handled in an innovative fashion in one British clinical program, where narcotics, including heroin and cocaine, are provided both to addicts and to users. The program, under the auspices of the Mersey Regional Health Authority, in Liverpool, England, is headed by Pat O'Hare and Allan Parry.

In a personal conversation with Parry in October 1988[3] he explained how the staff at the Mersey clinic deals with tolerance and the problem of patients arguing with prescribing physicians over the quantity of narcotics provided. In essence, the physician makes an initial evaluation and then provides paramedical personnel with the responsibility to interface with the user/addict population on a regular basis. The physician is spared the stress of interacting regularly with the addict/user, and the paramedical personnel, some of whom may be prior addicts or users themselves, are able to establish rapport with most of the individuals who come to the clinic for help. The Mersey clinic has been the subject of a paper in and of itself, but this example alone shows that innovative and flexible approaches to interfacing with the user/addict population are possible.

Legalization and AIDS

It seems probable that bringing the intravenous drug culture within the legal fold and providing free, sterile needles would greatly reduce the spread of AIDS. While the balance of the debate on drug regulatory reform unfolds, there should be immediate action to provide sterile needles to all intravenous drug users. It was encouraging to see New

York City embarking on a pilot needle exchange program in August 1988. Based on the Liverpool experience, however, it appears that the success of needle exchange programs in reducing HIV prevalence is closely linked to success in establishing a caring, nonthreatening context that encourages participation by the intravenous drug user (Parry and Newcombe, 1988).

Impact on Insurance and Health Care Costs

It is difficult, if not impossible, to project the impact of drug policy reform on either medical insurance or overall costs of health care. Perhaps as statistics accumulate, insurance companies would offer discounts for abstainers or moderate users as they do now for nonsmokers. Insurers in the nineteenth century did not penalize stabilized opiate addicts because they discovered they were not a costly health risk (Berridge, 1977). The same was *not* true for alcoholics.

Assuming the worst—that overall health care costs increased—there would be tremendous revenues available both from monies freed up from law enforcement and from funds produced through taxation of drugs. These funds would be earmarked for health care. Many solutions to complex problems involve trade-offs (Aldrich and Mikuriya, 1988; Church et al., 1988; Kupfer, 1988).

NOTES

1. Some of the information regarding prominent Vin Mariani users comes from a personal conversation with Paul Eddy, co-author of *The Cocaine Wars,* during the course of the Mike Cuthbert Show on WAMU Radio, Washington, D.C., on June 17, 1988.

2. I had a personal conversation with Morgan on October 21, 1988, at the International Conference on Drug Policy Reform, presented by the Drug Policy Foundation at the Hyatt Regency in Bethesda, Maryland. Morgan related that he heard Yesavage testify that his study on the carry-over effects of marijuana was highly inconclusive.

3. This information comes from a personal conversation with Allan Parry on October 21, 1988, at the International Conference on Drug Policy Reform, presented by the Drug Policy Foundation at the National Press Club, Washington, D.C. Parry is Drugs/HIV Coordinator for the Mersey Regional Health Authority in Liverpool, England.

REFERENCES

Aldrich,, M., & Mikuriya, T. (1988). Savings in California marijuana law enforcement costs attributable to the Moscone Act of 1976—a summary. *Journal of Psychoactive Drugs, 20* (1): 75-81.

Bearman, D. (1988). The medical case against drug testing. In J. Wrich (Ed.). Beyond testing: Coping with drugs at work. *Harvard Business Review, 88* (1): 126.

Bedford, J., et al. (1982). Comparative lethality of coca and cocaine. *Pharmacology, Biochemistry and Behavior, 17:* 1087-1088.

Berridge, V. (1977). Opium eating and life insurance. *British Journal of Addiction, 72:* 371-377.

Berridge, V., & Edwards, G. (1981). *Opium and the people: Opiate use in nineteenth-century England.* London: Allen Lane.

Boaz, D. (1988, October). The corner drugstore. In America after prohibition. *Reason.*

Brecher, E. M. (1972). *Licit and illicit drugs: The Consumers Union report on narcotics, stimulants, depressants, inhalants, hallucinogens and marijuana—including caffeine, nicotine, and alcohol.* Boston: Little, Brown.

Church, G. et al. (1988, May 30). Thinking the unthinkable. *Time, 131* (22): 14-15.

DeRopp, R. S. (1957). *Drugs and the mind.* New York: St. Martin's Press.

Drug Abuse and Drug Abuse Research. (1987). *The second triennial report to Congress from the Secretary, Department of Health and Human Services* (DHHS Publication No. ADM 87-1486). Washington, DC: Government Printing Office.

Furst, P. (1986). *Mushrooms: Psychedelic fungi.* New York: Chelsea House.

Gawin, F. H., & Kleber, H. D. (1984). Cocaine abuse treatment—open pilot trial with desipramine and lithium carbonate. *Archives of General Psychiatry, 41:* 903-909.

Gomez, L., et al. (1984, May). Cocaine: America's 100 years of euphoria and despair. *Life, 7* (5): 59

Grinspoon, L. (1988, September 29-October 2). *The harmfulness tax: A proposal for regulation and taxation of drugs.* Address to International Meeting of Antiprohibitionism, Brussels, Belgium. Manuscript provided by author.

Huxley, A. L. (1954). *The doors of perception.* New York: Harper.

Inciardi, J., & McBride, D. (1989). Legalization: A high-risk alternative in the War on Drugs. *American Behavioral Scientist, 32* (3): 259-289.

Kagan, A., et al. (1981). Alcohol and cardiovascular disease: The Hawaiian experience. *Circulation, 64* (Supp. 3): 27-31.

Kolata, G. (1988, June 25). Drug researchers try to treat a nearly unbreakable habit. *New York Times:* 1, 30.

Kolata, G. (1989, August 24). Experts finding new hope on treating crack addicts: In a shift, experts see users' environment as more vital than drug's qualities. *New York Times:* A1, B7.

Krippner, S. (1985). Psychedelic drugs and creativity. *Journal of Psychoactive Drugs, 17* (4): 235-245.

Kupfer, A. (1988, June 20). What to do about drugs. *Fortune, 117* (13): 40-41.

Kurland, A. (1985). LSD in the supportive care of the terminally ill cancer patient. *Journal of Psychoactive Drugs, 17* (4): 279-290.

Law, C. E. (1980). Yes, Virginia, drinking is good for your health. *MacLean's, 93* (6): 44.

Marmot, M. G., et al. (1981). Alcohol and mortality: A U-shaped curve. *Lancet, 1:* 580-583.

Mill, J. S. (1921). *On liberty.* Boston: Atlantic Monthly Press.

Morgan, J. (1987, February). Carry-over effects of marijuana. *American Journal of Psychiatry, 144* (2): 259-260.

Musto, D. F. (1987). *The American disease: Origins of narcotic control* (expanded edition). New York: Oxford University Press.

Nadelmann, E. A. (1988, Spring). U.S. drug policy: A bad export. *Foreign Policy, 70:* 92-95.

National High School Senior Drug Abuse Survey. (1989, February 28). Overview of national survey of drug abuse among the high school senior class of 1988. *HHS News.* U.S. Department of Health and Human Services.

National Institute on Alcohol Abuse and Alcoholism. (1988, June). *Liver cirrhosis mortality in the United States, 1971-1985.* (Surveillance Report No. 8). Public Health Service. Alcohol, Drug Abuse, and Mental Health Administration, U.S. Department of Health and Human Services, Washington, DC: Government Printing Office.

NNICC (1989, April). *The NNICC report of 1988.* National Narcotics Intelligence Consumers Committee, pp. 31-32.

O'Donnell, J. A. (1969). *Narcotics addicts in Kentucky.* (U.S. Public Health Service Publication No. 1881). Chevy Chase, MD: National Institute of Mental Health.

O'Driscoll, P. (1988, May 17). Smoking war blows up into drug battle. *USA Today:* 2A.

Parry, A., & Newcombe, R. (1988, October 22). *Preventing the spread of HIV infection among and from injecting drug users in the UK: An Overview with specific reference to the Mersey Regional Strategy.* Paper presented at International Conference on Drug Policy Reform. Bethesda, MD: Drug Policy Foundation.

Rangel, C. B. (1988a, May 17). Legalize drugs? Not on your life. *New York Times:* Op. Ed.

Rangel, C. B. (1988b, May 18). A lot of questions must be answered. *USA Today:* Guest columnist.

Ray, O. (1972). *Drugs, society and human behavior.* St. Louis: C. V. Mosby Company.

Reuter, P. (1987, Spring). Coda: What impasse? A skeptical view. *Nova Law Review, 11* (3): 1027.

Reuter, P. (1988, Summer). Can the borders be sealed? *The Public Interest, 92:* 51-65.

Riedlinger, J. (1986). The scheduling of MDMA: A pharmacist's perspective. *Journal of Psychoactive Drugs, 17* (3): 167-171.

Ruter, F. (1988, May 25). *The pragmatic Dutch approach to drug control—does it work?* Presentation to the Drug Policy Foundation, Washington, DC.

Siegel, R. K. (1978, March). Cocaine hallucinations. *American Journal of Psychiatry, 135* (3): 309-314.

Siegel, R. K. (1989). *Intoxication: Life in pursuit of artificial paradise.* New York: E. P. Dutton.

Siegel, S. (1986). Alcohol and opiate dependency: Re-evaluation of the Victorian perspective. *Research Advances in Alcohol and Drug Problems, 9:* 279-314.

Terris, M. (1967, December). Epidemiology of cirrhosis of the liver: National mortality data. *American Journal of Public Health, 57* (12): 2076-2088.

Von Glascoe, C., et al. (1977). Are you going to learn to chew coca like us? *Journal of Psychoactive Drugs, 9* (1): 209-219.

Weil, A. (1977). Why coca leaf should be available as a recreational drug. *Journal of Psychoactive Drugs, 9* (1): 75-78.

Weil, A. (1986). *The natural mind: An investigation of drugs and the higher consciousness.* Boston: Houghton-Mifflin.

Werth, J. A. (1980). A little wine for the heart's sake. *Lancet, 2:* 1141.

White, P. (1985, February). The poppy. *National Geographic:* 169.

Wisotsky, S. (1987, Spring). Introduction: In search of a breakthrough in the war on drugs. *Nova Law Review, 11* (3): 892.

Wolfson, P. (1986). Meetings at the edge with Adam: A man for all seasons? *Journal of Psychoactive Drugs, 18* (4): 329-333.

Yensen, R. (1985). LSD and psychotherapy. *Journal of Psychoactive Drugs, 17* (4): 267-277.

Yesavage, J. A., et al (1985). Carry-over effects of marijuana intoxication on aircraft pilot performance: A preliminary report. *American Journal of Psychiatry, 142* (11): 1325-1329.

4

Beyond the War on Drugs

STEVEN WISOTSKY

The world we have made as a result of the level of thinking we have done
thus far creates problems we cannot solve at the same level at which we
created them.

—Albert Einstein

This chapter proposes to answer three basic questions. What is the
state of the war on drugs? How did we get there? Where should we go
from here?

The current war on drugs began on October 2, 1982, with a radio
address by President Reagan to the nation: "The mood towards drugs is
changing in this country and the momentum is with us. We are making
no excuses for drugs—hard, soft, or otherwise. Drugs are bad and we
are going after them."[1] Twelve days later, in a speech delivered at the
Department of Justice, the President followed with an "unshakable"
commitment "to do what is necessary to end the drug menace" and "to
cripple the power of the mob in America."[2] He cited the "unqualified
success" of the Miami Task Force on Crime and Drugs as a model to
build on.[3]

It is important to note that President Reagan was not the first to
declare war on drugs. President Nixon had done the same in 1971. In a
message to Congress he had described drug abuse as a "national emergency," denounced drugs as "public enemy number one," and called for
a "total offensive."[4]

First drug war or not, President Reagan's statement about the mood
of the country seemed accurate. At the time of his October 1982
speeches, some 3,000 parents groups had already organized nationwide
under the umbrella of the National Federation of Parents for Drug Free
Youth.[5] Within the government, the House Select Committee[6] and the

Attorney General's Task Force on Violent Crime had urged the President to declare war on drugs.[7]

The President's October 14 speech called for and got more of nearly everything: (1) more personnel—1,020 law enforcement agents for the Drug Enforcement Agency (DEA), Federal Bureau of Investigation (FBI), and other agencies, 200 Assistant U.S. Attorneys, and 340 clerical staff; (2) more aggressive law enforcement—creating 12 (later 13) regional prosecutorial task forces across the nation "to identify, investigate, and prosecute members of high-level drug trafficking enterprises, and to destroy the operations of those organizations"; (3) more money—$127.5 million in additional funding and a substantial reallocation of the existing budget from prevention, treatment, and research programs to law enforcement programs; (4) more prison bed space—the addition of 1,260 beds at 11 federal prisons to accommodate the increase in drug offenders to be incarcerated; (5) more stringent laws—a "legislative offensive designed to win approval of reforms" with respect to bail, sentencing, criminal forfeiture, and the exclusionary rule; (6) better interagency coordination—bringing together all federal law enforcement agencies in "a comprehensive attack on drug trafficking and organized crime" under a Cabinet-level committee chaired by the attorney general; and (7) improved federal-state coordination, including federal training of state agents.[8] Energized by the hardening attitude toward illegal drugs, the Administration acted aggressively, mobilizing an impressive array of federal bureaucracies and resources in a coordinated, although largely futile, attack on the supply of illegal drugs—principally cocaine, marijuana, and heroin. The Administration hired hundreds of drug agents and cut through bureaucratic rivalries with greater vigor than any Administration before it. It acted to streamline operations and compel more cooperation among enforcement agencies. It placed the FBI in charge of DEA and gave it major drug enforcement responsibility for the first time in its history. And, as the centerpiece of its prosecutorial strategy, it fielded a network of Organized Crime Drug Enforcement Task Forces in 13 "core" cities across the nation.[9]

To stop drugs from entering the country, the Administration attempted to erect a contemporary antidrug version of the Maginot Line: the National Narcotics Border Interdiction System (NNBIS), an intelligence network designed to coordinate radar surveillance and interdiction efforts along the entire 96,000-mile border of the United States.[10] As part of the initiative, NNBIS floated radar balloons in the skies over Miami, the Florida Keys, and even the Bahamas to protect the nation's perimeter against drug-smuggling incursions.

The CIA joined the war effort by supplying intelligence about foreign drug sources, and NASA assisted with satellite-based surveillance of coca and marijuana crops under cultivation.[11] The Administration also initiated financial investigations, aided by computerized data banks and staffed by Treasury agents specially trained to trace money-laundering operations. The State Department pressured foreign governments to eradicate illegal coca and marijuana plants and financed pilot programs to provide peasant farmers with alternative cash crops.[12] It also negotiated Mutual Assistance Treaties to expose "dirty" money secreted in tax haven nations and to extradite defendants accused of drug conspiracies against the laws of the United States.[13]

The government also literally militarized what had previously been only a rhetorical war, deploying the armed forces of the United States to "assist" drug enforcement operations.[14] The Department of Defense provided pursuit planes, helicopters, and other equipment to federal civilian enforcement agencies, while Navy E-2C "Hawkeye" radar planes patrolled the coastal skies in search of smuggling aircraft and ships.[15] The Coast Guard, receiving new cutters and more personnel, intensified its customary task of interdicting drug-carrying vessels at sea.[16] In 1981 amendments to the Posse Comitatus Act relaxed the century-old ban on military enforcement of criminal laws and permitted Coast Guard boarding parties to sail on naval warships serving as "platforms" for Coast Guard interdictions.[17] Finally, for the first time in American history, navy vessels, including a nuclear-powered aircraft carrier, began directly to interdict—and in one case fired upon—drug-smuggling ships in international waters.[18] On a purely technical level, the Administration could rightly claim some success in focusing the resources of the federal government in a historically large and single-minded attack on the drug supply. What were the results of this extraordinary enforcement program? It set new records in every category of measurement—drug seizures, investigations, indictments, arrests, convictions, and asset forfeitures.[19] For example, DEA, FBI, and Customs seized nearly one-half billion dollars in drug-related assets in FY 1986. DEA arrested twice as many drug offenders in 1986 (12,819) as in 1982, and the percentage of high-level traffickers among arrestees also rose from roughly one-third to one-half. DEA, FBI, and other federal agencies seized more than 100,000 lbs. of cocaine in FY 1986.[20] From the end of 1980 to June 30, 1987, the prison population (counting felonies only) soared from 329,021 to 570,519.[21] Roughly 40% of new prison inmates now go in for drug offenses. In recognition of this boom, the FY 1989 budget submission of the President sought a 48% increase for the U.S. Bureau of Prisons to accommodate an anticipated increase in prisoners from 44,000 today to 72,000 by 1995.

Despite the Administration's accumulation of impressive statistics, domestic marijuana cultivation took off and the black market in cocaine grew to record size. In 1980 the supply of cocaine to the United States was estimated at 40 metric tons; by 1986 it had risen to 140 tons. As a result of this abundant supply and a more-or-less stable pool of buyers, prices fell dramatically.[22] In 1980 a kilo of cocaine cost $50,000 to $55,000 delivered in Miami; by 1986 it had fallen to the range of $12,000 to $20,000; $14,000 was typical for much of 1988. In 1980-1981, a gram of cocaine cost $100 and averaged 12% purity at street level. By 1986 the price had fallen to as low as $80 ($50 in Miami), and the purity had risen to more than 50%.[23] Around the nation, crack was marketed in $5 and $10 vials to reach the youth and low-income markets. More than 22 million Americans report having tried cocaine; and roughly 5.8 million reported having used it during the month preceding the 1985 National Household Survey.[24] Cocaine-related hospital emergencies rose from 4,277 in 1982 to 9,946 in 1985 to more than 26,000 in 1987.[25]

As if to mock the aggressive efforts of the war on drugs, this rapid market growth occurred in the face of President Reagan's doubling and redoubling of the federal antidrug enforcement budget from $645 million in FY 1981 to more than $4 billion in FY 1987.[26] Resources specifically devoted to interdiction rose from $399 million to $1.3 billion, one-third of the current budget; and military assistance rose from $5 million to $405 million, including the provision of (the services of) Air Force AWACS and Navy E-2C radar planes; Army Black Hawk helicopters used in Customs pursuit missions; and the Customs Service's own purchases of P-3 radar planes, Citation jet interceptors, and Blue Thunder interceptor boats. DEA personnel rose from 1,940 in 1981 to 2,875 special agents in 1988, with more on request for FY 1989, along with a 47-position air wing for DEA.[27]

This budgetary expansion seems all the more remarkable when compared to the antidrug budget for FY 1969 of $73.5 million.[28] Commenting specifically upon the interdiction budget, the Office of Technology Assessment concluded:

> Despite a doubling of Federal expenditures on interdiction over the past five years, the quantity of drugs smuggled into the United States is greater than ever. . . . There is no clear correlation between the level of expenditures or effort devoted to interdiction and the long-term availability of illegally imported drugs in the domestic market.[29]

The social "return" on the extra billions spent during that time has been a drug abuse problem of historic magnitude, accompanied by a drug trafficking parasite of international dimensions.

This latter point is crucial. It is not simply that the war on drugs has failed to work; it has in many respects made things worse. It has spun a spider's web of black market pathologies, including roughly 25% of all urban homicides, widespread corruption of police and other public officials, street crime by addicts, and subversive narco-terrorist alliances between Latin American guerrillas and drug traffickers.[30] In the streets of the nation's major cities, violent gangs of young drug thugs engage in turf wars and open shoot-outs with automatic rifles.[31] Innocent bystanders are often shot. Corruption pervades local police departments and foreign governments.[32] Some Latin American and Caribbean nations have been effectively captured by drug traffickers. Where capture is incomplete, intimidation reigns: one-third of the Colombian Supreme Court was assassinated in a (suspected) narco-terrorist raid. An estimated 60 Colombian justices have been murdered in a recent five-year period.[33]

Of course, these pathologies were foreseeable. They are a function of money. Drug law yields to a higher law: the law of the marketplace, the law of supply and demand. The naive attack on the drug supply through an aggressive program of enforcement at each step—interdiction, arrest, prosecution, and punishment—results in what Stanford Law School Professor Herbert Packer has called a "crime tariff." The crime tariff is what the seller must charge the buyer to monetize the risk he takes in breaking the law, in short, a premium for taking risks. The criminal law thereby maintains hyper-inflated prices for illegal drugs in the black market.[34]

For example, an ounce of pure pharmaceutical cocaine at roughly $80, just under $3 per gram, becomes worth about $4,480 if sold in the black market at $80 per diluted gram (at 50% purity). The crime tariff is $4,400 an ounce. This type of law enforcement succeeds to some unknown extent in making drugs less available—to the extent (probably slight) that demand is elastic or sensitive to price. But because the crime tariff is paid to lawbreakers rather than the government, it pumps vast sums of money into the black market, more than $100 billion a year by government estimate.[35] The flow of these illegal billions through the underground economy finances or supplies the incentives for such pathologies as: homicides, street crime, public corruption, and international narco-terrorism. If these phenomena were properly costed out, one might well conclude that the war on drugs makes a net negative contribution to the safety, well-being, and national security interests of the American people.

Confronted by these threatening developments, both the public and the politicians predictably react in fear and anger. The specter of uncontrolled and seemingly uncontrollable drug abuse and black marketeering lead to frustrated reaction against the drug trade. The zeal to "turn the screw of the criminal machinery—detection, prosecution and punishment—tighter and tighter" leads directly to the adoption of repressive and punitive measures that aggrandize governmental powers at the expense of individual rights.

This reactive, almost reflexive growth of governmental power and the correlated squelching of personal liberty occur as two closely related, if not inseparable, phenomena: (1) the government's sustained attack, motivated by the perceived imperatives of drug enforcement, on traditional protections afforded to criminal defendants under the Bill of Rights, and (2) the gradual but perceptible rise of "Big Brotherism" against the public at large in the form of drug testing, investigative detention, eavesdropping, surveillance, monitoring, and other intrusive enforcement methods.

It may be difficult for those not familiar with criminal law and procedure to understand the degree to which the war on drugs has disempowered the criminal defendant, especially in drug cases. Perhaps by focusing on a few of the most important of the many restrictions that have been imposed, one may begin to appreciate the severity of the crackdown on the rights of those accused of crime.

First, let us consider pretrial detention. It is important to understand that in the United States the law has always favored pretrial release to reinforce the presumption of innocence and to allow a defendant to aid counsel in his defense. The Eighth Amendment to the U.S. Constitution prohibits excessive bail; and while the cases do not establish a "right" to bail, the law has evolved as if there were a presumptive right to pretrial release on bail (or other conditions), except in capital cases where "the proof is evident or the presumption great."[36] This was changed radically by the Comprehensive Crime Control Act of 1984, which not only authorized pretrial detention[37] but created a statutory *presumption* in favor of it in any case in which, *inter alia*, the defendant is charged with a drug offense punishable by 10 years or more in prison.[38] Although the presumption is rebuttable, in the first seven months under the act, the government won 704 motions for pretrial detention while defendants won only 185.[39] Pretrial detention is a severe blow to the morale of defendants and to their ability to assist in the preparation of their defense.[40]

Another major erosion in the rights of defendants is the more permissive use of illegally seized evidence. Since 1914, the Fourth Amendment to the U.S. Constitution has been interpreted to exclude from use in court evidence obtained by federal law enforcement authorities in an illegal search and seizure.[41] Many states voluntarily adhered to that ruling, and in 1961 the remaining states were required to do so by the decision of the Supreme Court in *Mapp v. Ohio*.[42] But under the relentless pressure of drug prosecutions and the frequent attempts of Congress to repeal or restrict the exclusionary rule, the courts have whittled away at the protections afforded to individual privacy. Despite the independence of the judicial branch, the courts have in effect joined the war on drugs. Most notably, the U.S. Supreme Court has given its approval to just about every challenged drug enforcement technique. For example, the Court upheld the power of drug agents to use the airport drug courier profile to stop, detain, and question citizens without probable cause;[43] to subject a traveler's luggage to a sniffing examination by drug detector dogs without probable cause;[44] to make warrantless searches of automobiles and closed containers therein;[45] to conduct surveillance of suspects by placing transmitters or beepers in containers in vehicles;[46] to search at will without cause ships in inland waterways;[47] and to obtain a search warrant based on an undisclosed informant's tip.[48] The Supreme Court also adopted a "good-faith exception" to the exclusionary rule for evidence seized in searches made pursuant to defective warrants.[49] It authorized warrantless searches of open fields and barns adjacent to a residence.[50] It significantly enlarged the powers of police to stop, question, and detain drivers of vehicles on the highways on suspicion less than probable cause[51] or with no suspicion at all at fixed checkpoints or road blocks.[52] The Court also validated warrantless aerial surveillance, that is airplane overflights of private property,[53] the warrantless search of a motor home occupied as a residence,[54] and the warrantless search of the purse of a public school student.[55] In the realm of search and seizure, there is hardly a drug case that the government has failed to win. Indeed, the Supreme Court in *Albernaz v. United States* (1981) apparently placed its imprimatur on the turn-the-screw approach of the U.S. Congress. Thus, the crackdown mentality prevails not only in the political realm but, to use Madison's phrase, in "the least dangerous branch" as well.

One further example of the crackdown atmosphere prevailing in the United States comes from the Anti-Drug Abuse Act of 1986, in which Congress not only created new crimes but also added to the penalties that already existed. The effect of the Act is that drug crimes now rank among the most seriously punished offenses in the U.S. Criminal Code.

For example, the Act provides mandatory minimum penalties of 5 and 10 years in prison, depending upon drug and weight involved; in the case of possession with intent to distribute five kilograms of cocaine, the penalty is a minimum of 10 years up to a maximum of life imprisonment. Even as little as five grams of cocaine base requires not less than five years in prison and a maximum of 40 years. In both cases, the range of penalties rises to a minimum of 20 years to a maximum of life if death or serious bodily injury results from the use of such substances.[56] It should be emphasized that these penalties apply to *first-time* drug offenders; those with a prior state or federal drug conviction must receive a *mandatory life term* under these circumstances.

The facts that these penalties are so severe, more stringent in fact than sentences typically meted out to robbers or rapists,[57] illustrates one of the themes of this chapter: People in the United States are so fearful and angry about their inability to contain drug trafficking that they are resorting to extremist, desperation measures. More than one public official has proposed simply shooting suspected drug-carrying planes out of the sky. The atmosphere is perhaps best conveyed by the judicial opinion of a respected federal judge in Miami, who, in an order denying bail pending appeal, condemned drug dealers as "merchants of misery, destruction and death" whose greed has wrought "hideous evil" and "unimaginable sorrow" upon the nation. Their crimes, he wrote, are "unforgivable." And if drug crimes are literally "unforgivable," traditional constitutional and statutory protections for individual rights can be discounted or discarded.[58] One congressman complained about the extent to which legal protections interfered with the prosecution of drug cases: "In the War on Narcotics we have met the enemy and he is the U.S. code. I have never seen such a maze of laws and hangups."[59] In that spirit, and the spirit of the angry judge just quoted, the punitive measures I have described, along with dozens of others, such as forfeiture of defense attorney's fees,[60] have become "logical" measures in an endless cycle of crackdowns and failures.

Perhaps if these repressive laws applied only to drug defendants, who could be dismissed as an alien "them," few would care and fewer still would protest. But this kind of reactionary force cannot be contained, cannot apply only to those accused of drug crime. In fact, the tentacles of drug enforcement have already spread out to reach into the lives of ordinary people, not just to those involved in the drug underworld. These intrusions into the lives of civilian society take many forms. One of the most obvious is the rapid proliferation of mandatory drug testing of employees and job applicants in the U.S. Civil Service, state and local services, and in the private sector as well.[61] Some 40% of *Fortune*

500 companies now subject their applicants or employees to urinalysis.[62] Government surveillance is on the increase in the form of wiretaps and the maintenance of 1.5 million or more names in NADDIS, a drug investigative data bank. On a more prosaic level, the war on drugs hampers the mobility of travelers, who are subjected to road blocks and detained for questioning at airports, and whose luggage can be diverted for sniffing by drug detector dogs.

One of the latest repressive antidrug initiatives to emerge from Washington is called "zero tolerance," begun by the Customs Service on March 21. It means, in a nutshell, punishing drug users to promote "user accountability" and to reduce "the demand side of the equation." One manifestation of this policy is the effort to promote federal criminal prosecution of those found possessing personal-use amounts of drugs. They formerly would have either escaped prosecution or been referred to local authorities. On March 30, 1988, Attorney General Meese sent a memorandum to all U.S. Attorneys, encouraging the selective prosecution of "middle and upper class users" to "send the message that there is no such thing as 'recreational' drug use."

More widely known is the seizure or forfeiture of cars, planes, or boats of persons found in possession of even trace amounts of illegal drugs. In effect, these forfeited assets impose fines far greater than would ordinarily be imposed upon a criminal conviction for drug possession; but as civil forfeiture is *in rem,* no conviction or prosecution is required at all. Some examples: On April 30, the Coast Guard boarded and seized the motor yacht *Ark Royal,* valued at $25 million, because 10 marijuana *seeds* and two stems were found aboard. Public criticism prompted a return of the boat upon payment of $1,600 in fines and fees by the owner. The 52-foot *Mindy* was impounded for a week because of cocaine dust in a rolled-up dollar bill. The $80-million oceanographic research vessel *Atlantis II* was seized in San Diego when the Coast Guard found .01 ounce of marijuana in a crewman's shaving kit. It was returned also. But a Michigan couple returning from a Canadian vacation lost the wife's 1987 Cougar when Customs agents found two marijuana cigarettes in the husband's pocket. No charges were filed, but the car was kept by the government. In Key West, Florida, David Phelps, a shrimp fisherman, lost his 73-foot shrimper to the Coast Guard, which found three grams of cannabis seeds and stems aboard. Under the law, the boat is forfeitable regardless of whether Phelps had any responsibility for the drugs. Three weeks later, the boat had not been returned. There are many other ways, too numerous to mention in this chapter, that the war on drugs has choked off civil liberties in the United States.

In 1987 the United States celebrated the bicentennial of its Constitution. The framers of the Constitution were animated by the spirit of
William Pitt's dictum that "unlimited power is apt to corrupt the minds
of those who possess it." They therefore created a constitutional structure in which governmental power was limited in the first instance and
constrained in the second by the system of the Constitution. The Bill of
Rights was added in 1791 to further secure personal freedom from
governmental oppression.[63] The war on drugs has substantially undermined the American tradition of limited government and personal
autonomy. Since the early 1980s the prevailing attitude, both within
government and in the broader society, has been that the crackdown on
drugs is so imperative that extraordinary measures are justified. *The end
has come to justify the means.* The result is that Americans have
significantly less freedom than they did only five or six years ago.

THE LATEST DEVELOPMENTS IN 1988: POLARIZATION

Election year politics continued to ratchet the war on drugs machinery tighter and tighter. In June the Administration declared its goal
of a "drug free America."[64] During the month of April, the Senate voted
93-0 to adopt the Anti-Drug Abuse Act of 1988, creating a $2.6-billion
special reserve fund for antidrug programs over and above the regular
annual budget of $3-plus billion. (As noted above, the regular budget
represents a manifold increase in the level of funding that prevailed
when the war on drugs was declared.) The frustration of Congress with
drug-producing nations of Latin America, crystallized by the stalemate
with General Noriega in Panama, produced a number of controversial
proposals involving the threat of sanctions and the use of military
force to destroy coca crops or to capture fugitives from United States
drug charges.[65] Secretary Carlucci's opposition to arrest powers for
the military services might tone down the final bill, but an expanded
military surveillance role seemed likely. At the state level, the National Guard had already been deployed on antidrug search and destroy
missions.[66]

President Reagan, on April 19, "call[ed] upon the House and Senate
to vote promptly on my bill providing for capital punishment when a
death results from drug dealing, and when a . . . law enforcement officer
is murdered." In the latest piece of fundamentalist-style antidrug zeal-
otry, the House on September 22 voted 375-30 to: adopt capital punishment for a drug exception to the exclusionary rule, to deny college
student loans to anyone convicted of possessing drugs, to impose

without trial up to $10,000 in "civil fines" for a person caught in possession of drugs, and to impose a mandatory five-year prison sentence on those convicted of possessing crack cocaine. Other "zero tolerance" style bills abound. A House Republican task force introduced a bill calling for confiscation of 25% of the adjusted gross income and net assets of anyone caught possessing illegal substances. It would also cut off federal highway funds to states that do not suspend drivers' licenses of persons convicted of using drugs.

But at the same time there was movement in the opposite direction. Respected journalists and other opinion leaders began to break ranks with the war on drugs, in some cases suggesting that it be abandoned altogether. Here are some notable examples. David Boaz, Vice-President for Public Policy at libertarian-oriented CATO Institute, wrote an Op. Ed. piece for the *New York Times* (March 17), "Let's Quit the Drug War." In it he denounced the war on drugs as "unwinnable" and destructive to other values such as civil liberties and advocated a "withdrawal" from the war. Edward M. Yoder, Jr., of the *Washington Post* Writers Group called the war on drugs "dumb" and compared it to the prohibition of alcohol for "encouraging and enriching mobsters" (March 4, 1988). On March 10, 1988, Richard Cohen of the *Los Angeles Times* Syndicate published a piece endorsing government distribution of drugs in order to "recognize the drug problem is with us to stay—a social and medical problem, but not necessarily a law enforcement one. We've been making war on drugs long enough. It's time we started making sense instead." By May and June, articles of this type became a staple item in newspapers all over the country as editors hopped aboard the "legalization" bandwagon.

This sample of articles shows the emergence of a significant body of opinion opposed to the war on drugs. What is perhaps even more significant is that the opposition transcends the liberal/conservative split. Traditionally, conservatives have advocated strict law enforcement, and liberals have been identified with a permissive approach to the drug issue. But in a break with tradition, respected conservative spokesmen have also dissented from the war on drugs.

Even before the spate of articles described above, prominent conservative columnist William F. Buckley, Jr., had reversed his position and advocated the legalization of drugs as the only effective course of governmental action. Nobel Prize-winning economist Milton Friedman has made public statements advocating more market-oriented approaches to the regulation of drugs. *National Review,* the most prominent organ of conservative opinion, through its editor Richard Vigilante, published a piece (December 5, 1986) exposing the Anti-Drug Abuse Act in 1986 as a manifestation of public panic and criticizing the intrusiveness of drug testing and other enforcement measures. He also rejected the war on drugs as intolerant and politically unwise: "Embracing the drug hysteria requires a rejection of essential conservative principles." In the same issue was an article by Richard C. Cohen, titled "How the Narcs Created Crack," arguing as follows: "Any realistic approach to the drug problem must begin with the legalization of small scale cultivation and sale of marijuana so that it is separated from the other, more dangerous drugs. . . . We need not fear that if we stop the lying and hypocrisy, the American people are going to destroy themselves with drugs."

This debate has captured the attention of the mainstream media. Clearly, the challenge to the monopoly status of the war on drugs has gained ground. Nothing approaching this level of dissent had been seen or heard since the war on drugs started.

The dissent has also spilled over to the political sector. For example, the *ABA Journal* (January 1, 1988) reported that the New York County Lawyers Association Committee on Law Reform published a report advocating the decriminalization of heroin, cocaine, and marijuana. On April 18, New York State Senator Joseph L. Galiber, from a district in the drug-ravaged Bronx, introduced a bill in the New York State Legislature to decriminalize the possession, distribution, sale, and use of all forms of controlled substances under the aegis of a State Controlled Substance Authority. At a speech at the National Conference of Mayors and again on a May 10, 1988, broadcast of ABC's *Nightline*, the mayor of Baltimore called for congressional hearings to study the issue. Other mayors and a few congressmen supported him. And, surprisingly, Congressman Charles Rangel, Chairman of the House Select Committee on Narcotics Abuse and Control, scheduled a one-day hearing for September 29, 1988, clearly inadequate for the task at hand, yet perhaps a harbinger of the future.

There have also been pressures from abroad. For example, the Attorney General of Colombia said in a telephone interview with the *Miami Herald* (February 23, 1988) that Colombia's battles against drug trafficking rings had been a failure, "useless." He suggested that legalizing the drug trade is something that the government "may have to consider" in the future. *The Economist* magazine ran a cover story (April 2-8) called "Getting Gangsters Out of Drugs," advocating the legalized and taxed distribution of controlled substances. It followed up with similar commentaries on May 21 and June 4. *El Pais,* the most influential Spanish newspaper, also recommended "La legalizacion de la droga" in an editorial (May 22, 1988).[67]

What accounts for this trend? Negative experience with the war on drugs certainly plays a role. In the *Structure of Scientific Revolutions,* Thomas S. Kuhn argued that "the process by which a new candidate for paradigm replaces its predecessors" occurs "only after persistent failure to solve a noteworthy puzzle has given rise to crisis" (pp. 144-145). There is little doubt that the perception that the war on drugs is a failure at controlling drug supply has spread significantly. And the perception that it has negative side-effects, breeding crime, violence and corruption, has spread even to the comic pages of the daily newspapers.[68] In a more serious vein, Ted Koppel's *Nightline* broadcast a special three-hour "National Town Forum" on the subject of legalization. Perhaps we have already reached Kuhn's stage of "persistent failure and crisis," in which the war on drugs has been dislodged as the only conceivable paradigm for the control of drugs in the United States. What now should be done?

TOWARD A NEW BEGINNING IN DRUG CONTROL

One historically tested model of exploring policy reform is the appointment of a national study commission of experts, politicians, and lay leaders to make findings of fact, canvass a full range of policy options, and recommend further research where needed. The precedent set by the National Commission on Marijuana and Drug Abuse in the early 1970s offers a model that might be emulated in many respects. At the very least, a national commission performs a vital educational function: Its public hearings and attendant media coverage inform the public, bringing to their attention vital facts and a broader array of policy options. The level of public discourse is almost certain to be elevated. Only those who prefer ignorance to knowledge could possibly oppose the commission process.

What should be the agenda of such a commission? Its overriding goal should be to develop policies directed toward the objectives of (a) reducing drug abuse and (b) reducing the black market pathologies resulting from the billions in drug money generated by drug law enforcement. In pursuit of these dual goals, the commission's study might benefit from adherence to the following five points:

Define the Drug Problem. What exactly is the problem regarding drugs in the United States? The lack of an agreed-upon answer to this question is one of the primary sources of incoherence in present law and policy. People now speak of "the drug problem" in referring to at least five very different phenomena: (1) the mere use of any illegal drug;

(2) especially drug use by teenagers; (3) the abuse of illegal drugs, i.e., that which causes physical or psychological harm to the user; (4) drug-induced misbehavior that endangers or harms others, e.g., driving while impaired; and (5) drug trafficking phenomena (crime, violence, and corruption) arising from the vast sums of money generated in the black market in drugs. This confusion in the very statement of the problem necessarily engenders confusion in solving it. The "drug problem" as Edward Brecher reminds us in his classic *Licit and Illicit Drugs* is itself a problem. Therefore, as presently stated, it does not and cannot lead to the formulation of useful solutions. It would be a real breakthrough if the Congress or the president would generate a meaningful statement of the "drug problem." Otherwise, we are condemned to confirm the truth of Eric Sevareid's quip that the chief cause of problems is solutions.

State Your Goals. A creative definition or redefinition of the drug problem would carry us toward a (re)statement of goals. Rational policy-making is impossible without a clear articulation of the goals sought. Part of that impossibility arises from the inconsistency between, for example, pursuit of existing goal 1 by an attack on the drug supply and pursuit of goal 5, the suppression of drug money. Pursuit of the first creates a crime tariff, which makes pursuit of the last more or less impossible. Instead, the result of drug enforcement is a black market estimated by the government to be more than $100 billion per year, money that funds or gives rise to homicidal violence, street corruption by addicts, corruption of public officials, and international narco-terrorism. It is therefore essential to distinguish between problems arising from drugs and problems arising from drug money. For example, how much criminality is attributable not to the psychopharmacology of drugs but to the excessive prices intentionally caused by the prohibition of drugs? Rational policymakers have to distinguish between the two and acknowledge the trade-offs between the two lines of attack.

Set Realistic and Principled Priorities Based on Truth. The suppression of drugs as an end in itself is frequently justified by arguments that drugs cause addiction, injury, and even death in the short or long run. Granted that all drug use has the potential for harm, it is clear beyond any rational argument that most drug use does not cause such harm. DEA Director John Lawn's opinions notwithstanding ("Drugs are illegal because they are bad"), drugs are not harmful per se. Exposure to drugs is not the same as exposure to radioactive waste. Rather, the overwhelming majority of incidents of drug use are without lasting personal or societal consequence, just as the overwhelming majority of drinking causes no harm to the drinker or to society.

Accepting the truth of that premise means that not all drug use need be addressed by the criminal law, and that society might actually benefit from a policy of benign neglect respecting some forms of drug use. I have in mind the Dutch model—where nothing is legal but some things are simply ignored, cannabis in particular. NORML estimates that there are approximately one-half million arrests a year for marijuana, almost all for simple possession or petty sale offenses. Depending upon the age of consent chosen, most of these arrests could be eliminated from the criminal justice system, thereby achieving a massive freeing of resources for the policing of real crime.

Because we live in a world of limited resources, it is not possible to do everything. It is therefore both logical and necessary to make distinctions among things that are more or less important. Consider these differences in priority: (a) drug use by children (top priority) versus drug use by adults (low priority); (b) marijuana smoking (low priority) versus use of harder drugs (higher priority); (c) public use of drugs (high priority) versus private use of drugs at home (low priority); (d) drug consumption (no priority) versus drug impairment (high priority); (e) occasional use (low priority) versus chronic or dependent use (higher priority).

From these general criteria for drug policy, a national commission could formulate five specific goals for an effective, principled drug policy:

(1) *Protect the children.* This priority is self-evident and needs no discussion. This is the only domain in which "zero tolerance" makes any sense at all and might even be feasible if enforcement resources were concentrated on this as a top priority.

(2) *Get tough on the legal drugs.* It is common knowledge that alcohol (100,000 annual deaths) and tobacco (360,000 annual deaths) far exceed the illegal drugs as sources of death, disease, and dysfunction in the United States. Everyone knows that alcohol and tobacco are big business—the advertising budget alone for alcohol runs about $2 billion a year—and, what is worse, the state and federal governments are in complicity with the sellers of these deadly drugs by virtue of the billions in tax revenues that they reap.

This is not to suggest prohibition of these drugs. That is wrong in principle and impossible in practice, as experience teaches. Nonetheless, there are more restrictive measures that can and should be undertaken. One is to get rid of cigarette vending machines so that cigarettes are not so readily available to minors. A second is to require or recommend to the states and localities more restrictive hours of sale. A third is to levy taxes on these products that are consistent with their social costs—billions of dollars in property damage, disease, and lost productivity. Those costs should be financed largely by the sale of these products; at present prices, society is clearly subsidizing those products by providing police, fire, ambulance services for road accidents; Medicare and Medicaid reimbursement for therapy, surgery, prosthesis, or other medical care; and many other hidden costs effectively externalized by the industries from smoker and drinker to society as a whole. Precise numbers need to be derived from studies, but cigarettes at, say, $10 a pack and hard liquor at, say, $30 to $50 a bottle might be priced more consistently with their true social costs. Such taxes would have the additional salutary effect of reducing the consumption of these dangerous products to the extent that demand is elastic.

(3) *Public safety and order.* This means protection of the public from accident and injury on the highway, in the work place, and from unruly disruptions in public streets, public transport, parks, and other gathering places. Programs specifically tailored to accomplish this more focused goal make a lot more sense than futile and counter productive "zero tolerance" approaches. Street-level law enforcement practices need to be reviewed to see how much they may actually encourage hustling drugs in the street to avoid arrests and forfeitures that might follow from fixed points of sale.

Driving and workplace safety require more knowledge. Nothing should be assumed. Drug use, as the Air Force's and Freud's examples show,[69] does not automatically mean that a pilot or driver is impaired. Even with marijuana there is ambiguous evidence as to motor coordination.[70] Responsible research is required.

(4) *Protect public health.* The emphasis here is on the word "public." Policy should be directed toward (a) treatment of addicts on a voluntary basis and (b) true epidemiological concerns such as the use of drugs by pregnant women and the potential for transmission of AIDS by IV drug users. Addiction treatment is now shamefully underfunded, with months-long waiting lists in many cities.

Purely individualized risks are not in principle a public health matter and are in any case trivial in magnitude compared to those now accepted from alcohol[71] and tobacco. (Other long-term harms may result but are not systematically known at this time.) In any event, harmfulness is not the sole touchstone of regulation; the requirements of goal 5, listed below, require considerable deference to individual choice in this domain.

(5) *Respect the value of individual liberty and responsibility.* The current Administration's goal of a drug-free America, except for children, is both ridiculous—as absurd as a liquor-free America—and

wrong in principle. After all, this is not a fundamentalist Ayatollah Land. A democratic society must respect the decisions made by its adult citizens, even those perceived to be foolish or risky. Is it different in principle to protect the right of gun ownership, which produces some 10,000 to 12,000 homicides a year and thousands more nonfatal injuries? Is it different in principle to protect the right of motorcyclists, skydivers, or mountain climbers to risk their lives? Is it different to permit children to ride bicycles, which "cause" tens of thousands of crippling injuries and deaths per year? To say that something is "dangerous" does not automatically supply a reason to outlaw it. Indeed, the general presumption in our society is that competent adults, with access to necessary information, are entitled to take risks of this kind as part of life, liberty, and the pursuit of happiness. Why are drugs different?

It would be truly totalitarian if the government could decide these matters. After all, if the government is conceded to have the power to prohibit what is dangerous, does it not even have the power to compel what is safe? More specifically, if one drug can be prohibited on the ground that it is dangerous to the individual, would it then not be permissible for the government to decree that beneficial doses of some other drug must be taken at specified intervals?

The freedom of American citizens has already been seriously eroded by the war on drugs.[72] More civil liberties hang in the balance of the 1988 Omnibus Anti-Drug Abuse Act and further legislation in years to come. Is the defense of Americans from drugs to be made analogous to the defense of the Vietnamese from Communism, i.e., that it was necessary to destroy the city of Hue in order to save it? A national commission should give serious weight to this value in its policy recommendations.

Focus on the Big Picture. Present drug policy suffers from a kind of micro-think that borders on irresponsibility and is sometimes downright silly. This typically manifests itself in proud Administration announcements or reports to congressional committees of a new initiative or new accomplishment without regard to its impact on the bottom line. The examples are endless—a joint strike force with the government of the Bahamas; shutdown of a source of supply; the Pizza Connection case, the largest organized crime heroin trafficking case ever made by the federal government; a new bank secrecy agreement with the Caymans; a new coca eradication program in Bolivia or Peru, and so forth. But none of these programs or "accomplishments" has ever made any noticeable or lasting impact on the drug supply. Even with the Godfather of Bolivian cocaine residing in a Bolivian prison, was there any observable reduction in the supply of cocaine?

The lack of insistence that enforcement programs should make a difference in the real world produces fatuous reports like this 1979 report by GAO to the Congress: "Gains made in Controlling Illegal Drugs, Yet The Drug Trade Flourishes."[73] In what sense is it meaningful to say that gains are made if the bottom line grows worse and worse? This is reprehensible double-talk that should not be tolerated by responsible public officials.

The whole drug enforcement enterprise needs to be put on a more business-like basis, looking to the bottom line and not to isolated "achievements" of the war on drugs. In fact, the investor analogy is a good one to use: If the war on drugs were incorporated as a business enterprise, with its profits to be determined by its success in controlling drug abuse and drug trafficking, who would invest in it? Even if its operating budget were to be doubled to $6 billion a year, or doubled again to $12 billion a year, would it be a good personal investment? If not, why is it a good social investment?

This kind of hard-headed thinking is exactly what is lacking and has been lacking throughout the war on drugs. No attention has been paid to considerations of cause and effect, or to trade-offs, or to cost-benefit analysis. New antidrug initiatives are not subjected to critical questioning: What marginal gains, if any, can be projected from new programs or an additional commitment of resources? Conversely, how might things worsen? For example, many law enforcement officials believe that the Coast Guard's "successful" interdiction of marijuana coming from Jamaica and Colombia in the early 1980s had two negative side-effects: the substitution of domestic cultivation of more potent marijuana in California (and throughout the United States) and the diversion of smugglers into more compact and more readily concealable cocaine. Was that interdiction initiative truly successful? Weren't those side-effects reasonably foreseeable? There are other examples. Drug gangs are probably far more ruthlessly violent today than in the 1970s because they have learned to adapt to aggressive law enforcement methods. The friendly governments of Colombia, Peru, and Bolivia are far weaker today, far more corrupt, and far more subject to narco-terrorist subversion because of similar adaptations there by the drug cartel and its associates. Has our national security been thus advanced by the war on drugs?

For these reasons, it is important to abjure meaningless, isolated "victories" in the war on drugs and to focus on whether a program or policy offers some meaningful overall impact on the safety, security, and well-being of the American people. In this respect, does it really matter that the DEA doubled the number of drug arrests from 6,000 to

12,000 during the 1980s? Or that the Customs Service dramatically increased its drug seizures to more than 100,000 pounds of cocaine? Or that kingpins like Carlos Lehder Rivas have been convicted and imprisoned for life plus 135 years? Might it not be that the resources devoted to those antidrug initiatives were not merely wasted, but actually counter-productive?

Similarly, it is critical to pay scrupulous attention to cause and effect. Throughout the war on drugs, Administration officials have been making absurd claims about the effects of antidrug policies. President Reagan frequently asserted that the war on drugs was working. His evidence? Marijuana smoking is down to 18 million per year and experimentation with cocaine by high school seniors in the University of Michigan survey declined by 20%.[74] Everyone trained in logic knows that this is the fallacy of *post hoc ergo propter hoc*. But one need not be trained in logic to realize that there is no provable correlation between law enforcement initiatives and levels of drug consumption. Indeed, the same University of Michigan survey shows that marijuana consumption peaked in 1979, three years before the war on drugs even began. Cocaine is purer, cheaper, and more available than ever before. If use is down, it is not because of successful law enforcement. Most categories of drug use are down and will likely continue to go down as people become more educated and more concerned about health and fitness, fueled in some immeasurable degree by media reports of celebrity overdose deaths such as David Kennedy, John Belushi, Len Bias, and Don Rogers.

Another important factor is the aging of the Baby Boom generation. That demographic bulge leaves fewer young people behind and thus contributes to the aging of the population as a whole. An older population is simply one that is less likely to use cocaine, marijuana, and heroin.

To attribute these changes to law enforcement levels is at the least unprofessional. The liberalization of marijuana laws in California, Oregon, Maine, and elsewhere in the early 1970s produced no observable rise in consumption (either new users or increased frequency) of marijuana compared to other states.[75] The connection between law and individual behavior at this level is remote. Government policies are no more responsible for the current decline in drug use than they were for the boom in the 1970s and early 1980s. Drug use will almost certainly decline in the 1990s, no matter what law enforcement does, for roughly the same reasons that cigarette smoking has declined dramatically without any change in the law.[76]

Substitute Study for Speculation. The war on drugs has produced a siege mentality. Senators from large states speak of invasions and national security threats. Even professionals who should know better succumb to antidrug hysteria. A former director of the National Institute of Drug Abuse claimed that without the war on drugs to restrain the people, we would have 60,000 to 100,000,000 users of cocaine in this country. Now this is extremely unlikely; because of the stimulant nature of the drug, it appeals mostly to younger people; the population is aging, and there is already a downward trend in cocaine use except for crack, and so forth. But rather than trading assertion and counter-assertion, the real question is epistemological: How does the director know what he "knows." Clearly, there is no empirical basis for his claim. It must therefore be an expression of fear or perhaps political maneuver, but clearly it is something other than a statement of fact. Why would the director of the public agency most responsible for informing the public on drugs take that tack? Whatever his reasons, wild speculation is not the path to informed judgment and intelligent, workable policy. Why not truly confront the question of what less-restricted availability of cocaine would mean in terms of increased drug use, taking into account both prevalence and incidence.

There are a number of ways in which this might be done if we truly want to know the answers. One way is market research. A standard technique of market research is to conduct surveys and ask people about what they desire in a product in terms of price, quality, and other features. How much will they buy at various prices? The same techniques are adaptable, *mutatis mutandis*, to illegal drugs.

What about the effects of the drug? Is it addictive? Longitudinal studies of the kind pioneered by Ronald Siegel of UCLA should be encouraged.[77] NIDA Household Surveys register only gross numbers and do not track users. (They do not even cover group quarters, such as college dormitories and military barracks, where drug use may be higher than average.) At present we have almost no real-world knowledge of the experience of past and present cocaine users, except those unrepresentative few who come forward as former or recovering addicts. Even NIDA has conceded that we lack any estimate of the relative proportions of addictive use versus experimental or other non-consequential use in the total population of cocaine users.[78] Isn't that critical information in regulating the drug? (Drug users should be systematically interviewed, but they will be loathe to step forward in the current climate of repression.) Useful experiments might also be performed using volunteers from the prison population (e.g., those serving life sentences without parole) and perhaps volunteers from the military services. How would men behave and how would their health fare with abundant access to cocaine? Would it be used widely or intensively or both? Finally, comparative studies from countries such as the Netherlands can tell us a great deal about the effects of more freely available cannabis and heroin, although not so with respect to cocaine. We have a lot to learn from the Dutch.

CONCLUSION

This chapter endorses a substantial measure of relaxation of drug laws in some respects simultaneously with a substantial measure of intensification in other respects: the enforcement of laws to protect children, along with more stringent laws regarding the sale of liquor and tobacco. As to the first point, some measure of relaxation of drug laws is both correct in principle and pragmatically necessary in the real world of limited resources. But this is not a "surrender" in the war on drugs. There is a paradox here, i.e., that the use of less force may actually result in producing more control over the drug situation in this country.

Consider the analogy of a panic stop in an automobile. In a typical scenario, a driver observes a sudden obstruction in his path and slams on the brakes in order to avoid a collision. If he uses too much force on the pedal, the sudden forward-weight transfer will very likely induce front-wheel lockup. At that point, the car starts skidding out of control. If the driver turns the wheel left or right, the car will simply keep on skidding forward toward the very obstacle that he is trying to avoid. In this moment of panic, the "logical" or instinctive thing to do is to stomp the brake pedal even harder. But that is absolutely wrong. The correct thing to do to stop the skid is to modulate the brake pedal, releasing it just enough to permit the front wheels to begin rolling again so that steering control is restored. Thus, the correct and safe response is counter-intuitive, while the instinctive response sends the driver skidding toward disaster. The reader can decide whether this has any relevance in the remaking of drug policy.

NOTES

1. *President's radio address to the nation.* (1982, October 2). 18 Weekly Comp. Pres. Doc. 1249, 1249. (Hereinafter "Radio Address").

2. *President's message announcing federal initiatives against drug trafficking and organized crime.* (1982, October 14). 18 Weekly Comp. Pres. Doc. 1311, 1133-14.

3. *New York Times.* (1982, October 15). p. A20.

4. Epstein, E. (1987). *Agency of fear.* pp. 173, 179. Nixon consolidated agencies and created DEA as the lead agency in drug enforcement. See note 8.

5. The war on drugs. (1982, April). *Playboy,* p. 134.

6. House Select Committee on Narcotics Abuse and Control. (1982). *H. R. Rep. No. 418,* pp. 1-2. 97nd Cong., 2d Sess. 50.

7. Attorney General's Task Force on Violent Crime, Final Report 28. (1981).

8. The call for the buildup in the size and scope of the federal drug enforcement bureaucracy also occurred under the Nixon Administration. At the end of June 1968, the Bureau of Narcotics and Dangerous Drugs had 615 agents. By June 1970 this number had increased to more than 900, with authorization for at least 300 more agents during 1971. See *H. R. Rep. No. 1444,* 91st Cong., 2d Sess. 18, reprinted in *1970 U.S. Code Cong. & Admin. News,* 4566, 4584.

9. See 28 C.F.R. §0.85 (a), 0.012 (1986). Authority for federal drug law enforcement is distributed among several agencies, including the DEA, the Customs Service, the Coast Guard, the FBI, and the IRS. Supporting roles are played by the Immigration and Naturalization Service (INS), the CIA, and the Department of Defense. See: *National and international drug law enforcement strategy.* (1987, January). National Drug Enforcement Policy Board.

10. See: Organized crime drug enforcement tasks forces: Goals and Objectives. (1984). *11 Drug Enforcement 6; New York Times.* (1982, October 15).

11. *Ft. Lauderdale News & Sun-Sentinel.* (1983, June 18). A, at 1, col. 3. See also: Office of Technology Assessment, U.S. Congress. (1987). *The border war on drugs,* pp. 33-39. (Hereinafter "Border War").

12. *Miami Herald.* (1983, June 23). p. 11A.

13. For a description of Operation Greenback, the prototype money-laundering investigation, see: *Financial investigation of drug trafficking: Hearing before the House Select Committee on narcotics abuse and control.* (1981). 97th Cong., 1st Sess. 65.

14. See: *International narcotics control: Hearings before the House Committee on foreign affairs.* (1982). 97th Cong., 2d Sess. 156; *International narcotics trafficking: Hearings before the permanent subcommittee on investigations of the Senate Committee on governmental affairs.* (1981). 97th Cong., 1st Sess. 201-02.

15. See: President's Commission on Organized Crime. (1986). *America's habit: Drug abuse, drug trafficking and organized crime,* pp. 412-19.

16. *Miami Herald.* (1982, March 13). p. 1B.

17. Congress has likened the drug smugglers to an invading army, complete with generals, soldiers, and an armada that operates over the unpatrolled coastline and unmonitored airspace of the United States. See note: Posse Comitatus Act restrictions on military involvement in federal law enforcement. (1986). *54 George Washington Law Review 404,* 417 & pp. 140-42.

18. Stein. (1983, August 4). Naval task force enlists in drug war. *Miami Herald,* p. 13A; Balmaseda. (1983, July 17). Navy bullets riddle pot-smuggling ship. *Miami Herald,* p. 1A.

19. National Drug Policy Board. (1986). *Federal drug enforcement progress report, 1986.* Exhibit II-2, pp. 19-20. (Hereinafter "Progress Report").

20. Ibid., Exhibit II-11, p. 35.

21. Ibid., Exhibit III-1, pp. 74-78.

22. Data on price, purity, and supply are taken from the annual reports of the National Narcotics Intelligence Consumers Committee (NNICC), titled *The supply of illicit drugs to the U.S. from foreign and domestic sources.*

23. "Progress Report," p. 7.

24. Ibid., p. 5.

25. Ibid., p. 6., 1987 data from 1987 NNICC Report.

26. Congressional Research Service, Library of Congress. (1987, February 27). *Drug abuse and prevention control: Budget authority for federal programs.* FY 1986-FY 1987 [IP334D]. The budget dropped to $3-plus billion in FY 1988.

27. Leen. (1988, September 11). Drug war proving a costly failure. *Miami Herald,* p. 18A.

28. Select Committee on Narcotics Abuse and Control, 95th Cong., 2d Sess. (1976). *Congressional resource guide to the federal effort on narcotics abuse and control,* 250. (Comm. print).

29. "Border War," p. 3.

30. These phenomena are described in some detail in Wisotsky, S. (1986): Chapters 7-9.

31. The drug gangs. (1988, March 28). *Newsweek,* p. 20.

32. The leader of Panama, General Manuel Noriega, is under two separate federal indictments for drug trafficking offenses. The Chief Minister and the Commerce Minister of the Turks and Caicos were convicted in the United States of drug-smuggling charges in 1985. Top officials in Haiti, Honduras, and Nicaragua are also under investigation in the United States. Oppenheimer. (1988, February 14). U.S. urged to step up drug fight. *Miami Herald,* p. 14A. George Baron, a U.S. government witness in the Carlos Lehder Rivas cocaine conspiracy trial, testified that he paid $3 million to $5 million in bribes to Bahamian Prime Minister Lynden O. Pindling. Baron testified that he paid Pindling $15 for each pound of marijuana smuggled through the Bahamas to protect the boats from Bahamian police. Associated Press. (1988, February 17). *Miami Herald,* p. 10A.

33. See: Bin. (1986). Drug lords and the Colombian judiciary: A story of threats, bribes and bullets. *5 Pacific Basin L. J. 178.*

34. Packer (1968): 277-282.

35. *House Select Committee on narcotics abuse and control annual report for the year 1984.* (1985). H. R. Rep. No. 1199, 98th Cong., 2d Sess. 9.

36. *Albernaz v. United States,* 450 U.S. 333, 343 (1981).

37. Publ. L. No. 98-473, Tit. II, ch. 1, §203 (a), 98 Stat. 1976 (1984). (Codified as 18 U.S. C. §3142). (Supp. 1986).

38. 18 U.S. C. §3142 (e). (Supp. 1986).

39. Kennedy. (1984). Forward to symposium on the Crime Control Act of 1984. *22 American Criminal Law Review vi,* viii n. 4.

40. Wald. (1964). Pretrial detention and ultimate freedom: A statistical study. *39 New York University Law Review 631.*

41. *Weeks v. United States,* 232 U.S. 383 (1914).

42. 367 U.S. 643 (1961).

43. *Florida v. Royer,* 460 U.S. 491, 493 (1983). See also: *United States v. Montoya,* 473 W.S. 531 (1985); *Florida v. Rodriguez,* 469 U.S. 1, 5 (1984). Drug courier profiles are based on an informal compilation of traits commonly associated with drug smugglers; they have been criticized for allowing impermissible intrusions on Fourth Amendment rights based solely on an agent's "hunch." See note: "Drug courier profiles in airport stops." (1984). *14 S.U.L. Rev. 315,* 316-317 & n. 23. For further criticisms, see note:

"Search and seizure: Defining the outer boundaries of the drug courier profile." (1985). 17 Creighton Law Review 973.

44. *United States v. Place,* 462 U.S. 696, 706 (1983).

45. *United States v. Ross,* 456 U.S. 696, 706 (1982); see also: *Colorado v. Bertine,* 107 S. Ct. 738 (1987).

46. *United States v. Knotts,* 460 U.S. 276, 282 (1983).

47. *United States v. Villamonte-Marquez,* 463 U.S. 579, 593 (1983).

48. *Illinois v. Gates,* 462 U.S. 213 (1983). *Gates* replaced the principles of probable cause established in *Aquilar v. Texas,* 378 U.S. 108 (1964) and *Spinelli v. United States,* 393 U.S. 410 (1969) with a more loosely structured "totality of the circumstances" test. *Gates,* 462 U.S. at 230.

49. *United States v. Leon,,* 468 U.S. 897, 905 (1984). To similar effect are *Illinois v. Krull,* 107 S. Ct. 1160 (1987) and *Maryland v. Garrison,* 107 S. Ct. 1013 (1987). For criticism of the good faith exception, see: LaFave, W. (1987). *Search and seizure: A treatise on the Fourth Amendment* §1.3 (c)-(d), at 51, 58-59. This argues that the *Leon* court overestimated the costs of adherence to the exclusionary rule based on "intuition, hunches, and occasional pieces of partial and often inconclusive data."

50. *United States v. Dunn,* 107 S. C. 1134 (1987) (barn); *Oliver v. United States,* 466 U.S. 170 (1984) (open fields).

51. *United States v. Sharpe,* 470 U.S. 675 (1985).

52. *Texas v. Brown,* 460 U.S. 730 (1983).

53. *California v. Ciraolo,* 106 S. Ct. 1809, 1813 (1986).

54. *California v. Carney,* 471 U.S. 386, 390 (1985).

55. *New Jersey v. T.L.O.,* 469 U.S. 325, 333 (1985).

56. Pub. L. No. 99-750, reprinted in 1986 *U.S. Code Cong. & Admin. News* (No. 10A). (Codified as amended in scattered sections of U.S.C.)

57. A not untypical example comes from a prominent 1988 news story. Larry Singleton had been convicted of raping a teenager and hacking off her arms between the wrist and elbow. He was convicted in California and given the maximum sentence of 14 years, of which he served eight. In Florida a person convicted of possession of 400 grams of cocaine, or another similar drug-trafficking offense, would receive a non-parolable mandatory term of 15 years. With typical gain time and work credits, he might serve approximately seven years in prison.

58. *United States v. Miranda,* 442 F. Supp. 786, 795 (S.D. Fla., 1977).

59. *Financial investigation of drug trafficking: Hearings before the House Select Committee on Narcotics Abuse and Control.* (1981). 97th Cong., 1st Sess. 58. (Statement of Congressman Hutto.)

60. *United States v. Caplin & Drysdale,* 814 F. 2d 905 (4th Cir., 1987)

61. *President's message announcing the goals and objectives of the national campaign against drug abuse.* (1986, August 4). 22 Weekly Comp. Pres. Doc. 1040, 1041.

62. General Dynamics, General Motors, Greyhound, E. F. Hutton, IBM, Mobil, the *New York Times,* the Teamsters, and the United Auto Workers are but a few of the enterprises that have instituted some type of workplace drug testing. Ross (1985). Drug testing at work spreading—and likely to spread further. *L. A. Daily J.,* p. 4.

See generally: Testing for drugs in the American workplace. (1987). *11 Nova Law Review 291;* Wisotsky, S. (1987). The ideology of drug testing. *11 Nova Law Journal 763.*

One rationale for requiring that urinalysis be predicated upon individual suspicion is the not-unlikely possibility of a false positive result:

Two Navy doctors were almost drummed out of the service (in 1984) because they tested positive for morphine, the result of having eaten too many poppyseed bagels.

Indeed, the Navy program has seen huge errors—more than 4,000 men and women were recalled at full back pay (in 1985) because they were discharged on the basis of a (false positive). [Ross, supra].

63. Speech. (1770, January 19). Case of Wilkes.

64. National Drug Policy Board. (1988). *Toward a drug free America.*

65. In February, the House Foreign Affairs Committee Task Force on International Narcotics Control demanded that the State Department impose sanctions against Colombia, Peru, Bolivia, and other nations to force them to intensify their drug enforcement efforts.

66. *The drug enforcement report.* (1988, June 23). p. 2.

67. *Time* magazine ran a May 30, 1988, cover story on the debate, titled "Thinking the Unthinkable." *Newsweek* did a similar piece; both the *New York Times* and the *Miami Herald* ran front-page stories on the same subject in May.

68. For example, the syndicated strip, "Bloom County," satirized the issue on at least two separate occasions. The April 18, 1988, strip portrayed a scenario in which a lobbyist for smugglers makes contributions to antidrug political candidates as a way to keep drug prices high. "Nothing makes us madder than some liberal talking drug legalization."

69. Truth-based legislation will also have to acknowledge that "recreational" drugs also have beneficial uses, most notably medicinal ones. Respectable authorities in the United States and abroad endorse heroin for pain relief in terminally-ill patients. Francis Young, the chief administrative law judge of DEA, recommended this summer that marijuana be reclassified to permit doctors to prescribe it for relief of nausea from chemotherapy and for other purposes. His opinion concludes the marijuana is "far safer than many foods we commonly consume" and that its medical benefits are "clear beyond any question." Judge Young had previously recommended that MDMA ("ecstasy") be removed from Schedule I and be made legally available to psychiatrists for treating patients.

Medical uses are not the only beneficial effects of drugs. An AP wire from Frankfurt, West Germany, reported that the Air Force allows its pilots to take Dexedrine "so that they are able to fly when they haven't gotten enough sleep or don't feel fit enough." Hundreds of thousands of "drug abusers" similarly stimulate themselves with amphetamines and cocaine. More than a century ago, Sigmund Freud discovered in self-experiments that moderate doses (1/10 gram) of cocaine improved his muscular strength and reaction time. See: Byck (1974): 98, 103.

70. The Research Triangle Institute estimated the annual costs of alcohol abuse to society at $116 billion in 1983. See: Axel. (Ed.). (1986). *Corporate strategies for controlling substance abuse.* Conference Board. p. 13. With 1,000 deaths daily from lung cancer and other diseases often preceded by years of medical treatment, there must be billions more in social costs attributable to tobacco.

71. See, Knepper (1980, June). Puff the dangerous drug. *Car and Driver,* p. 43.

72. See, Wisotsky, S. (1987).

73. GGD-80.4. (October 25, 1979).

74. About the only category of drug use that appears to be up is crack, and even that may be confined in large part to urban ghettos. *New York Times,* July 10, 1988. The overall decline, of course, is a positive development as long as it is not offset by a correspondng rise in other drug use, e.g., alcohol or tobacco, or suicide or other forms of health-endangering behavior. In this respect, a national commission should fund research directed toward the development of some meaningful index of health and well-being by somehow combining total morbidity/mortality data from all major causes. It would be a

true "Big Picture" accomplishment if we could somehow confirm that specified demo-graphic segments not only were using drugs less but also were happier and healthier.

75. Maloff. (1981, Fall). A review of the effects of the decriminalization of marijuana. *Contemporary Drug Problems, 132.*

76. To speak of a rise or fall in drug use is simplistic. It is important to distinguish between prevalence (the number of users) and incidence (the frequency of use). In terms of measurable health consequences, it may be meaningless if the number of people who try cocaine goes up or down; conversely, a change in the amounts and frequency of consumption may significantly alter morbidity and mortality.

77. In a 1984 paper for NIDA (Research Monograph 50), Siegel concluded that the "hypothesis that long-term use of cocaine is inevitably associated with an escalating dependency marked by more frequent patterns of use is not supported by the finding." Instead, he found that "social recreational drug users maintained relatively stable patterns of use" in the face of ready supplies and increased income as they aged.

78. Jaffe, J. H. (1985). Foreword in *Cocaine use in America: Epidemiologic and clinical perspectives.* NIDA. Other research agendas should include the possibility of addiction maintenance treatment and other therapeutic uses of cocaine.

REFERENCES

The reader who wants to study U.S. drug policy in depth is advised to consult: Wisotsky, S. (1986). *Breaking the impasse in the war on drugs.* Westport, CT: Greenwood Press, p. 263. For convenience, reprinted below is a short introductory bibliography taken in part from a Nova Law Center Symposium, "The War on Drugs: In Search of a Breakthrough." *11 Nova Law Journal 891,* 1050 (1987).

AN ESSENTIAL BIBLIOGRAPHY ON DRUG LAW AND POLICY

Bakalar, J. B., & Grinspoon, L. (1985). *Drug control in a free society.* Cambridge: Cambridge University Press.

Brecher, E. (1973). *Licit and illicit drugs: The Consumers Union Report on narcotics, stimulants, depressants, inhalants, hallucinogens & marijuana—including caffeine, nicotine and alcohol.* Consumers Union.

Byck, R. (Ed.). (1974). *Cocaine papers: Sigmund Freud.* New York: New American Library.

Grabowski, J. (Ed.). (1984). *Cocaine: Pharmacology, effects, and treatment of abuse.* (Research Monograph No. 50). National Institute on Drug Abuse.

Grinspoon, L. (1977). *Marijuana reconsidered.* (2nd ed.). New York: Bantam Books. (Previously published by Harvard University Press, 1971).

Grinspoon, L., & Bakalar, J. B. (1985). *Cocaine: A drug and its social evaluation.* (Revised ed.). New York: Basic Books.

Institute of Medicine, Division of Health Promotion and Disease Prevention. (1980). *Alcoholism, alcohol abuse, and related problems: Opportunities for research.* National Academy Press.

Institute of Medicine, Division of Public Sciences Study. (1982). *Marijuana and health.* National Academy Press.

Kaplan, J. (1983a). *Marijuana—the new Prohibition.* World Publishing.

Kaplan, J. (1983b). *The hardest drug: Heroin and public policy.* Chicago: University of Chicago Press.

Kozel, N. J., & Adams, E. H. (Eds.). (1985). *Cocaine use in America: Epidemiology and clinical perspectives.* (Monograph No. 61). Rockville, MD: National Institute on Drug Abuse.

Lee, D. (1980). *Cocaine handbook: An essential reference.* And/Or Press.

Liaison Task Panel on Psychoactive Drug Use/Misuse. (1978). *Task panel reports submitted to the President's Commission on Mental Health.* (Vol. IV, Appendix 2103-40). Washington, DC: Government Printing Office.

Moore, M. (1977). *Buy and bust: The effective regulation of an illicit market in heroin.* Lexington, MA: Lexington Books.

Musto, D. F. (1973). *The American disease: Origins of narcotic control.* New Haven: Yale University Press.

National Commission on Marijuana and Drug Abuse. (1972). *Marihuana: A signal of misunderstanding.* Washington, DC: Government Printing Office.

National Drug Enforcement Policy Board. (1986). *Federal drug enforcement progress report, 1985-86.* Washington, DC: Government Printing Office.

Packer, H. (1968). *The limits of the criminal sanction.* Palo Alto, CA: Stanford University Press.

Phillips, J., & Wynne, R. (1980). *Cocaine: The mystique and the reality.* Avon Books.

President's Commission on Organized Crime. (1986). *America's habit: Drug abuse, drug trafficking, and organized crime.* Washington, DC: Government Printing Office.

Szasz, T. (1976). *Ceremonial chemistry: The ritual persecution of drugs, addicts, and pushers.* Doubleday Anchor.

Trebach, A. (1982). *The heroin solution.* New Haven: Yale University Press.

Weil, A. (1972). *The natural mind: A new way of looking at drugs and the higher consciousness.* Boston: Houghton Mifflin.

Wisotsky, S. (1983). Exposing the war on cocaine: The futility and destructiveness of prohibition. *Wisconsin Law Review,* 1305.

Wisotsky, S. (1986). *Breaking the impasse in the war on drugs.* Westport, CT: Greenwood Press.

Wisotsky, S. (1987). Crackdown: The emerging "drug exception" to the Bill of Rights. *38 Hastings Law Journal,* 889.

Wisotsky, S. (1987). The ideology of drug testing. *11 Nova Law Journal,* 763.

Zinberg, N. E. (1984). *Drug, set and setting: The basis for controlled intoxicant use.* New Haven, CT: Yale University Press.

5

War Is Not the Answer

KARST J. BESTEMAN

President Nixon was the first elected leader of the country to declare "war" on drugs. He did this in 1971 with a strong initiative against drug dealers and a rapid expansion of drug treatment facilities with the priority drug being heroin. Presidents Ford, Carter, and Reagan have continued this effort, with each promising to increase the war effort against drugs but with different priorities.

In the middle of the 1988 campaign to elect the next president of the United States, both candidates pledged to continuing and expanding the "war on drugs." Both appeared before law enforcement groups to claim the issue and promised to increase federal efforts to interdict and to support stricter enforcement penalties.

The nature of the federal role in interdiction activities has led to the promise of more potent weapons, faster pursuit craft, and greater international cooperation. As an afterthought to these commitments, each candidate mentioned the importance of reducing the demand for drugs. The specific actions that would result in a reduction in demand were not described.

In examining this emphasis and its 20-year history, it is my conclusion that the war on drugs is not the answer to the many problems of drug abuse in this country. I reach this point by realizing that during the entire time the country has been at war against drugs there has been no attempt in any administration to place the federal government and the American people on a wartime status. There are several characteristics of war that have not been met. These are:

- the lack of total mobilization
- the lack of unlimited resources
- the lack of expendable personnel and willingness to take casualties

- the lack of strategic leadership by professionals
- the lack of a national will for victory at any cost

Drug abuse is not monolithic. It is not the problem or a problem to be solved. Drug abuse manifests itself in a multitude of problems. Some of these drug problems are the direct result of the physiological impact of the drug. Some of the problems are the result of psychological impairment and decrement of performance. One of the problems is the impact of a lethal dose in causing premature death. Virtually none of the direct drug abuse effects causes a response of urgency in our society. Urgency is generated by the host of problems associated with drug abuse.

There is an acute concern about driving a vehicle while under the influence of a drug. Drugged drivers are subject to a number of punitive measures designed to assure the safety of the motoring public. The neighborhood gets upset with the seemingly random and unprovoked violence that is associated with the use and distribution of illicit drugs. Communities now keep score of homicides as "drug related." Drug abuse is viewed as the cause and motivation for family dysfunction and disruption. Drug abuse is condemned as a cause of damage to newborns. An entire industry has developed to control and remove drug abuse from the workplace. Pre-employment testing, laboratory standards, for-cause testing, and false positives have become an important part of the discussion for major employers. Congress has legislative proposals to test employees who are part of the nation's transportation system. Industry is concerned about potential losses in productivity due to reduced and impaired capacity of workers.

Local communities and courts are angered and overwhelmed at the realization that an addicted criminal is likely to escalate the number of criminal acts fivefold while taking drugs when compared to crimes committed while abstinent. Surveys by arresting authorities repeatedly report that more 60% of the suspects arrested and arraigned test positive for the presence of illicit drugs.

Periodically, reports make us aware that law enforcement officials, bankers, and other highly respected community leaders have been corrupted by the larger amounts of money that fuel this illegal enterprise. The amount of corruption in the United States is usually under-reported as our media pursues the impact of public corruption in supplier nations.

As all these items accumulate in our public debate the country seems frozen into a single repetitive response. The elected legislators reflexively seek to pass more punitive and restrictive laws. The failure of previously enacted criminal penalties to deter the use and trafficking in illicit drugs is used as an excuse to pass more and similar laws as a strategy to accomplish this goal. There is a body of knowledge in the criminal justice literature that speaks to certain and swift punishment as having an impact on criminal behavior. Yet the legislative effort is to construct more severe penalties with no action taken to ensure the swift and certain application of the law.

In my opinion the country has passed the point of benefit from increased criminal penalties. The sole weapon in the declared but unwon "war" has been more legal sanctions. It is time to consider that the many problems of drug abuse do not respond to hostile combat but are solved by engaging in a concerted public health approach. This approach is not a mystery. It requires patience. It requires much more precise information to craft an effective response and intervention.

First let us consider the accuracy and appropriateness of the data that our government now collects. There are three major mechanisms that are used to guide the country in assessing the scope and nature of its drug problems. They are the High School Senior Survey, the Household Survey, and the Drug Abuse Warning Network. Each of these data sources has limited value. None defines the extent or nature of the drug problems found in our society. There is no comparably inadequate estimate of any other disease area in the Public Health Service at the national level. Today we know more of the presence and patterns of measles and chicken pox, which we count to the precise case number by county, than we do of any of the destructive drug-taking patterns within any jurisdiction. The excuse given for not mounting a comprehensive epidemiologic study of drug consumption patterns is that it is too expensive. Yet the federal investment in responding to these ill-defined problems exceeds $1 billion annually.

The technical and professional skills exist to accomplish the task of defining and identifying the problems of drug abuse. The public policy leaders within the federal government prefer to approach the issues from a position of ignorance and rely on their common sense. The sad fact is that our legislative leaders enter into this charade by cooperating in generating solutions to unknown and undefined problems. The Congress, through its committees of jurisdiction, has not held an oversight hearing to define the problems and develop the solutions for almost a decade. During the years in which there has been no election, the committee staff members emphasize the large agendas on more important health matters that must be held. However, these other priorities seldom have major legislative action without full and extensive hearings.

When the agencies of the executive branch are approached on this same issue of a lack of definition and understanding of the extent and nature of the problems of drug abuse, the answer most often given is that to define the problems properly will take too much of the appropriated funds for solving the problem, and thus hurt the ongoing agency activities. There is rarely any desire to be self-aware and certain that the activity of the agency does contribute to solutions. This issue is assumed in the belief that if an agency was not solving a problem it would not get public funds.

Once a major area of concern such as drug abuse is properly defined, the individual problems identified can be addressed. One very specific problem of drug abuse is the administration of a lethal overdose. The study of the data we have on overdose deaths in this country from the Drug Awareness Warning Network would lead a person interested in reducing drug-caused overdose deaths to concentrate on some factors that are often neglected in our war on drugs. The drugs that are very lethal are frequently prescription compounds and are often taken in combination with alcohol when they prove to be the cause of death.

A second illustration of the benefit of approaching drug abuse with comprehensive and specific data can be illustrated by analyzing the impact of marijuana and the patterns of consumption. There are no data to directly identify marijuana as a lethal drug. This drug's negatives are subtle and long-term. The acute problems of marijuana are often discovered when it is used in combination with alcohol or other illicit drugs. The accurate and factual demonstration with solid research findings of the risks of impairment in performance and lung pathology can be powerful tools in educating people to avoid this drug, which at the time of ingestion appears innocuous. It is also well documented that the segment of the population that abuses marijuana is separate in age and life-style from that in the previous reference to people who overdose on prescription drugs.

To use the public health approach in solving the many problems of drug abuse would have an additional positive feature when compared to our present policies of criminal sanctions. The arrest, apprehension, trial, and incarceration of the abuser for the criminal acts committed are by definition the sole responsibility of the police and the criminal justice system. Issues of public health are by definition the responsibility of each of us as members of the community with obligations to protect one another. In the interest of public health we participate in immunization programs, assist the city in disposing of garbage, and accept and uphold rules designed to avoid the spread of communicable diseases.

The prohealth life-style movement is an outgrowth of the understanding that public health is the sum of a vast number of individual decisions and actions. The public has demonstrated its responsiveness to improving health practices. The public has not demonstrated its approval of war against inanimate substances. The public has the desire to understand and experience the connection between an action required and an outcome desired.

There are several other features of the public health approach that, if followed, would assist the nation's leaders and the public to join in an agreed-upon goal and specific strategies for solution. The history of public health is to understand with great precision how and why a disease spreads. There is great emphasis on how an individual can avoid the disease. Failing to avoid the disease, intense study is given to raising resistance to the disease. And in the event all else fails, there is a major effort to treat the condition.

This country has not pursued any of these alternatives. We have tried defining drug abuse as a moral flaw. We have given the drug itself evil attributes. We have defined the addicted person's actions as illegal. We have declared a war. We have not solved the problems. It is time for a fundamental reassessment of our federal policies and approach. War against our citizens is unthinkable. War against drugs is unwon.

Until our elected leaders and the officials who develop national policies regarding drug abuse abandon their reflexive reliance on hostile symbols, we will experience little progress in the healing and restoring needed to solve the problems of drug abuse. At the core of the addicted person's dilemma is an attempt to deal with personal loneliness, alienation, and depression. The motivation and effort needed to rejoin the community will not come when every message from society proclaims the status as enemy.

6

Why MDMA Should Not Have Been Made Illegal

MARSHA ROSENBAUM
RICK DOBLIN

The most recent "recreational" drug to be made illegal is MDMA, or "ecstasy."[1] Its criminalization never should have happened. MDMA had a beneficial therapeutic use prior to scheduling. Hundreds of therapists and psychiatrists used MDMA-assisted psychotherapy with thousands of patients suffering from terminal illness, trauma, marital difficulties, drug addiction, phobias, and other disorders. MDMA was also used outside of therapeutic circles. With many anecdotal claims of benefits, users showed little evidence of problematic physiological or psychological reactions or addiction.

Scheduling and the attendant media attention on the controversial public hearings *created* an expanded market. But the scheduling process was fraught with problems, with the Drug Enforcement Administration's emergency scheduling itself declared illegal by the courts and its scheduling criteria overturned. Ultimately, criminalization had little deterrent effect on the recreational user population while substantially reducing its therapeutic use. Perhaps the most profound effect of MDMA's illegality has been the curtailment of scientific research and experimentation with a drug that held therapeutic potential.

The information to be presented here is taken from a recently completed NIDA-funded study of MDMA conducted by the lead author.[2] Using a qualitative methodology, this was an exploratory study in which 100 MDMA users were interviewed in depth between 1987 and 1989.[3] The second author was involved in the scheduling process and had done physiological research on MDMA.

This chapter begins with a short history of MDMA's use and the scheduling process. Ultimately, it presents an argument critical of criminalization.

A SHORT HISTORY OF MDMA USE

Early Therapeutic Use

Although first synthesized by Merck Pharmaceuticals in Germany in 1912, MDMA was almost completely unknown until the mid-1970s. In 1973, the first study in the literature mentioning MDMA was published, based upon toxicological research conducted in the early 1950s by the Army's Chemical Center (Hardman et al., 1973). Around this time, MDMA began to be explored by a small group of therapists and researchers who were part of the human potential movement. MDMA was typically called "Adam," and its use, by individuals interested in self-actualization, was therapeutic. MDMA encouraged the experience of emotions by reducing the fear response to perceived emotional threats. There were no direct observable harmful physical effects. For example, couples who were having marital problems were treated with MDMA-assisted psychotherapy by psychiatrists and psychotherapists who believed that MDMA could facilitate communication. Trauma victims were treated with MDMA-assisted psychotherapy to help them delve into the source of their problems, experience a healing catharsis, and subsequently function more effectively.

In sum, prior to 1982-1983, the major distribution networks had a "mindful" attitude. The handful of chemists who produced MDMA were more concerned with making a meaningful contribution to psychological health than with making money. Roughly 500,000 doses had been consumed between the early 1970s and the early 1980s, with no publicity and little notice taken by drug abuse officials or police. Use grew by word of mouth, with occasional periods of greater supply than demand.

Distribution Changes and Recreational Use

By 1983, with an eye toward enlarging the market, a member of a Los Angeles distribution network coined the term "ecstasy" because, "it would sell better than calling it 'empathy'." "Empathy," he said, "would be more appropriate, but how many people know what it means?" (Eisner, 1989). Simultaneously, a more aggressive marketing campaign took place in Texas. "Ecstasy" was distributed openly in bars and nightclubs in Dallas. There were pyramid sales structures, 800-numbers and credit card purchase options. It became a "phenomenon" among Dallas yuppies, college students, and gays, who would go out "X-ing" on Friday and Saturday nights. Distribution grew and recreational, as opposed to the more therapeutically oriented, use increased dramatically.[4]

Enter the DEA

But there was a war going on—the War on Drugs. In 1982, the DEA's Drug Control Section began collecting information on MDMA. Although there was not much data, as one DEA spokesman said, "If we can get enough evidence to be sure there's potential for abuse, we'll ban it" (Dye, 1982). By 1984, the open sales in Texas resulted in a request from Senator Lloyd Bentsen to the DEA for scheduling, and in July 1984 the DEA filed a formal notice in the Federal Register, announcing its intention to place MDMA in Schedule I.

But just as the DEA had been slowly gathering its forces, so had the MDMA-using therapeutic community. Psychiatrists and therapists from around the country formally requested that the DEA hold a hearing on MDMA's scheduling. This request surprised the DEA, which had no idea that MDMA had any use other than "recreational." The press was immediately interested in this group of respectable professionals, who had emerged from a decade of secret work into the courtrooms of the Drug Enforcement Administration and were ready to engage in the legal defense of the medical use of MDMA. As a publicity avalanche started rolling, several monks and rabbis testified about their beneficial use of MDMA, complicating the DEA's efforts to portray MDMA as a wholly dangerous drug.

While a guest on a *Phil Donahue Show* devoted to the MDMA controversy, a DEA official heard physiological brain researcher Dr. Charles Schuster (now head of the National Institute on Drug Abuse) discussing a study by one of his students, which showed changes in the brains of rats as a result of the injection of large, frequently repeated doses of MDA, a chemical "cousin" of MDMA. The fate of MDMA was sealed with this piece of information. Within a few weeks, the DEA called a press conference to announce that it was placing MDMA in Schedule I on an emergency basis. This action was justified by reference to MDMA's potential brain-damaging effect and its widespread use (that was partially the result of publicity about the original hearing).

THE SCHEDULING PROCESS

In order for a drug to be placed in Schedule I, the Controlled Substances Act of 1970 stated that it must have a high potential for abuse *and* have no accepted medical use *and* no accepted safety for use under medical supervision.[5] The only legal uses of a Schedule I drug are those that are specifically authorized by the federal authorities for limited medical or scientific purposes.[6] Schedules II-V are used for drugs that have some accepted medical uses and accepted safety and have potential for abuse ranging from high to medium or low. The appropriate schedule for drugs that have no accepted medical use but only medium or low potential for abuse is extremely unclear.

The DEA Administrative hearing process began in the fall of 1984. DEA Administrative Judge Young planned to hold hearings in three separate cities, with lawyers arguing over scientific data, governmental statistics, and expert witnesses. At issue was whether or not MDMA had: (a) a high potential for abuse, (b) no accepted medical use, and (c) no accepted safety for use under medical supervision.[7]

Defenders of MDMA's medical use argued that MDMA should be placed into Schedule III, whereby physicians could legally prescribe MDMA. All recreational use would be criminalized, but medical treatment and scientific research could still be conducted. The arguments were based on the rejection of each of the three basic criteria for Schedule I placement. The attorney argued that MDMA did not have a *high* potential for abuse, but rather a medium or low potential. This argument was based on the minimal number of mentions (8) for MDMA in the National Institute on Drug Abuse's Drug Abuse Warning Network (DAWN), particularly in view of the roughly 3,000,000 doses that had been consumed both therapeutically and recreationally by the time of the hearings. Numerous psychiatrists asserted that MDMA did have an acceptable medical use.[8] The claim that MDMA had accepted safety for use under medical supervision was supported by three studies.[9] The MDMA attorney also cited the lack of alleged harm to any patient as evidence of the safety of MDMA under medical supervision.

The DEA chief attorney made three basic allegations. He claimed that a drug need not have caused any actual harm before being placed into Schedule I, merely that the drug had to have a high *potential* for abuse. He further argued that only the FDA could accept a drug for medical use, and without FDA approval, no drug could have accepted safety under medical supervision.

In May 1986, after almost two years of hearings, Judge Young issued his final ruling, recommending that MDMA be placed in Schedule III.

He made three basic findings: that MDMA had a low potential for abuse; that it had an accepted medical use; and that there was accepted safety for use under medical supervision. Furthermore, Judge Young ruled that the Controlled Substances Act contained a logical inconsistency and was written in such a way as to preclude drugs, which had no accepted medical use but only medium or low potential for abuse, from being scheduled at all. Despite Judge Young's ruling, the DEA administrator placed MDMA into Schedule I.

WHY MDMA SHOULD NOT HAVE BEEN CRIMINALIZED

There are a number of reasons why MDMA should not have been made illegal. In the following paragraphs we discuss problems with the scheduling process; the media and its role in the spread of MDMA; the lack of a deterrent effect on users; the loss of research that may have illuminated MDMA's therapeutic benefits; and the continuing lack of evidence that MDMA use is socially and personally problematic.

Problems with the Scheduling Process

The decision to place MDMA in Schedule I was immediately appealed to the U.S. Court of Appeals, First Circuit. In September 1987, after appellate review, the decision of the DEA to place MDMA into Schedule I was found to be flawed. The court sidestepped the logical inconsistency in the Controlled Substances Act, finding that MDMA did have a high potential for abuse. It agreed with the DEA's decision to focus on the word *potential* rather than on the word *high*. However, the court disagreed with the DEA's assumption that Congress intended that FDA approval determine accepted medical use. As a result, the court voided the DEA's placement of MDMA into Schedule I and remanded the decision back to the DEA for reconsideration.

The DEA, after several months of reflection, had placed MDMA into Schedule I once again. Rather than a rationale requiring FDA approval (that had been overturned by a court order), the DEA devised a new rationale. But it was Catch 22. A series of criteria were used that were virtually identical to current FDA approval.[10] Since only a pharmaceutical company could afford the required studies, for which FDA permission would be impossible to secure, the DEA's new criteria was of dubious legality. Rather than simply requiring FDA approval, the DEA broke down FDA approval into a series of criteria that looked identical to FDA approval, and then required virtually all the criteria.

DEA arguments that "currently accepted medical use" implies FDA approval have been clearly and repeatedly repudiated by the courts. Since essentially the same issues were at stake in the current legal debate over the medical use of marijuana, the defenders of MDMA's medical use, who were drained of both patience and money, decided to lodge no further appeal. They accepted the fact that MDMA would remain in Schedule I until the legal definition of "currently accepted medical use" was resolved in the context of the medical marijuana lawsuit, or until research had satisfied the FDA that MDMA was both safe and efficacious for human use.

The stonewalling of the rescheduling process was an attempt by the DEA to continue to promote the message that all illegal drugs are inherently "bad." Scheduling has effectively eliminated all approved medical uses of Schedule I drugs. The costs of this loss of medical access[11] may vastly exceed the benefits in reduced drug abuse, if any, that result from the government's continued decision to propagandize the American people about the unqualified harmfulness of these drugs.[12] Judge Young himself calls the DEA refusal to accept the medical use of Schedule I drugs disingenuous, arbitrary, and capricious.

MDMA's emergency scheduling itself was found to be illegal in the courts. Congress gave the attorney general the power to criminalize certain drugs through the use of an emergency scheduling process. Yet the attorney general never formally subdelegated those powers to the DEA. Therefore, the DEA had no legal authority to declare the emergency scheduling of any drug. Thus, MDMA was actually legal until the Designer Drug Law of 1986 went into effect.[13]

In sum, the scheduling process itself was flawed, marred by illegal and inappropriate government actions.

The Media's Role in the Spread of MDMA

The popular media loved MDMA. They loved the name "ecstasy"; they loved its users—a white, affluent contrast to the popular stereotype; they loved the bar scene in which it was distributed in Texas. And they wrote glowing reports about it in nearly every popular publication, including *Newsweek, Time,* and the *Washington Post.* This was not the first time the media helped to advertise a "new" drug. In 1972, Edward Brecher detailed the media's role in publicizing glue sniffing in his "How to Launch a Nationwide Drug Menace." (Brecher, 1972). More recently, Reinarman and Levine exposed the media's contribution to spreading the crack epidemic (Reinarman and Levine, 1989).

MDMA received free advertising as a result of media publicity, which was beneficial for those MDMA distributors interested in expanding their markets. News accounts, which were primarily favorable reports (the nickname alone was enough), piqued the interest of casual recreational (as opposed to therapeutic) drug users. Many of these individuals had started using illegal drugs such as marijuana and psychedelics in the 1960s. They had dabbled with cocaine in the late 1970s and early 1980s and continued to use marijuana on occasion. As busy, "conventional," productive individuals, most had long since given up psychedelics as too time-consuming and debilitating. Few were interested in experiencing the lack of control and related difficulties they associated with LSD. But reports of the "ease" and euphoria of "ecstasy" made this drug sound different. And while media reports did not cause this group to rush out and try to find MDMA, if it did appear in their social worlds, they now, because of the publicity, had some familiarity with the drug. As a result of the publicity and the scheduling, recreational interest and use of MDMA among non-therapeutically oriented professionals, students, and yuppies appears to have greatly *increased*. Had it not been for the scheduling controversy that first attracted the media, it is very likely that the use of MDMA would have followed the earlier diffusion pattern of its first decade (the 1970s), growing slowly by word of mouth.

The Non-Deterrent Effect of Criminalization

Making MDMA illegal did not significantly deter its recreational use. It did increase demand, raise prices, and limit availability.[14] In the study population, most individuals who had started using MDMA after it was scheduled had already had experience with illegal drugs. The younger (under 35) users had discounted government information about drugs as propaganda, not to be taken seriously. The older (over 35) users had been alienated from the conventional view of drugs since the 1960s and saw government decisions about drugs as wholly political. When asked if MDMA's illegality made a difference, one 42-year-old physician said: "That didn't make any difference. My friends were using drugs before—smoking dope certainly. I think that's one way that one selects their friends. You sort of seek out people who, like you, are a little extra-legal."

Most respondents had ceased the use of "heavy" psychedelics such as LSD, but MDMA offered excitement without the "Who am I?" dilemma and other challenges associated with "acid." In general, recreational, post-1985 MDMA users had turned the notion of illegality on its head: "If it's illegal, it's probably good."

End of Research on Therapeutic Benefits

Scheduling did have a deterrent effect on the therapeutic use of MDMA. As a result of its illegality, there have been far fewer "guided" sessions with professional therapists and instrumental use of MDMA. Therapists almost uniformly abandoned their clinical use of MDMA, since their licenses and careers were at stake. These same people were among the most cautious users of MDMA, producing the greatest benefits. Only a few psychiatrists, who reported to us their continued use of MDMA in the psychological treatment of AIDS patients, have chosen to risk their licenses for the benefit of their patients.

Many respondents reported on the therapeutic benefits of MDMA. They had used it to uncover painful childhood memories and experiences that had been repressed; to decrease fear and defensiveness; to increase communication and empathy with one's spouse; to get through traumatic experiences such as rape and incest; to live with the pain of cancer; to resolve oneself to dying.

Formal therapeutic use and human research of MDMA has been deterred by its Schedule I status. This is perhaps the most regrettable aspect of its illegality, as argued by the therapists during the hearings. Though the FDA claims that its refusal to permit experimentation is based on concern for the health of the volunteers, after more than 11 million doses of MDMA have been taken in the United States, the literature does not contain even one case of an individual suffering neurological symptoms linked to MDMA-related brain damage. In Switzerland, psychiatrists have used MDMA successfully in hundreds of cases.[15] Even the animal data shows that primates receiving doses equivalent to amounts used in psychotherapy show no evidence of any physiological changes. When excessive doses sufficient to cause changes are given to primates or rats, all evidence shows that such changes are temporary and without observable behavioral significance (Battaglia, Yeh, and DeSouza, 1988; Ricaurte, 1988).

MDMA Use as Non-Problematical

MDMA should not have been made illegal because it never was, and continues not to be, a significant social problem. "Ecstasy" use has not surfaced as a significant problem because there are properties of MDMA itself that contain its use. Respondents reported that frequent use of MDMA almost invariably produces a strong dysphoric reaction that is only exacerbated with continued use. Many respondents described how too frequent use resulted in an increasing number of unpleasant aftereffects (i.e., muscular tension, particularly in the jaw, and anxiety), coupled with an almost total loss of desired effects. These effects occurred with greater rapidity than those experienced with other more commonly abused substances such as cocaine. Unlike classic addictive drugs such as opiates, increasing the dose of MDMA after a tolerance has built up will not result in desired effects. Therefore, although some individuals use MDMA frequently at the beginning, they eventually taper their use in order to derive the maximum benefit (Beck et al., 1989).

MDMA's use primarily by middle-class devotees has also limited potential problems. These individuals contain and control their use of all drugs because they have viable life investments (such as jobs, families, homes) to protect (Rosenbaum, 1989). Secondly, they tend to be well informed about MDMA and recognize that overuse greatly diminishes the drug's positive effects. The majority of individuals in this study population used MDMA infrequently, as "time-out" behavior (Rosenbaum et al., 1989).

Manufacturers and distributors of MDMA tend to be white, middle-class men and women, most of whom have legitimate occupations outside their dealing enterprise. Because they are conventional citizens and wish to remain so, the distribution network is extremely closed. These individuals sell MDMA "on the side" and very rarely sell other drugs. They do not refer to themselves as dealers and, in fact, look down on those who sell drugs such as cocaine and heroin. Unlike successful crack dealers, they do use their own product and have little problem with abuse. Violent enforcement of debts and murderous competition for markets are unknown. Most lower-level distributors sell MDMA as a service to their friends, making little or no money in the process. There is virtually no interest among these distributors to expand in more "traditional" drug circles to build a business. This helps explain the absence of MDMA in the inner cities.

MDMA's absence in the inner cities may be considered by some to be a sign of the success of the criminalization of MDMA. Pharmacological reasons are more likely to explain this absence, since legal status has nothing to do with a drug's popularity among the "underclass." MDMA is a drug that promotes self-reflection, can only be used enjoyably every few weeks, and is unpleasant to overuse. It is not likely to be attractive to classes of individuals whose life options are so limited that they feel they need to use anesthetizing drugs on a daily basis.

CONCLUSIONS

This chapter has attempted to show that criminalization of MDMA was unjustified. The scheduling process itself had numerous problems and was of dubious legality. We concur with the administrative law judge's concerns about the DEA's and FDA's interpretations of scheduling criteria as applied to MDMA. We also agree with the judge's broader critique of the denial of medical use and research with Schedule I drugs.

These considerations, together with the problems that can result from the criminalization of any drug, lead the writers to conclude that the DEA acted counterproductively in scheduling MDMA. It should have spent more time gathering information before making a reactive, largely blind decision. Given its problematic implications, the scheduling of substances should be viewed as a last resort to be implemented only after determining that, (1) there are real problems associated with a drug, (2) these problems can be remedied by legislation, and (3) legislation will not impede the development of a drug's potential benefits.

NOTES

1. Structurally similar to both mescaline and amphetamine, MDMA produces a mild psychedelic affect and is almost always taken orally, with effects lasting from four to six hours. An average dose (100-150 mgs.) costs from $10 to $25. MDMA typically produces a very euphoric effect, often leading users to feel both optimistic and relaxed. While experiencing the effects of MDMA, communication between individuals can be enhanced, with counterproductive ego defenses lessened.

2. NIDA Grant No. R01 DA 04408, "Exploring Ecstasy: A Descriptive Study of MDMA Users," Marsha Rosenbaum, Principal Investigator; Patricia Morgan, Co-Principal Investigator; Jerome Beck, Project Director; Beatrice Rouse, NIDA Project Officer.

3. Project staff also did ethnographic fieldwork, traveling to Dallas, Bali, Grateful Dead concerts, and accompanying users during their MDMA experiences. Members of MDMA distribution networks were also interviewed in an effort to trace trends in production and sales of the drug.

4. MDMA's recreational use further increased after several cocaine dealers had MDMA experiences, which convinced them to abandon cocaine and its attendant harms and turn their attentions instead toward distributing MDMA.

5. For a detailed discussion of the scheduling process, see Beck and Rosenbaum, 1990.

6. In the United States, both the DEA and the FDA regulate all scientific and medical use involving human subjects. The DEA regulates the researchers and the FDA regulates research protocols. No federal scientific review is required for nonhuman studies, although researchers must have DEA approval before it is legal to be in possession of a Schedule I drug.

7. Judge Young's ruling would not be final, however, but would be merely a recommendation to John Lawn, the Administrator of the DEA. The actual scheduling recommendation of John Lawn would not necessarily be final either, but could be appealed in the Federal Court of Appeals. Nor was United States scheduling completely an independent decision. The United States was a signatory to the International Convention on Psychotropic and Narcotic Drugs, administered by the World Health Organization, and was bound to place internationally scheduled drugs into domestic schedules at least as restrictive as the Convention's. In May, 1985, an Expert Committee on Drug Dependence for the International Convention was scheduled to issue a ruling on MDMA and a large number of other similar substances for possible inclusion in the treaty.

8. Among those testifying were Dr. Morris Lipton, a psychiatrist and associate editor of the *American Journal of Psychiatry;* Dr. Robert Lynch, the chief statewide psychiatric consultant for two cabinet departments in California; Dr. Lester Grinspoon of Harvard Medical School.

9. Dr. George Greer cited a study he conducted with 29 of these patients; Dr. Jack Downing cited a study in which 21 healthy volunteers were extensively monitored before, during and one day after an MDMA experience. Also cited were animal toxicity studies conducted by Dr. Charles Frith of Toxicology Pathology Associates.

10. This includes multiyear double-blind placebo studies and multimillions of dollars of animal toxicity studies.

11. Legal, medical research in Switzerland suggests that MDMA has a beneficial role in the treatment of reactive depression, addictive disorders, phobias, obsessive-compulsion, and anorexia. U.S. patients with these disorders number in the millions. As for marijuana, almost 100,000 U.S. citizens were treated with THC for nausea associated with cancer chemotherapy last year, even though all studies comparing THC and marijuana find marijuana more effective while producing fewer side effects.

12. Dr. David Blum, brain specialist at the UCLA Neurophysiology Clinic, as well as other physicians, criticized the television ad of the Partnership for a Drug-Free America, which purported to contrast the EEG of a person on marijuana with that of a "normal" person. Blum pointed out that the 1982 National Academy of Sciences report found that marijuana had no marked effects on EEG and that the EEG in the ad was from a person either asleep or in a coma.

13. At that time, several people who had been arrested for MDMA as a result of the 1985 emergency scheduling had their cases dropped.

14. While the scheduling frightened some of the original distributors, who then curtailed business, other producers increased their output. They hoped to take advantage of the expanded profit potential caused by (1) the increased demand caused by the media blitz, and (2) the increased price caused by scheduling. Average price per dose went from about $10 to about $15, while consumption rose from about 200,000 to about 400,000 doses per month.

15. Personal communication, Dr. Jorg Roth, Research Director, Swiss Association of Physicians for Psycholytic Therapy.

REFERENCES

Battaglia, G. Yeh, S. Y., & DeSouza, E. B. (1988). MDMA-induced neurotoxicity: Parameters of degeneration and recovery of brain serotonin neurons. *Pharmacology, Biochemistry and Behavior, 29:*269-274.

Beck, J., Harlow, D., McDonnell, D., Morgan, P., Rosenbaum, M., & Watson, L. (1989). *Exploring ecstasy: A description of MDMA users* (Grant No. 1 R01 DA04408). Final report to the National Institute on Drug Abuse.

Beck, J., & Rosenbaum, M. (1990). The scheduling of MDMA ("Ecstacy"). In J. Inciardi (Ed.), *The handbook of drug control in the United States.* Westport, CT: Greenwood.

Brecher, E. M. (1972). *Licit and illicit drugs.* Boston: Little, Brown.

Crackdown on ecstasy, A. (1985, June 11). *Time.* p. 64.

Dye, C. (1982). XTC: The chemical pursuit of pleasure. *Drug Survival News, 10* (5):8-9.

Ecstasy: The lure and the peril. (1985, June 1). *Washington Post,* p. 1, 4.

Eisner, B. (1989). *Ecstasy: The MDMA story.* Berkeley: Ronin.

Getting high on "ecstasy." (1985, April 15). *Newsweek.* p. 96.

Hardman, H. F., Haavik, C. O., & Stephens, M. H. (1973, June). Relationship of the structure of mescaline and seven analogs to toxicity and behavior in five species of laboratory animals. *Toxicology and Applied Pharmacology, 25* (2):229-309.

Reinarman, C., & Levine, H. (1989). The crack attack: Media and politics in America's latest drug scare. In J. Best (Ed.), *Images and issues: Current perspectives on social problems.* New York: Aldine deGruyter.

Ricuarte, G. (1988). *Abstract.* Annual meeting of Society of Neurosciences.

Rosenbaum, M. (1989). *Just say what?* San Francisco: National Council on Crime and Delinquency.

Rosenbaum, M., Morgan, P., & Beck, J. (1989). Ethnographic notes on "ecstasy" use among professionals. *International Journal on Drug Policy, 1* (2).

7

Marijuana Legalization: The Time Is Now

DOUGLAS McVAY

The concept of marijuana legalization has gone in and out of vogue over the past 20 years, as several states, either de jure or de facto, have decriminalized its possession and use. Some describe the cause of decriminalization in the 1970s as a wave of permissive liberalism. This is hardly the case, however.

In the early 1970s, a presidential commission chaired by the former Republican governor of Pennsylvania, Raymond P. Schafer, called for federal decriminalization and eventual legalization, regulation, and control of marijuana (National Commission on Marihuana and Drug Abuse, 1972).

The commission concluded that marijuana should be decriminalized. This was not interpreted as a license to abuse substances. In fact, the Shafer Commission's overriding concern was reducing substance abuse. According to the report, "On the basis of our findings, discussed in previous Chapters, we have concluded that society should seek to discourage use, while concentrating its attention on the prevention and treatment of heavy and very heavy use. The Commission feels that the criminalization of possession of marihuana for personal use is socially self-defeating as a means of achieving this objective" (National Commission on Marihuana and Drug Abuse, 1972).

In 1977, Senator Jacob Javits and Representative Edward Koch introduced a bill to federally decriminalize marijuana. Although both congressmen were Democrats, their motivation for this bill had as much to do with the economics of pursuing marijuana users, then estimated at 13 million, as the undesirability of seeking to imprison such a large portion of the national population (Koch, 1977).

Today, government surveys estimate the number of regular marijuana users at about 11.8 million (NIDA, 1988). The cost of pursuing and punishing 11.8 million marijuana users, if that is all there are, would be enormous, both financially and societally.

NORML and others are skeptical of the government's ability to take an accurate survey of any criminal behavior. Such estimates inevitably underreport the actual number of users for several reasons, including agency bias and respondents' fear of disclosure. This will present problems when marijuana is legalized. The number of reported users will appear to skyrocket. The number of users may in fact increase slightly; however, the biggest increase will come from those who failed to report their use while it was illegal. The difference between truly new users and users previously hidden in the general population will not be immediately apparent. Thus estimates of the impact of legalization will have to be tempered appropriately.

Currently, only a small fraction of offenders are actually caught. The public concern over violence stems largely from the trade in crack cocaine, methamphetamine, and other dangerous drugs. The question becomes, do we have the luxury to continue sending police after marijuana bushes, or is there a more effective, less wasteful means to control marijuana use?

The alternatives include: (1) continue the present system of catching a few and making examples of them; (2) fully decriminalize the possession and use of marijuana in private by adults, as 11 states have attempted to do; or (3) legalize, regulate, and control marijuana, a substance that DEA Administrative Law Judge Francis Young called "the safest therapeutically active substance known to man" (Young, 1988).

Another option, actually only an expansion of the current system, would mean arresting, prosecuting, and punishing a significant percentage of the estimated 11.8 million regular marijuana offenders. This idea should be discarded as impossible and undesirable. In 1988, law enforcement authorities made 1,155,200 criminal arrests for all drug offenses (FBI, 1989). Of these, more than 324,000 arrests were for simple possession of marijuana (FBI, 1989).

It is unreasonable to increase by 12 times the number of drug arrests made annually, and add the proportionate amount of resources to the criminal justice system, simply to crack down on marijuana users. There are higher priorities for the criminal justice system and for society as a whole. Significant expansion of criminal justice efforts directed solely against occasional marijuana use would be unworkable because of the cost. It would also further compound crime problems, since resources would be diverted from pursuit of violent criminals toward marijuana users, sellers, and growers.

The ethics of any society that criminalizes and seeks to punish 5% of its population over a simple plant must be called into question. The rationale behind such a scheme must be questioned critically, and the costs of both dollars and lives ruined by a criminal drug arrest must be considered.

There is also the question of how to enforce the prohibition. Marijuana is simply the dried leaves and flowers of the cannabis plant. The cannabis plant grows easily almost anywhere in the world, and is produced and sold in all 50 states. It grows wild as a weed throughout the United States and in many other parts of the globe. The plant may be grown either outdoors or indoors, using very simple gardening techniques. It is possible for any individual to violate the current marijuana prohibition with very little chance of detection.

For these reasons among others, criminalization of marijuana must be discarded as an option. How can society control marijuana? This article argues that the best available option is regulation of the market through civil means. This civil regulation could take any of several forms. NORML has developed a system for such regulation, and several others have been proposed in the past. Existing methods for control of legal drugs (e.g., alcohol, tobacco, aspirin) could serve as models for a marijuana regulation system. Both positive and negative experiences with legal drugs could be used to help formulate the best possible system.

Specifics are important, but a lack of consensus among law-makers on an agreed-upon model should not end the discussion. Rather, it should serve as a touching-off point for discussion. The question should not be, as it has been legislatively, "How can we best proceed within the limited constraint of prohibition as decided several decades ago?" but rather "How can we best regulate, control, and discourage the use and abuse of marijuana?" The answer to that question is simple: Legalize marijuana, regulate it, and tax the commerce.

CURRENT STATE OF MARIJUANA PROHIBITION

The goals of a particular program or policy and its success or failure at meeting these goals must be reviewed in order to analyze the policy. In terms of marijuana as with other illegal drugs, the goal of current policy is twofold: (1) halt use, and (2) suppress production and trafficking. How successful has the government's war on marijuana been? A number of indicators give a contradictory view.

For example, the 1988 NIDA Household Survey of drug use in the noninstitutionalized population referred to above estimates that 11.8 million people use marijuana once per month or more. This is a decrease of roughly 37% from 1985, when an estimated 18 million were regular users (NIDA, 1988).

Other indicators tell a different story, however. The National Narcotics Intelligence Consumers Committee, for example, estimates that in 1985 there were 6,400-8,300 metric tons of marijuana available for consumption (NNICC, 1988). NNICC reports that in 1988, 12,130-16,710 metric tons were available for consumption (NNICC, 1989). The NNICC also reports that domestic production of marijuana has increased and notes that marijuana prices have risen in the last 5 to 10 years (NNICC, 1989). NORML contends, and many formal and informal indicators support the contention, that the NNICC estimate is itself an underestimate. The extent is difficult to determine because of the illegal nature of the trade; however, it is substantial.

Emergency room mentions of marijuana and hashish have also increased dramatically, from 3,818 in 1985 to an estimated 8,200 in 1988 (NNICC, 1989). Note that there is a very high degree of concomitance associated with these figures. More than 80% of the mentions are in combination with other drugs (NIDA, 1988).

Without a reliable count of the number of marijuana users, the full extent of the prohibition policy's failure is difficult to determine. The fact that 33% of the U.S. population 12 years of age or older, 65,748,000 people, admit to using marijuana at some time in their lives (NIDA, 1988), indicates that the policy has failed at its primary goal of stopping use. How badly the policy has failed must remain a matter for conjecture until prohibition is repealed.

The question thus must be, where do we go from here? The federal government has pushed since 1981 for increases in fines, penalties, and other criminal justice sanctions for marijuana use. Combined federal, state, and local expenditures were estimated at more than $10 billion in 1987 (Nadelmann, 1989), and the costs continue to escalate. The federal antidrug budget alone for 1990 totals $9.4 billion (*Washington Post,* 1989).

In addition, countless lives and reputations are ruined by giving otherwise lawabiding citizens an arrest record. For example, 28% of the 1,115,200 total estimated drug arrests performed in 1987 were for simple possession of marijuana (FBI, 1989). Calls by Drug Policy

Director William Bennett, President George Bush, Senator Joseph Biden, and others from both ends of the political spectrum for increased efforts by law enforcement indicate that the number of arrests will be likely to increase in the future.

The other two alternatives, decriminalization and legalization/regulation, must be explored. Decriminalization of possession of marijuana is a good idea, yet without ensuring a noncriminal method of acquiring the drug, the policy falls short of the promise implied in the very term "decriminalization."

Alaska is the only state that has truly decriminalized marijuana use by allowing cultivation for private personal use. The other 10 states that decriminalized marijuana laws simply reduced the penalty classification and punishment for possession.

Under the "decriminalized" system, the user is forced to choose between either committing a major felony by cultivating plants for personal use, or purchasing marijuana from a criminal drug dealer, which perpetuates the black market and exposes the marijuana user to other drugs being peddled by the same dealer. Decriminalization does not necessarily remove the marijuana consumer from the criminal market, since the user must rely on that market to avoid committing a major felony.

Two of the alternatives for control of the marijuana market, continued prohibition and decriminalization, are inadequate. If only to reserve precious court time and jail space, decriminalization is preferable. The remaining option, marijuana legalization, regulation, and control, must be explored as the only remaining viable option.

LIKELY EFFECTS OF LEGALIZATION

Prohibitionists frequently argue that marijuana legalization would not be a panacea for the United States's drug problems. In addition, problems arising from illicit trafficking in cocaine, heroin, PCP, methamphetamine, and other drugs might still occur, as would problems arising from simple use of marijuana. The prohibitionists also argue that legalization would send the message that marijuana is good for young people to use and abuse. These may be legitimate concerns and should be addressed. The question, however, remains: what would be the real effect, on the individual and on society, of legalizing marijuana?

There are four areas of concern that must be addressed in assessing any proposal to legalize marijuana: what might a model legalization scheme look like; the effect on the criminal justice system; the financial impact; and the impact on society from legal availability of marijuana, especially as regards the use of drugs.

A MODEL SYSTEM

One of the most frequent arguments heard against legalization is the speculation over what Madison Avenue would do with drugs like marijuana or cocaine. The most important point to stress is that the system of legal marijuana need not resemble the system for either tobacco or alcohol. Those models of legalization are examples of how not to regulate and discourage use and abuse.

The American experience with these drugs and their legalization is largely responsible for the bitter taste left by discussion of drug legalization. The spectre of a marijuana "Marlboro Man" or "Buds McKenzie" attracting young people, minorities, and other populations at highest risk for drug abuse into using marijuana is frightening for most citizens. Of course, the actual blame legitimately belonging to these advertising icons is debatable. Yet, the imagery forms a frightening picture for many average citizens.

A comparison of the effects of the repeal of alcohol prohibition in the United States and in England may shed some light on how best to avoid an explosion in marijuana use. It is true that, in the United States, when alcohol prohibition was repealed, the death rate from liver cirrhosis rose dramatically. This leading indicator of alcohol abuse, by contrast, remained steady in the United Kingdom for several years following repeal of their wartime prohibition. An analysis by Milton Terris, M.D., contends that a combination of strict limits on hours of availability, increasingly high taxes, anti-alcohol education, and treatment of alcoholics, was responsible for the success of the British system. In the United Kingdom, the death rate from cirrhosis actually declined for several years after prohibition's repeal (Terris, 1967).

In contrast, the American system of laissez-faire legalization, combined with the alcohol industry's largely successful opposition to anti-alcohol education efforts, seemed to create an immediate, continuing increase in the number of cirrhosis deaths in the United States. This is not an absolute gauge of the success or failure of either the British or the American system, yet it does give an indication that more effective approaches exist.

Applying the lessons of history to the marijuana laws, we can observe that any attempt to repeal marijuana prohibition must be approached carefully. For instance, granting the existence of problems with alcohol and tobacco legalization, it may be appropriate to first reform those systems of regulation and control in order to facilitate the effort to discourage use of those two drugs. Then, after making these changes, a similar system should be put in place that would regulate and control the use, production, and distribution of marijuana, while at the same time discouraging abuse and first use of marijuana.

Such discouraging mechanisms include, yet are not limited to, the following: age limits; restrictions against some forms of marketing and merchandising that may be seen as glamorizing the drug; a complete ban on advertising; prominent display of medically legitimate health warnings; and pricing structures that discourage consumption while denying criminal drug dealers market supremacy.

The system for legal marijuana would need to be flexible, since the effects of marijuana legalization, pro and con, can only be guessed at. Yet, it is vital to get past initial objections and begin coming to grips with the practical necessities of dealing with drugs. It is easy to dismiss the notion of marijuana legalization as long as no plan has been officially formulated at the federal level to handle such a change in policy.

Efforts at the federal level should thus be directed toward developing a scheme for marijuana distribution, regulation, and control that would be acceptable to a plurality of the public. States would then have the option of adopting such a system or maintaining some sort of prohibition, much as states have the option of prohibiting alcohol sales and production.

Appropriate taxes and user fees would be levied in order to fund substance abuse prevention efforts. Such a system, with appropriate discouraging mechanisms built in, would send the message that marijuana is no more acceptable when legal than it was when illegal. It is only the current methods of control that are inappropriate and must be altered.

Once the stigma of criminalization is removed, the relatively few users who develop abuse or dependence problems could come forward and get help. Taking the marijuana market out of criminal hands would ensure purity, quality controls, and the like. It would also eliminate the possibility that the dealer, motivated by greed, would entice the marijuana user to try harder, more dangerous (and more profitable) drugs.

CRIME/PRISONS

The most obvious area to feel the impact of the legalization of marijuana is the criminal justice system. There are two groups of offenses that must be looked at in this context: (1) actual drug offenses, e.g., possession, cultivation/production, sale; and (2) drug-related offenses, e.g., theft and other property crimes for gain, and trafficking-related violence.

In terms of the first group of offenses, the role of marijuana is unusual. The number of persons actually incarcerated for simple possession of marijuana is small compared to the total number of prison and jail inmates in the United States. Yet, arrests for simple marijuana possession make up a large part of total annual drug arrests (see above). A great deal of police and court time is squandered pursuing throwaway arrests.

One of the most pressing problems that this situation creates is the impression of selective enforcement of the laws. This problem was noted as early as 1972 in the Shaffer Commission's report. It states: "On top of all this is the distinct impression among the youth that some police may use the marihuana laws to arrest people they don't like for other reasons, whether it be their politics, their hair style or their ethnic background. Whether or not such selectivity actually exists, it is perceived to exist" (National Commission on Marihuana and Drug Abuse, 1972).

This impression is inevitable when the number of marijuana arrests is compared to the number of marijuana users. Even using the government's conservative estimate of marijuana users (12 million regular users), only 2% or 3% of these people are arrested each year. The law is violated with impunity, the only harm done being directed against the offender herself or himself. It is thus questionable what business the state has interfering in the private affairs of some individuals based on their use of a weed.

The other aspect of drugs and crime—crimes committed under the influence of a drug—is one about which there is some confusion. A great deal of concern is expressed over the involvement of illegal drugs in crimes. As the U.S. Bureau of Justice Statistics reported in 1988, "Concern over the use of drugs and a belief that such use leads to criminal activity has long been an issue in American society" (Innes, 1988). Yet, the government's own statistics contradict, not support, this relationship.

A new program for measuring the prevalence of drug use among arrestees, the Drug Use Forecasting (DUF) program of the Department of Justice, reveals that anywhere from 53% to 90% of male arrestees test positive for illicit drugs. This statistic is of dubious value, however, since only a fraction of the nation's total annual arrests result in adjudications of guilt (U.S. Department of Justice, 1989). No data is available on the disposition of the cases included in the DUF program. It is thus impossible to know the number of persons testing positive who are actually guilty of any crimes. It is also possible that DUF's results are skewed by the inclusion of a number of small-scale drug arrests, including possession offenses, in the DUF program reports.

Studies on state prison inmates reveal some connection between daily use of heroin or cocaine and property crime, although only about one-third of the total number of these offenders was reported to be under the influence of these drugs at the time of their offense. A far stronger connection was found between use of alcohol and crime, particularly violent crime. At least 40% of the violent offenders were reported to have been under the influence of alcohol at the time of their offense (Innes, 1988).

The chicken-and-the-egg discussion over which comes first also arises when discussing drug use and crime. As the Bureau of Justice Statistics notes:

> An alternative view of the relationship between drugs and crime holds that drug use does not directly cause criminal behavior, but the same circumstances that might lead a person to begin committing crimes may also contribute to the development of drug habits. For example, social conditions, including poverty and discrimination, may limit opportunity and reduce an individual's investment in society, leading to both drug abuse and criminal behavior. Also, some people enjoy taking risks and are willing, for whatever reasons, to violate laws or norms, or they seek possessions or experiences that are not available by legitimate means. The use of drugs, especially on a regular basis, may not occur among such persons until after they have begun a career of criminal activity. Drug use may thus be only part of a more general lifestyle that also includes other types of criminal activity. . . . (F)or some prison inmates drug use began prior to other criminal activity and may have contributed, either by lowering inhibitions or by generating a need for money, to a developing criminal career. For many others, drug use, particularly regular use of a major drug, started only after their criminal careers had begun. (Innes, 1988)

TAX REVENUE

The impact marijuana legalization would have on tax revenues would be felt in two ways. First, the tax money currently funding efforts at marijuana suppression and eradication would be redirected. This much is obvious, since marijuana would no longer be contraband.

How this funding redirection would effect overall antidrug spending is difficult to gauge. There might not necessarily be a "peace dividend." The funds would need to go to enforcement of other drug laws; those against cocaine, heroin, PCP, and hard drugs, and whatever other drugs are still illegal.

In addition, some funds would need to be devoted to the regulatory system set up to control production and distribution, at the state and federal levels. This funding need would eventually be offset by taxes on both the marijuana sales as well as taxes on the income derived from such sales, licensing fees, and so on.

It is also difficult to measure just how removing marijuana from the list of crimes that our police enforce would effect police functions and efficiency. Noting the tremendous number of marijuana possession arrests performed each year, it is evident that some police time could be redirected toward dealing with serious problems and violent crimes. This also means clearing the courts, jails, and prisons of marijuana offenders—not only users, who would no longer be criminals, but also dealers and cultivators, who would be outmoded and put out of business.

· Currently, control over the marijuana market is left in the hands of the criminal black market. As such, proceeds from marijuana sales are kept in the underground economy. The profits go untaxed, and the money generated is kept off the books. *Fortune* magazine estimated the potential tax earnings from legal marijuana sales at $11 billion per year, and that only accounts for taxes on the marijuana, not including taxes on the income generated by the legal sellers, distributors, and producers (Kupfer, 1988).

Some opponents of legalization argue that it is inappropriate for society to profit from drug use. Such a policy, it is argued, puts the state into the position of promoting drug use.

Legalization supporters counter that people in general use drugs of one kind or another, mostly legal ones. Thus, the responsibility of society is to ensure that relatively safe drugs are available, although discouraged, while the relatively dangerous drugs should be less available and more actively discouraged. The United States already taxes alcohol and tobacco, the two worst public health problems our society faces. Society would profit tremendously from legal marijuana sales if we decide to take advantage of the market already in existence.

IMPACT ON SOCIETY, DRUG USE

Finally, what would a society with legal marijuana look like, and what would be the impact on drug use in general? We can look toward The Netherlands for part of the answer, although we would certainly not get the full picture since marijuana and hashish are still officially illegal in The Netherlands. Their policy of tolerance toward soft drugs has, however, resulted in effective decriminalization of use and transfer of small amounts of cannabis.

In spite of this acceptance of cannabis, use rates by both youth and adults are much lower than the reported rates in other European countries or in the United States (van der Wal, 1985; van de Wijngaart, 1987). In addition, the rate of heroin addiction in The Netherlands is reported to be slowly decreasing from its current estimated rate of 0.14% (much lower than the United States), and the crime rate, stable since 1984, may be falling (Drug Abuse Education Newsletter, 1988).

While it is true that the United States is not The Netherlands, the example of the Dutch system provides at least an indication that marijuana legalization would not be the disaster that opponents say it would be. Indeed, if marijuana legalization means people would avoid use of alcohol or hard drugs and would use marijuana instead, the net result would be positive, since the harm both to the user and the society would be less. Critics claim that the number of marijuana users would increase after legalization. It must be conceded that this claim may be true in some respects, although the net result would hardly be the disaster opponents predict. After marijuana legalization there will be an increase in the number of people willing to admit that they are marijuana users, because a significant number of users will no longer fear admitting their use. NORML estimates that there are currently some 30 to 50 million regular marijuana users in the United States, many more than the government's reported 11.8 million. Thus, an initial explosion in the number of users is likely, is no cause for alarm, and is easily understood.

Some "new" users who really would be using marijuana for the first time may formerly have been users of alcohol, a drug that is more dangerous than marijuana. Although these people would still be using a drug, they would be doing less damage to themselves than they would have otherwise. Thus, less harm would result from their drug use than would have occurred under marijuana prohibition.

It is likely that a period of a few years would be needed to stabilize the marijuana using population, and to begin reducing the number of users. Yet as the example of The Netherlands proves, it is possible to reduce the number of users without imposing criminal or even civil penalties against them. The first problem is getting a true handle on the extent of marijuana use.

There would probably be a need for a vigorous campaign to reduce the risk of abuse and to discourage first use. The experience of American society with reduction of tobacco use should provide the groundwork for setting up a discouragement campaign against marijuana use.

It is difficult to predict the effects of legalization precisely because we have so little experience at legalizing a social drug. The example of the repeal of alcohol prohibition, as noted above, left a bitter taste because of the immediate rise in abuse indicators, specifically cirrhosis deaths. Arguably, American society has learned a great deal in the more than 50 years since alcohol became legal. NORML contends that the United States has matured since then, and that a responsible plan for production, distribution, and regulation of marijuana can be developed; indeed, such a plan was formulated in 1981 (Evans et al., 1981).

The concern over what message is being sent by legalizing a drug is understandable, and legitimate. The message, however, is not a negative one. The drug suggested for legalization is marijuana, a reasonably safe drug if used responsibly, a drug that has never caused an overdose death (Grinspoon, 1987; Young, 1988).

Legalization with age limits for purchase and use is the only way to prevent underage use; few criminal dealers ask for proof of I.D. before making a sale. Indeed, the concern should be over what message is sent when society makes alcohol and tobacco, both deadly and addictive, legally available, and prohibits marijuana, a relatively less dangerous drug. The message is obviously not one of concern for the society at large, nor for the health of the individual user. At best, no intelligible message is discerned. At worst, the society is thought of as hypocritical and culturally biased.

CONCLUSIONS

What, then, is the future of marijuana in America? The direction in which our government is currently heading is toward more enforcement and tougher penalties. This direction, however, leads inevitably to a dead-end. In more than 50 years, prohibition of marijuana has failed to stop marijuana use and abuse. It has instead created a large criminal class out of citizens who are otherwise law-abiding, peaceful, productive members of society. Those citizens who have not had their lives and careers ruined by an arrest have to live in fear and mistrust of their own government and the police. Meanwhile, the problems created by the legal drugs alcohol and tobacco go largely unabated. Citizens who decide to use a drug recreationally have little legal recourse except these very dangerous drugs. Something must change.

A better system for managing marijuana use would involve civil regulation, taxation, and control. Such a system could take one of many forms. The system would be set up to guarantee the licit availability of good-quality marijuana at reasonable prices (below criminal market levels), while at the same time discouraging first use and abuse with age restrictions, honest health warnings, restrictions on availability, and other mechanisms. The financial impact from legalized marijuana would be positive, from enhanced tax revenue as well as redirection of current antidrug expenditures. The effect on criminal justice would be to free considerable police time to deal with other, more serious problems. The experience of The Netherlands shows that the societal impact would not be negative overall, and in fact would be positive in reducing rates of abuse of marijuana and other substances.

Marijuana legalization is a good idea, whether in fashion or not. American society needs sensible, rational answers to such pressing problems as the nation's drug problems. Legalizing marijuana can help. It is time to take a fresh look.

REFERENCES

Evans, R., et al. (1981, December 12). The regulation and taxation of cannabis commerce. *Task Force on Cannabis Regulation.*

Expert cites success of Dutch policy; "war on drugs" creates "entrepreneur's paradise." (1988, June). *Drugs & Drug Abuse Education Newsletter,* p. 52.

Federal Bureau of Investigation. (1988). Sourcebook of criminal justice statistics—1988. *Uniform Crime Reporting Statistics,* p. 519.

Federal Bureau of Investigation. (1989). Crime in America, 1988. *Uniform Crime Reporting Statistics.*

Grinspoon, L. (Ed.). (1987, November). Marijuana. *Harvard Medical School Mental Health Letter,* p. 2.

Innes, C. (1988a, January). Profile of state prison inmates 1986. *Bureau of Justice Statistics.* Washington, DC: U.S. Department of Justice.

Innes, C. (1988b, July). Drug use and crime. *Bureau of Justice Statistics.* Washington, DC: U.S. Department of Justice.

Koch, E. (1977, March 15). Testimony on decriminalization of marijuana. *Hearings before the U.S. House Select Committee on Narcotics Abuse and Control.*

Kupfer, A. (1988, June 20). What to do about drugs. *Fortune,* 117(13): 40.

Nadelmann, E. A. (1989, September 1). Drug prohibition in the United States: Costs, consequences, and alternative. *Science,* p. 940.

National Institute on Drug Abuse (NIDA). (1988a). *Annual data 1987: Data from the Drug Abuse Warning Network (DAWN).* Series I, No. 7. p. 1.

National Institute on Drug Abuse. (1988b). *Household survey on drug abuse.*

National Commission on Marihuana and Drug Abuse. (1972). Marihuana: A signal of misunderstanding. *First Report of the National Commission on Marihuana and Drug Abuse,* p. 154.

NNIC. (1988, April). *The NNICC report 1987: The supply of illicit drugs to the United States.* National Narcotics Intelligence Consumers Committee, p. 18.

NNIC. (1989, April). *The NNICC report 1988: The supply of illicit drugs to the United States.* National Narcotics Intelligence Consumers Committee, p. 18.

Senate votes $9.4 billion drug plan. (1989, September 28). *Washington Post,* p. A1.

Terris, M. (1967, December). Epidemiology of cirrhosis of the liver: National mortality data. *American Journal of Public Health,* 57 (12): 2076-2088.

U.S. Department of Justice. (1989a). FY 1988 report on drug control. *Bureau of Justice Statistics,* p. 1.

U.S. Department of Justice. (1989b, February). Felony sentences in state courts, 1986. *Bureau of Justice Statistics,* p. 3.

van der Wal, H. J. (1985, March). Forward to Sylbing, G. *The use of drugs, alcohol and tobacco.* Foundation for the Scientific Study of Alcohol and Drug Use.

van de Wijngaart, G. F. (1987, June). *The normalization of cannabis use.* Paper presented at the 16th International Institute on the Prevention and Treatment of Drug Dependence, Lausanne, Switzerland.

Young, F. L. (1988, September 6). Opinion and recommended ruling, findings of fact, conclusions of law and decision of administrative law judge. *In The Matter of Marijuana Rescheduling Petition, Docket No. 86-22, Administrative Law Court of the Drug Enforcement Administration,* p. 58-59.

8

The U.S. Drug Problem and the U.S. Drug Culture: A Public Health Solution

STEVEN JONAS

In the United States the use and abuse of both legal and illegal recreational drugs have been recognized as the causes of serious health, social, and economic problems for more than 100 years. Much time, effort, and money have been spent trying to solve the recreational drug problem and the associated crime problem created by the illegalization of certain recreational drugs. To date, only the public education program that has led to the decline in the proportion of adults smoking cigarettes is known to have been even modestly successful.

The degree to which the use of the more intensely psychoactive drugs, such as alcohol, heroin, marijuana, and cocaine, is affected by public interventions, whether educational or punitive, is unknown. Yet society presses on relentlessly, trying to achieve success. The present principal focus of public drug policy is on the use of law enforcement to deal with the currently illegal drugs. However, even if the law enforcement approach does result in a lower level of use than if they were legal, the cost in crime, corruption, money, disease, and ruined lives is high. And there is no responsible authority who claims that the "war on drugs" (which is, in fact, a war on only certain drugs) has been a success. In fact, most consider it to be a failure.

In part, this failure is because the right questions have not been asked. To design and implement a successful recreational drug use and abuse reduction program, there are several questions not on the current drug policy agenda that must be asked and answered. *First,* what is the real nature and scope of the drug problem? *Second,* what are its principal causes? *Third,* what is wrong with the current approaches? *Fourth,* in light of the answers to these three questions, what constitutes a workable, effective program, and what needs to be done to implement it? In this chapter, answers are provided in some detail to the first two questions, in outline to the latter two. (The third and fourth questions are dealt with in some detail elsewhere [Jonas, 1990, 1991].)

It is postulated here that a primary cause of the drug problem in the United States is a Drug Culture that is a major feature of American society. There are other causes, to be sure. But if this one is not dealt with, nothing else stands much chance of success. To diminish the importance of the Drug Culture, it will be necessary to significantly reduce the influence of the tobacco and alcohol industries. Given their economic, political, and social power, that will be a very difficult task. However, after examining the reality of the place of drugs in our culture, it becomes clear that to decrease the deleterious effects of the recreational drugs on our society, that is precisely what must be done.

THE DRUG PROBLEM

There are five major recreational drugs used in the United States that cause health problems: tobacco (when smoked in cigarettes), alcohol, heroin, cocaine, and marijuana. The mortality data (Table 8.1) show clearly that in health terms the principal *drug* problems in the United States are the use and abuse of cigarette tobacco and alcoholic beverages, not the use and abuse of the currently illegal drugs (for more detail, see the section "Epidemiology" below). (The principal *drug-related crime* problems are caused by cocaine, currently illegal, and alcohol, currently legal.)

All of the drugs are addicting or potentially addicting. Cigarette tobacco is known to be (Office on Smoking and Health, 1988), and heroin (when used intravenously in a relatively pure form) is thought by many to be, almost invariably addicting. There are very few if any "weekend users" of cigarettes (Schoenborn and Cohen, 1986). Alcohol, cocaine, and marijuana are all potentially addicting. However, they all may be used safely on an occasional basis (except that cocaine, when smoked as "crack," is apparently an obligatory addictive drug, like cigarette tobacco and heroin). As far as is known, most users of each of these drugs (except, apparently, for crack) is only an occasional user (Bradley, 1987). However, addiction to each is a well-known and serious problem for up to 20% of users.

As mentioned regarding heroin, there is a serious risk of unintentional injury to self and others associated with intoxication with any of

Table 8.1
The Five Major Recreational Drugs Estimated Annual Mortality, 1988

Tobacco	Alcohol	Cocaine, Heroin, Marijuana
390,000	100,000 (direct)— 200,000 (direct plus indirect)	6,000

NOTE: See text references for sources.

these drugs. Long-term heavy use of alcohol causes many serious health problems. It is unclear whether there are any long-term serious physical health problems associated with either occasional or heavy use of cocaine, other than those related to acute intoxication. However, a constellation of serious mental health problems are associated with cocaine addiction (Gawin and Ellinwood, 1988). Regular smoking of marijuana appears to be associated with respiratory system disease (Wu et al., 1988). It is unclear whether either occasional use of or addiction to marijuana is associated with any other serious physical health problems.

Epidemiology

About 56 million U.S. adults (approximately one-third of the adult population) were cigarette smokers in 1988 (U.S. Bureau of the Census, Table 13; U.S. Department of Health and Human Services, Table 46). Cigarette smoking is the leading cause of preventable death in the United States (Office on Smoking and Health, 1989). The Surgeon General's current estimate is that approximately 390,000 deaths were attributable to cigarette smoking in 1988 (Office on Smoking and Health, 1989). Since cigarette smoking kills more people each year than all of the other drugs combined and is virtually always addicting, cigarette tobacco ought to be considered a very dangerous drug indeed. There is, in fact, no safe way to use cigarette tobacco. It is the most harmful to health of the recreational drugs currently in common use.

In contrast, alcohol may be consumed safely, and is, by most of its users (Bradley, 1987). Regular consumption of small amounts of alcohol may actually be beneficial for health (Breslow and Enstrom, 1980). However, because of its deleterious effects on the minority of persons who use it regularly, alcohol is certainly not a safe drug in terms of its health, social, and economic effects on the society as a whole.

In 1985 there were approximately 115 million adult users of alcohol, 65% of the total population 18 years of age and older (U.S. Bureau of the Census, Table 9; U.S. Department of Health and Human Services, Table 49). About 15% of them were classified as "heavy users," "problem drinkers," or "alcoholics." (There is some overlap in these definitions.) The 18 million or so adult heavy alcohol users in the United States consume about 50% of the ethyl alcohol sold (Bradley, 1987). That means that 50% of the industry's total sales of the chemical alcohol, and presumably a significant proportion of its profits, are generated by alcoholism and problem drinking.

Alcohol consumption is a major cause of death in the United States (Harwood et al., 1984: Table III-7; Bradley, 1987). The total number of direct alcohol-related deaths has been estimated at 100,000 annually. In an additional 100,000 deaths alcohol consumption is "a contributing factor" (Nadelmann, 1988b). Cirrhosis of the liver was the eighth leading overall cause of death in 1988 (*Monthly Vital Statistics Report,* 1988). Alcohol intoxication is associated with almost half of automobile injury deaths; one-third of drowning, homicide, boating, and aviation deaths; and one-fourth of suicide deaths. Close to half of all prisoners convicted of a crime were "under the influence" of alcohol at the time the crime was committed, and half of those were intoxicated at the time. More than half of all persons convicted of violent crime had been drinking at the time of the crime (Bradley, 1987).

The alcohol problem may be getting worse. Data indicate that younger people are drinking more now than did their forebears (Schoenborn). Further, the more that attempts are made to control, by user penalties, the use and abuse of the currently illegal drugs, the more people who like drugs will turn to alcohol. Thus, alcohol morbidity and mortality may be expected to increase in the coming decades.

In part because of their currently illegal status, epidemiological data on heroin, cocaine, and marijuana are much more difficult to come by than for cigarette smoking and alcohol. In 1984, there were an estimated 24 million regular users of marijuana. How many of these are habituated or addicted is unknown. An estimated 20 million people have tried cocaine, of whom between 10% and 20% are thought to be addicted (Wisotsky, 1986). The current rough guess for the number of heroin addicts is 500,000. In 1980, it was reported that the illegal drugs caused about 1,000 deaths annually (Harwood et al., 1984: Table III-8). The estimate for 1987 was about 6,000 (Nadelmann, 1988c).

Heroin addiction has destroyed many lives, although the number is certainly far less than that for cigarette smoking and alcohol. Yet it is unclear whether the destruction caused by heroin is related to the drug itself or to the life-style that is created by its status as an illegal drug. In the United States there are many people currently leading happy, productive lives who are addicted to methadone, a close chemical relative of heroin. In Great Britain, at least during the period when heroin was legally available on prescription from any general practitioner, it was said that there was a considerable number of "middle-class" addicts who lived reasonably normal lives, aside from their addiction. It is not known for certain whether long-term use of heroin, when administered in its pure form under sterile conditions, has any long-term deleterious health effects, other than the risk of unintentional injury to self and others associated with intoxication.

Thus, the data demonstrate clearly that, for the population as a whole, the health problems caused by the currently legal recreational drugs are far more serious than those caused by the currently illegal recreational drugs.

The Interrelationships Among the Drugs

This is a subject that has not been rigorously studied; yet it is an important one, worthy of more research. There is a "gateway theory" that use of certain, presumably less dangerous drugs leads to the use of other, more dangerous drugs. Former Attorney General Meese was fond of applying that theory to marijuana (Trebach, 1987). (Apparently he didn't apply the theory to alcohol, even though the District of Columbia has the highest annual per capita alcohol consumption rate in the country, 5.34 gallons of absolute alcohol per person in 1984 [*Statistical Bulletin,* 1987], as well as a massive illegal drug and drug-crime problem.) As analyzed by Professor Trebach, the data do not offer a strong case for marijuana as a gateway drug. Others believe that it is (Clayton, 1989). There certainly is evidence that cigarette tobacco and alcohol are gateway drugs to the use of the currently illegals (Schoenborn and Cohen, 1986; Casement, 1987; Trebach, 1987).

Multiple drug use and following pathways from one to another are certainly problems. Approximately one-fifth of all cocaine abusers are also alcohol abusers. Ninety-five percent of more than 2,000 cocaine addicts treated in one practice were adult children of parents who themselves were alcoholics or addicted to other drugs (Casement, 1987). In a study of the relationship between cigarette smoking and other unhealthy personal behaviors, it was found that a higher proportion of smokers than nonsmokers are classified as "heavy drinkers" (Schoenborn and Cohen, 1986).

There are many anecdotes on the subject. Consider the stories of two prominent New York professional athletes. In 1987 Dwight Gooden, the celebrated pitcher of the New York Mets baseball team, tested positive for cocaine on a voluntary urinalysis and immediately entered a cocaine rehabilitation program. He was almost universally condemned in the media. The assumption was made that he was a cocaine addict who would possibly be out for the season. The truth was rather different. Joseph Durso of the *New York Times* (1987) quoted a (presumably reliable) source at the treatment program: "There's no indication he's addicted to cocaine. [But] he definitely started on beer." In the late summer of 1988, Lawrence Taylor, the legendary linebacker for the New York Giants relapsed into cocaine use and likewise entered a drug treatment program. He said that under the pressure of training camp, he went to a bar, had a couple of beers, progressed to champagne, and before he knew it, was back using "coke" again.

Questions abound here. In persons who may have a genetic predisposition to alcoholism, is there also a genetic predisposition to other drug addictions? If there is a link, is it familial rather than genetic? Is it social? Are there risk factors that make persons susceptible to becoming addicted to one or more drugs? If so, what are they? Most smokers and most drinkers do not become cocaine or heroin addicts or alcoholics, but do the social acceptance and corporate promotion of cigarette smoking and alcohol consumption lead the more susceptible to try other drugs? Given the strong prodrug messages that abound in our society (see below), is there a certain proportion of people who will just naturally move from using the drugs that happen to be promoted to using those that happen not to be?

Economic Cost

The comparative costs of the principal recreational drugs are shown in Table 8.2. It must be borne in mind that estimating drug costs is a tricky business. Some experts think that the figures cited are much too high. Some figures are quite old. But at least the true order of magnitude relationship among the costs for the various drugs is probably as its appears in Table 8.2. Whatever the actual numbers are, the use and abuse of the recreational drugs cost the society a great deal of money.

For 1980 the costs of abuse of the currently illegal drugs were put at about $47 billion (Harwood et al., 1984). Less than $1.5 billion of that total was spent on treatment. The estimated mortality and morbidity cost was about $28 billion. The estimated crime cost was about $15 billion. With the explosion in the cocaine market that accompanied the expansion of the Reagan "war on drugs" in the 1980s, the estimated crime costs have skyrocketed as well. For 1985 the cocaine economy in the United States was estimated to be worth $80-$100 billion

Table 8.2
The Five Major Recreational Drugs Estimated Dollar Costs, in Billions

Costs	Tobacco (1984)	Alcohol (1983)	Cocaine, Heroin, Marijuana (1980, 1988)
health care	23	15[a]	1.5 (1980)[b]
lost productivity/ premature mortality and morbidity	31	98	
direct (drug-induced) crime and property loss	nil	4	> 100 (1988)[c]
drug-commerce crime (value of the illegal trade; tax losses)	0.3	nil	140 (1988)[d]
Total	54	117	241.5[e]

a. This figure includes only alcoholism and alcohol abuse treatment services. It does not include general health services costs incurred by alcohol-related or caused morbidity/mortality.

b. For 1988, this figure is significantly higher. For neither year does it include general health services costs incurred by illegal drug-related or caused morbidity/mortality.

c. This figure is for the value of illegal drug-related crime and lost productivity taken together.

d. This is the **commercial** value of the illegal drug market, in addition to the crime costs.

e. This figure combines 1980 data for treatment costs with 1988 data for crime and lost productivity costs.

NOTE: This table is based on the referenced work of: ADAMHA, 1986: 22; Harwood et al., 1984: 3; Nadelmann, 1988a; Office of Technology Assessment, 1985: Table 2; Rice et al., 1986: Table 9; *New York Times,* September 30, 1988; and Wisotsky, 1986: 6.

(Wisotsky, 1986). For 1988, Mayor Kurt L. Schmoke of Baltimore estimated that the illegal drug market was worth $140 billion and that the value of lost productivity and illegal drug-related crime was $100 billion (*New York Times*). These figures apparently include heroin. Because of the criminal nature of the cocaine market, cocaine exacts the highest economic cost of any of the recreational drugs.

The second most costly drug is alcohol. For 1980 it was estimated that alcohol abuse cost the nation about $80 billion. Of this, about $10 billion was for treatment services (Harwood et al., 1984). The balance represented lost future productivity due to premature mortality ($14.5 billion), reduced productivity and lost employment due to morbidity ($54.7 billion), and the direct costs of crime ($2.5 billion), motor vehicle crashes, incarceration, and the like. For 1983 the estimated total was increased to $117 billion (ADAMHA, 1986).

Next in terms of economic cost comes cigarette smoking. For 1984 it was estimated that cigarette smoking cost the nation about $54 billion (Rice et al., 1986: Table 9). About 43% ($23 billion) was spent for health services, the balance for lost production and premature mortality. Using a slightly different methodology, the Office of Technology Assessment (1985: Table 2) estimated that for 1985 total cost was $65 billion, with $22 billion attributed to health services. Cigarette smoking thus appears to be the most expensive drug in terms of health care costs. There is a relatively minor crime cost for cigarettes, about $300 million per year, lost to tax-avoidance bootlegging operations (Nadelmann, 1988a). (Of course, no income or sales taxes are collected on any portion of the illegal drug trade.)

The marijuana economy, which appears to involve organized crime to a much lesser degree than do heroin and cocaine, is counted separately. Since marijuana is fairly bulky, it is somewhat easier to stop its importation than it is to stop the importation of heroin and cocaine. However, demand remains high. So much of it is now grown in the United States that marijuana has become the country's third-largest cash crop. For 1985 its value was estimated at $14 billion per year (Wisotsky, 1986).

THE LEGAL STATUS OF THE DRUGS

Legal Classification

The history of narcotics control in the United States is convoluted (Musto, 1973; Wisotsky, 1986). In legal terms there are two classes of major recreational drugs in the United States. The first is those that are currently legal, alcohol and tobacco. The second is those that are currently illegal, primarily heroin, cocaine, and marijuana. Each of the latter three, has however, been legal at times in the past (Nadelmann, 1988b); and of course, alcohol possession and sale were illegal in the United States for 14 years from 1919. Even tobacco was almost illegalized in the past. In early Colonial times, the British government gave serious consideration to outlawing tobacco, characterized by King James I as a "noxious weed."

All five drugs are potentially dangerous both to personal health and the social fabric; however, their current legal status bears little relationship to their relative degrees of potential danger. It is cigarette tobacco that has the most serious negative effects on personal health, while it is alcohol abuse that claims the most noninvolved, innocent victims (in motor vehicle crashes). Recall that cigarette tobacco and (probably) heroin when administered intravenously in a relatively pure state are obligatory addictives; alcohol, marijuana, and cocaine are not, although all have an addiction potential.

It is ironic that the bulk of the vast social harm presently done by cocaine use results from its status as an illegal drug, not its direct biomedical or mood-altering effects. Considering personal health and societal disruption risks, the safest overall of the currently popular recreational drugs appears to be marijuana, although that is not entirely clear.

Going through this kind of analysis (which certainly should be done in much more depth), one must conclude that the legal status of the primary recreational drugs has been determined chiefly by (changeable) economic, political, and moral considerations. Logic, biomedical and epidemiological knowledge, and considerations of true social and economic costs appear to have played little role in the decision-making process.

Drugs and Crime

There are five classes of crime associated with the five major recreational drugs. Their relative severity ratings are shown in Table 8.3

(1) First is the crime that necessarily accompanies the distribution and sale of the currently illegal recreational drugs, shown in the table as "Drug-Commerce." There are four subsets of this class. *First* is the violation of laws against the importation, distribution, sale, and possession of the currently illegal drugs. *Second* is the corruption of the criminal justice system. *Third* is the corruption of otherwise legitimate businesses and banks as they become involved in aiding and abetting trade in the currently illegal drugs, engaging in such activities as "fronting" and "money-laundering." *Fourth* is the violent crime that sometimes accompanies the acts of importation, distribution, sale, and possession of the currently illegal drugs. (When crack dealers kill each other over market share, one wonders just how much demand for the drug there really is.)

(2) The second crime class includes the violent, nonviolent property-intrusive, and "white-collar" money-raising crime committed by persons who need additional funds to buy currently illegal drugs. Heroin and cocaine use and addiction produce a great deal of this sort of crime. Most of it is secondary to the high cost of the drugs, which is created only by their illegality. (The actual cost of production, refinement, and physical transportation is very low.) Thus, as is well known, addicts need to steal to support their addiction.

Table 8.3
The Five Major Recreational Drugs Crime, Ranking by Severity[a]

Type of Crime	Cocaine	Heroin	Marijuana	Tobacco	Alcohol
1. Drug commerce					
a. Importation, sale, and possession	High	High	Medium	Nil	Nil
b. Corruption of the criminal justice system	High	High	?	Nil	Nil
c. Corruption of legal commerce	High	High	?	Nil	Nil
d. Violent crime, commerce-related	High	Medium	Low	Nil	Nil
2. Money-raising crime	High	High	?	Nil	Nil
3. Violation of motor vehicle statutes	?	?	Low	Nil	High
4. Violent crime, not commerce-related	?	?	?	Nil	High
5. Income and excise tax evasion	High	High	High	Low	Low

a. Using a four-level scale: high, medium, low (but measurable), nil. "?" means "unknown."

(3) & (4) Third and fourth are the classes of crime not directly related to commerce in the currently illegal drugs committed by persons under the influence of a drug: violation of motor vehicle statutes and regulation, and interpersonal violence. These classes of crime for the currently illegals are similar to those associated with alcohol use. (5) Finally, there is income, sales, and excise tax evasion.

In terms of crime, marijuana appears to be a special case among the currently illegals. Its use causes many people to become lawbreakers solely to obtain the drug or raise their own. But since marijuana is relatively inexpensive, it is likely that there is not too much crime caused by the need to raise money to buy it. And unlike in the cocaine trade, there seems to be little violent crime related to the commerce in marijuana. There is an unknown amount of motor vehicle statute violation associated with use of the drug.

Interestingly enough, the currently legal drugs also are intertwined with crime. As noted above, alcohol use and abuse are associated with about half of all domestic and other types of interpersonal violent crime, and are also a major factor associated with the violation of motor vehicle law and regulations. In terms of lives lost—about 25,000 per year, four times the number of deaths from all causes associated with the currently illegal drugs—violation of motor vehicle statutes and regulations caused by alcohol abuse is the most serious crime problem caused by any recreational drug. Even cigarette tobacco is related to crime: uneven excise taxation among the states leads to bootlegging.

In summary, considering violation of motor vehicle statutes to be a crime, the most serious current recreational drug crime problem in terms of morbidity and mortality is that associated with alcohol abuse. In terms of burglary and robbery, mortality secondary to the drug trade itself, distortions of the criminal justice system, the wrecking of many lives by involvement with drug-distribution crime, and disruption and distortion of the life in many neighborhoods secondary to illegal drug distribution-related crime, the most serious recreational drug crime problems are obviously those of heroin and cocaine.

Some Foreign Policy Considerations

There are many foreign policy issues connected with the illegal status of certain recreational drugs in the United States (Nadelmann, 1988a). In certain cases, our response to the currently illegal drugs has produced major distortions in our foreign policy. Certain countries are condemned (for example, Bolivia, Colombia, and Mexico) for allowing the cultivation of drugs. In other countries (such as Pakistan), it is ignored when a second national interest (e.g., supporting guerrilla war in Afghanistan) is felt to outweigh the national interest in controlling drug production. The drug trade is actively ignored in certain countries (as in Panama under Noriega before actions of this original U.S. creation became too much to bear), or actively participated in with certain forces (as with the Nicaragua "contra" rebels) when we conclude that such activity will help achieve another foreign policy goal (e.g., the overthrow of the government of Nicaragua).

Dealing with the currently illegal drug trade and the U.S. illegal drug problem, which seems to be much worse that that of any other country, is a major item of our foreign policy agenda. It seems to divert U.S. policy from many more important foreign policy issues, given that the bulk of the health-related drug problems are caused by the two legal recreational drugs heavily promoted and sold in the United States.

LEGALIZING DRUGS

A major topic of current political debate is: "Should the currently illegal recreational drugs be legalized?" In considering this question, it should be understood that no one proposes to "solve" the problem of the crime directly caused by the *use* of alcohol, heroin, marijuana, and cocaine by legalizing murder, assault, rape, or violation of motor vehicle statutes. Nor does anyone propose to "solve" cigarette tax evasion by eliminating cigarette taxes. However, some classes of the crime associated with the *distribution, sale, purchase, and possession* of heroin, cocaine, and marijuana (see Table 8.3) would be sharply reduced by making them legal.

Further, legalization would help to curtail the current trend in the country to limit personal liberty. It would sharply reduce the corruption of the criminal justice system and free many resources to be used in combating other types of crime. However, it should also be understood that legalization of the currently illegals will not solve the drug problem.

The exact outcome of legalization in terms of drug use would be determined in part by just what "legalization" would mean in practice: which drugs would be legalized; how and where they would be sold; how much they would cost; advertising and promotion policies; what, if anything, would be done to control the distribution and sale of the currently legal recreational drugs; taxation policy; what, if any, responsible drug use educational programs would be instituted.

Legalization of the currently illegals might lead to an increase in the use of those drugs. It would do so especially if it were not accompanied by a strong, well-planned, comprehensive program to reduce the use and abuse of *all* recreational drugs. Legalization of the currently illegals would certainly do nothing to deal with the major health, social, and economic problems caused by tobacco and alcohol.

It may be, in the end, that society will decide not to deal with the drug problem. As with the repeal of Prohibition, by legalizing the currently illegal drugs, it could deal solely with the crime problem. But in any case, before that decision is to be made, serious attention should be paid to dealing with the drug problem. Thus, it is suggested that the question "Should the currently illegal recreational drugs be legalized?" be considered for the present not independently, but in the context of dealing with the drug problem.

A great deal of personal suffering and a huge cost to society are caused by all the recreational drugs. At the same time, all of them, with the exception of cigarettes, can bring pleasure to many individuals when used in moderation. The problem we face is how to reduce the bad effects of the drugs while preserving the good ones. If the goal is to reduce the use and abuse of the recreational drugs in the United States, legalization will not do the job. To accomplish that goal, the true causes of the problem must be examined first.

THE DRUG CULTURE

There are many causes of drug use and abuse. One is simple availability of the drugs. Present policy for the currently illegals focuses almost entirely on that factor, while present policy for the currently legals almost completely ignores it. There are social and economic causes: poverty, stress, disruptions of family and personal life by external factors. There are individual causes: inability to take responsibility for one's own life and health, blaming others for personal problems, the need to rely on outside stimulus rather than inner strength in order to succeed in life, genetic susceptibility to drug addiction. In the United States, however, an overarching cause appears to be a powerful and very influential Drug Culture.

It is postulated that this Drug Culture has four components:

- the patterns of promotion, sale, and use of the currently legal recreational drugs
- the manner in which over-the-counter medications are promoted, sold, and used
- the ways in which vitamins are promoted, sold, and used
- the mode of medical practice

The Recreational Drugs

The use of recreational drugs is heavily promoted and encouraged in our society. In 1985, expenditures for magazine advertising of "smoking materials" ranked third among 16 advertising product groups ($375 million), while beer, wine and liquor ranked ninth ($239 million) (U.S. Bureau of the Census, 1986: Table 927). As for network television, beer and wine advertising expenditures ranked fifth ($428 million) among 27 product groups (U.S. Bureau of the Census, 1986: Table 928). Among 24 product groups employing local spot television advertising, beer and wine ranked sixth ($218 million) (U.S. Bureau of the Census, 1986: Table 929).

How these drugs are sold is fascinating. The messages are almost invariably associational, virtually never a description of what the drug actually does to the user, even the positive aspects. Beer is touted as:

- the apogee of life: Miller's "That Says It All."
- a reward for a day's work well done: "Now it's Miller Time," "This Bud's for you."
- associated with prominent former professional athletes: "Miller Lite is less filling. No, it tastes great."
- associated with fast cars and fast boats: Budweiser promotions (particularly ironic in light of the high auto and boating crash death rate associated with alcohol)
- associated with humor: "No, I asked for a *Bud* Light"; "Miller Lite is less filling. No, it tastes great"; Stroh's wonderful dog Alex (who in one ad impersonates Rin-Tin-Tin, Benji, and even Bud Light's Spuds McKenzie); Schaefer's Mr. Celsius Fahrenheit; Bud Light's famous rival, Bimbelman's Beer
- associated with sex and glamour: "Michelob Light is the Beer of the Night"; "Spuds McKenzie, the Party Animal," and the Budweiser party girls who show up in the most unusual places; Colt 45's black sex and power ads; Lowenbrau, "The Lions' beer, brewed since 1383" (glamour but no sex)
- a way to learn a foreign language: Beck's
- associated with the great outdoors: Coors, and "Head to the mountains of Busch—beer."

Anheuser-Busch crowned its drug promotion efforts during the 1988 Olympics and inadvertently (one hopes) underlined its view of the place of the drug culture in American life. Its most prominent television ad for Bud Light concluded with the following line: "Spud and Bud Light—Now that's the American Dream." Just like Miller, "That says it all," doesn't it?

A similar profile can be drawn for the promotion of cigarettes. The tobacco companies associate their product with sporting events (the Virginia Slims tennis tournament, the Marlboro Australian Open), glamour (Benson and Hedges), strength and toughness (the Marlboro Man), achievement ("You've come a long way, baby"), youth and sex (many brands), and a healthy appearance.

They have used economic arguments too. In 1988, Phillip Morris initiated a strong pro-smoking campaign by pointing out the following:

America's 55.8 million smokers are a powerful economic force. If their household income of $1 trillion were a gross national product, it would be the third largest in the world. The plain truth is that smokers are one of the most economically powerful groups in this country. They help fuel the engine of the largest economy on the globe. (*New York Times,* June 28, 1988).

This is a fascinating argument in favor of selling and using a drug that now kills approximately 400,000 Americans each and every year.

The Over-the-Counter Drugs

The promotion of drug use is not confined to the recreational drugs. Over-the-counter drugs for the treatment of various ills and ailments are also heavily advertised. In 1985, $700 million was spent on network television advertising for "proprietary medicines," putting them in the fourth rank among television advertisers (U.S. Bureau of the Census, 1986: Table 928). Using the same basic message, these drugs are sold primarily as instant problem-solvers: "If something is wrong with your health, fix it by using this pill (or this lotion, this solution, this spray)." If you have a cold, take Anacin (or "Give your cold to Contac"); a headache, take aspirin; a backache, Bufferin; an itch, this salve. Relief of a stomach ache is spelled R-O-L-A-I-D-S. Diarrhea can be stopped with Pepto-Bismol, while constipation can best be treated by M-O-M: Milk of Magnesia. If you've overeaten, try Alka-Seltzer.

The message never is: "If you have a problem, why not try to figure out what caused it (and here are some helpful hints for doing that), so that you can prevent it next time, and in the meantime, here are some things that you can do other than taking drugs that will help you deal with the problem now." But over-the-counter drug companies, like the purveyors of the recreational drugs, whether currently legal or currently illegal, are in the business of selling drugs, instant fix-it problem-solvers, not long-range, gradual change, drug-free alternatives.

Vitamins

It has been said that the United States has the most expensive urine in the world. It is produced by the wasteful, widespread, heavily advertised and promoted use of vitamin supplements. There is no evidence in the scientific literature that general vitamin supplements are of any benefit to anyone who eats a reasonably balanced diet and has no identified specific vitamin deficiencies (Halpern, 1979; Aronson, 1984). Multivitamins benefit very few of their users; however, they are sold as a way to get a "better you" without working at it. Just like the vitamin supplement users, new users of cocaine and heroin are recruited with the promise that "they will make you feel better, and make you a better you."

The Practice of Medicine

Finally, medicine as it is currently practiced in the United States relies heavily on drugs. It pays little attention to disease prevention or the promotion of health as means of avoiding many of the problems that drugs are used to treat. It reinforces the national ethic: "Have a problem? Take a pill (or a swallow, or a shot, or a smoke). Want to do better, be better, feel better? Take a pill (or a swallow, or a shot, or a smoke). Want to be in the in group? Well, you know what to do."

What the Drug Culture Does

The Drug Culture promotes and sanctions the use of recreational drugs to solve problems, feel good, and become a better person. The Drug Culture glamorizes drug use by making the user appear to be a more "with-it" person than the non-user. It is the Drug Culture that links all of the drugs, which makes it difficult for the problem user to distinguish among them.

The bulk of persons who abuse, overuse, or become addicted to one or more of the recreational drugs does so between the ages of 10 and 25. For example, more than 80% of smokers born since 1935 started smoking before they were 21 (Office on Smoking and Health, 1989). As clearly demonstrated by tobacco and alcohol company advertising, the Drug Culture aims heavily at this group, and for its own good reasons. For example, the tobacco companies must recruit more than 1,000 new nicotine addicts a day just to replace those smokers who die every year, to say nothing of those who quit. And those 1,000 are easiest to find, and addict, among our young.

Most present prevention efforts for all drugs focus on public education. But what impact can a "Don't do cocaine" ad, delivered during a football game telecast by a serious, active football player, have when it is followed a few minutes later by a "Do do alcohol" ad, delivered by a group of jolly ex-football players? "Don't do cocaine" is a request not to do something, something that seems glamorous and appears to be virtually the same as the behavior that is actively encouraged and promoted in another ad.

The fundamental inconsistency of the negative message dooms it to failure for most beholders. Young people, especially, find logic and consistency impelling and the lack thereof repelling, in a word, a turn-off. They cannot be expected to readily say no to crack when they are bombarded with messages imploring them to say yes to alcohol and tobacco. It is the Drug Culture that makes the "Don't do it" and "Just Say No" messages virtually worthless. The Drug Culture certainly is not the only cause of the use and abuse of the five major recreational drugs in this country. But it is a major cause. Regardless of what else is done, it will not be possible to successfully deal with the drug problem unless the Drug Culture is dealt with first.

DEALING WITH DRUGS: A PROPOSED PROGRAM

There is presently no effective program in this country to solve either the crime problem or the drug problem caused by the use and abuse of recreational drugs. The prohibition/law enforcement approach simply does not work (Wisotsky, 1986; Trebach, 1987). It creates overwhelming crime problems. It may also modestly reduce overall drug use, but that is by no means clear. Even in the face of potential imprisonment, there is still much sale and use of the currently illegals. Actually, illegalization may make the drug problem worse by interfering with both measurement of the problem and treatment of individual sufferers.

Improved treatment alone is not the answer. This medical model approach does nothing to reduce the load of new cases. So-called antidrug education alone cannot be effective in the context of the Drug Culture. Nor does it do anything to deal with supply, distribution, and sale of recreational drugs, whether currently legal or currently illegal.

A multifaceted problem like drug abuse requires a multifaceted program for its amelioration if it is to be dealt with effectively. In brief, such a program would include the following:

1. research on the magnitude of the Drug Culture's impact on drug use in U.S. society and its precise role in the promotion and use of the recreational drugs.
2. measures to diminish the influence of the Drug Culture. First would be a comprehensive drug advertising and promotion policy. A ban on all recreational drug advertising would be considered, but other alternatives would also be examined, e.g., the creation of an advertising code, which might be voluntary in the first instance, and the institution of a permanent, national anti-legal drug use advertising campaign comparable in size to pro-drug use advertising and funded in part by a tax on that advertising.

   Proposals to replace the Drug Culture in part with a Health Culture would be developed. Alternate personal behaviors to drug use that might meet some of the personal needs currently met by drug use for some people include: taking control of one's life, positive personal assertiveness, self-responsibility, sports and exercise, and positive nutrition.

3. a system for classifying the recreational drugs by danger to health and well-being. This, rather than the currently used system of historical accident, economic power, and prejudice, would be used to decide the legal status of the several recreational drugs.

4. the institution of a primary common retail source system for the distribution and sale of the legal drugs, whichever ones they might be. This "drug store" would have much in common with the "package store" now used to sell alcoholic beverages in certain states. A common national policy on minimum age for drug sales, hours of availability, and sales through locations other than the "drug stores" would also be developed and recommended to the states.

5. a national pricing policy for the legal drugs, whichever they might be. It would be designed to discourage the use of the legal drugs without creating a significant black market in them. Developing a rational tax policy would be part of this effort. Tax policy can be effective in controlling recreational drug use (Terris, 1967; Bradley, 1987). Drug taxes would be used to discourage drug use as well as to fund, at least in part, the comprehensive prevention, treatment, and rehabilitation drug control program. Taxes would be applied not solely to consumption but also to promotion activities by the producers.

6. a research program to evaluate the role of drug-oriented personal and professional medical practice in the promotion of recreational drug use. Consideration would be given to how the promotion and use of over-the-counter medications, vitamins, and prescription drugs might be changed to ameliorate the recreational drug use and abuse problem.

7. a comprehensive national public, personal, and school health education program to discourage the use of drugs and encourage the participation in alternative behaviors.

8. a comprehensive job-training and employment program for those who use and/or deal in the currently illegal drugs at least in part because they have no other meaningful employment opportunities or prospects.

9. subsidies and job retraining programs for workers and farmers in this and other countries who would become un- or underemployed with the decline of both the legal and the currently illegal drug trade.

10. focused law enforcement to deal with negative and antisocial behaviors associated with drug abuse, and the violation of statutes governing promotion, distribution, sale, and use of all the recreational drugs, such as sale to minors, black market sales, tax evasion, and criminal actions while intoxicated.

11. a comprehensive use-cessation and abuse-treatment program would be developed for abusers and users who wish to stop using all of the recreational drugs.

THE POLITICS OF CHANGE

It is the usual inclination of public health physicians to be optimistic about the prospects for change, given that that change will produce better health for the people. However, given the components needed for an effective program to significantly reduce recreational drug use and abuse in the United States, one is here forced to conclude that it is highly unlikely, although not entirely out of the question, that it will be possible to develop and implement one in the foreseeable future. There are many powerful special interests arrayed against such a development. As a result, it would be extremely difficult to organize an effective political movement in its favor. One can hardly imagine that many cars would sport "I smoke dope and I vote" bumper stickers. It is more likely that major reductions in nuclear weapons will be agreed to by the United States and the Soviet Union than that drug use will be significantly reduced in the United States.

The opposition from the tobacco, alcohol, advertising, publishing, electronic media, and professional sports industries to any comprehensive antidrug program would be intense and immense. They already respond vigorously and negatively to such limited measures as calls for a ban on cigarette advertising (Warner, 1986), or controls on the advertising of alcohol (*Bulletin on Alcohol Policy,* 1986-1987), or providing health warning labels on alcoholic beverages (Sands, 1986), or modestly restricting the sale of beer in professional sports arenas (*Newsday,* 1988). While the pharmaceutical industry, the medical profession, and the medical education establishment would certainly not publicly oppose most of the elements of the program, they each would be privately arrayed against those pieces of it that affected their special interests and concerns and required them to make any significant changes in their policies.

Finally, very strong, if not public, opposition to a comprehensive drug abuse control program would come from the currently illegal drug industry itself. Presently, it is the most profitable enterprise on the face of the earth. The real cost of producing and distributing the currently illegal drugs is very low. The street prices charged bear absolutely no relationship to those costs (Wisotsky, 1986). The Drug Cartel would not want to see any significant reduction in demand for its products, cutting into their profits, any more than the alcohol and tobacco industries would.

As a subset of this reality, it should be recognized that legalization of the currently illegal recreational drugs, should that prove desirable as part of a comprehensive drug use and abuse reduction/control program, or prove safe from the public health point of view following the implementation of a successful program, is a virtual impossibility. The Drug Cartel has shown its ability to corrupt the political and law enforcement sectors to make sure that the current trade is not stopped under the law (Wisotsky, 1986; Shenon, 1988). But it is that law that makes the currently illegal drug trade so profitable.

At the same time that the Drug Cartel makes sure that its commerce is not significantly interfered with by the law enforcement system, it likely supports as many "antidrug" political figures as may be necessary to ensure that its oh-so-profitable commodity is *not* legalized. (By reducing prices, legalization would reduce profits. There is no guarantee that there would be enough increase in demand to make up for such a profit reduction.) Through campaign contributions from private individuals and dummy corporations, the Cartel could do this even without the knowledge of the politicians whom it chooses to support. It might also be the case that the tobacco and alcohol industries would privately oppose legalization of the currently illegals as well, anticipating that if it were to occur, competition with their products might increase and profits fall.

This is a grim note on which to conclude a health policy paper. There is but one glimmer of hope that may change the situation. Solution is possible only if the two principal U.S. drug industries, tobacco and alcohol, drastically change, or are made to drastically change, their goals and ways of doing business.

It must be recognized that this objective would be extremely difficult to achieve. The movement would have to either come from within the alcohol and tobacco industries themselves or be forced upon them by an aroused citizenry. The tobacco industry would have to recognize that it is a killer enterprise and would have to plan and implement its own gradual self-destruction, aided by government subsidy. The alcohol industry would have to recognize that when 50% of its sales are made to 10% of its consumers, it is making its profits from alcoholism. It would have to decide, or be forced to decide, to seriously do something about that.

Any development of this nature would require the active cooperation of everyone from the professional athletes and athletic club owners whose high salaries and profits are in part derived from the Drug Culture, to the advertising agencies, the print media, and the electronic media that promote and profit from the Drug Culture and the human misery it produces. Production for profit is what presently drives the American economy. As long as the free market economy is in place, it will be difficult to put production for use in its stead. But anything is possible if the people's political will can be organized and given voice.

REFERENCES

ADAMHA. (1986, September). *Towards a national plan to combat alcohol abuse and alcoholism.* Rockville, MD: Alcohol, Drug Abuse, and Mental Health Administration.

Aronson, V. (1984). *Thirty days to better nutrition.* Garden City, NY: Doubleday.

Alcohol use in the United States. (1987). *Statistical Bulletin, 68* (1).

Baltimore mayor supports legalization of illicit drugs. (1988, September 30). *New York Times.*

Beer sales at arenas restricted by law. (1988, September 4). *Newsday.*

Births, marriages, divorces, and deaths for May 1988. (1988, August 15). *Monthly Vital Statistics Report, 37* (5).

Blackout of RID, The. (1986-1987). *Bulletin on Alcohol Policy:* 1.

Bradley, A. M. (1987, Summer). A capsule review of the state of the art: The sixth special report to the U.S. Congress on alcohol and health. *Alcohol Health and Research World:* 4.

Breslow, L., & Enstrom, J. E. (1980). Persistence of health habits and their relationship to mortality. *Preventive Medicine, 9,* 486.

Casement, M. R. (1987). Alcohol and cocaine. *Alcohol Health and Research World, II* (4), 18.

Clayton, R. R. (1989). Commentary. Legalization of drugs: An idea whose time has not come. *American Behavioral Scientist, 32,* 316.

Durso, J. (1987, April 24). Gooden in treatment. *New York Times,* p. 1.

Gawin, F. H., & Ellinwood, E. H. (1988). Cocaine and other stimulants. *New England Journal of Medicine, 318,* 1173.

Halpern, S. L. (1979). *Quick reference to clinical nutrition.* Philadelphia: J. B. Lippincott.

Harwood, H. J., Napolitano, D. M., Kristiansen, P. L., & Collins, J. J. (1984, June). *Economic costs to society of alcohol and drug abuse and mental illness: 1980.* (RTI/2734/00-01FR). Research Triangle Park, NC: Research Triangle Institute.

Highlights of the 1975 national household survey on drug abuse. (1986, November). *NIDA Capsules.* National Institute on Drug Abuse.

Jonas, S. (1990). A public health program to reduce the use and abuse of both the legal and the recreational drugs. *Hofstra Law Review.*

Jonas, S. (1991). The public health approach to substance abuse. In J. Lowinson et al. (Eds.), *Comprehensive textbook of substance abuse.* Baltimore, MD: Williams and Wilkins.

Musto, D. (1973). *The American disease: Origins of narcotics control.* New Haven: Yale Univ. Press.

Nadelmann, E. A. (1988a, Spring). U.S. drug policy: A bad export. *Foreign Policy, 70* (83).

Nadelmann, E. A. (1988b, Summer). The case for legalization. *Public Interest, 92* (3).

Nadelmann, E. A. (1988c, August 4). Presentation at *Drug policy workshop,* Office of Mayor Kurt Schmoke, Baltimore, MD.

Office on Smoking and Health. (1979). Smoking and health: A report of the Surgeon General. (DHEW Publication No. (PHS) 70-55566). Washington, DC: Government Printing Office.

Office on Smoking and Health. (1988). *The health consequences of smoking: Nicotine addiction.* Rockville, MD.

Office on Smoking and Health. (1989). *Reducing the health consequences of smoking.* (DHHS Publication No. (CDC) 89-8411). Washington, DC: Government Printing Office.

Phillip Morris advertisement. (1988, June 28). *New York Times,* p. 7.

Rice, D. P., Hodgson, T. A., Sinsheimer, P., Browner, W., & Kopstein, A. N. (1986). The economic costs of the health effects of smoking, 1984. *The Milbank Quarterly, 64,* 489.

Sands, S. (1986). Researching the alcohol industry. *Bulletin on Alcohol Policy, 5,* 10.

Schoenborn, C. A., & Cohen, B. H. (1986, June 30). Trends in smoking, alcohol consumption, and other health practices among U.S. adults, 1977 and 1983. *Advance Data,* No. 118.

Shenon, P. (1988, April 11). Enemy within: Drug money in corrupting enforcers. *The New York Times,* p. 1.

Statistical abstract of the United States: 1987. (107th Edition). (1986). Washington, DC: Bureau of the Census.

Terris, M. (1967). Epidemiology of cirrhosis of the liver: National mortality data. *American Journal of Public Health, 57,* 2076.

U.S. Department of Health and Human Services. *Health United States: 1987.* (1988, March). (DHHS Publication No. (PHS) 88-1232). Washington, DC: Government Printing Office.

Warner, K. *Selling smoke.* (1986). Washington, DC: American Public Health Association.

Wisotsky, S. (1986). *Breaking the impasse.* New York: Greenwood Press.

Wu, T-C., Tashkin, D. P., Djahed, B., & Rose, J. E. (1988). Pulmonary hazards of smoking marijuana as compared with tobacco. *New England Journal of Medicine, 318,* 347.

9

Hidden Paradigms of Morality in Debates About Drugs: Historical and Policy Shifts in British and American Drug Policies

JOHN JAY ROUSE
BRUCE D. JOHNSON

A comparison of British and American drug policies over the past century-and-a-half reveals certain hidden moral paradigms that have governed public policy approaches toward drugs, either singly or jointly. These moral paradigms include commercial morality, prohibition-criminalization, vice regulation, public health, and rehabilitation. Both Britain and the United States were dominated by the commercial paradigm in the nineteenth century. International opium conventions (1912-1913) greatly restricted the commercial morality and developed a successful public health approach to opiates. The United States shifted toward a prohibition-criminalization approach for drug addicts, whereas Britain maintained a public health approach. This chapter examines the shifts in moral paradigms and policy differences that have evolved in these two countries.

INTRODUCTION

Moral standards guide personal conduct in many spheres of behavior, particularly drug use. Moral standards adopted by society may become "invisible clothing" and an integral part of the self. Other standards of morality do not seem possible or worthy and are essentially hidden from public view and discussion. Old moral standards are forgotten; only current standards can be continuously reaffirmed. The current debate about drug legalization in 1990 falls squarely in this tradition.

Imagine living in Britain or America a century ago and living within the morality of that period. In 1890 most pharmacies and/or other stores sold opium pills, pure morphine, opium for smoking, coca leaf products, pure cocaine, cocaine cigarettes (like crack today), a variety of beverages containing either alcohol plus opiates or alcohol plus cocaine, and patent medicines whose effective ingredients were opiates. A new soft drink contained coca leaf extract in its contents and name: Coca-Cola. People could purchase these commodities at a low price (even at 1890 wages) and use them with less stigma than drinking alcohol or smoking tobacco. Those who used large quantities of these substances or who overindulged might be thought of as having a bad habit, but would not likely commit crimes to obtain their drug(s) of choice. Opium smoking was a vice peculiar to the Chinese people, and perhaps a few criminals in America. A few British citizens who supported missionaries in China were proclaiming the almost absurd notion that the Indo-Chinese opium (smoking) trade was morally indefensible and should be stopped immediately. Furthermore, they proclaimed that opiates should be provided only by doctors for medical reasons, thus depriving the average citizens of their favorite patent medicines or opium pills or opiate wines. Surely such reasons were not sufficient either to restrict profits of merchants or to prevent the populace from using their favorite remedies for most maladies. Virtually no one (including the proponents of such restrictions) mentioned, much less advocated, criminal penalties and actually confining persons in jail or prison for opiate use or sales. Only in China had the barbaric practice of strangling opium smokers occurred—and that was more than 150 years ago (1830-1850).

In fact, the isolation of morphine from the poppy and cocaine from coca plants, and the invention of the hypodermic needle in the latter half of the nineteenth century, were major advances in alleviating pain and suffering from a multitude of diseases that had long plagued mankind. New professions had emerged since 1850: scientific chemists were replacing alchemists; physicians had training and skills that doctors and medicine men did not; pharmacists were replacing the friendly patent medicine salesmen. In Vienna, young Sigmund Freud had published some laudatory essays about a newly discovered drug, cocaine, to alleviate morbid depression. In short, physicians, doctors, pharmacists, entrepreneurs, and ordinary shopkeepers could sell their patients and customers the best that modern medicine had to offer which would actually alleviate (but not cure) the pain and suffering of many dreaded diseases. If a few persons overindulged and had an opium or morphine habit, this was a minor problem, not nearly as "morally wrong" as being a drunkard, or smoking pipes, or chewing snuff. Why should the average citizen either be concerned about the Chinese problem or restrict the income of doctors or businessmen? In 1890, the reasons were insufficient. But this changed rapidly in the next 40 years.

This is a brief historical examination of American and British approaches to the control of opiates, which reveals important similarities and differences. The differences, however, reveal even more about the hidden assumptions and implicit moral paradigms behind policy formulation and debates, as well as the choices made via legislation, regulation, and enforcement at critical points in history. This chapter examines policy toward drugs, especially opiates, as an evolving process that shifted over time and responded to different moral standards in these two countries.

PROMOTING MORALITY

Morality has its origins in religion and history and defines various behaviors as moral, or right, and immoral in various degrees (other terms include: vice, deviance, crime). Compared with definitions of normal physical health, much less agreement exists about appropriate moral behavior of citizens, and much disagreement exists within the polity about appropriate definitions for the degree and seriousness of behavior defined as immoral.

A major function of government is the promotion of moral behavior and good health practices among its citizens. So many exceptions from approved practices occur, however, that all governments have established laws. Legislators must socially construct definitions of the disapproved or questionable behaviors, define laws that provide a framework for enforcement, and establish and fund bureaucracies responsible for issuing regulations and enforcing them. The process by which such laws are passed has been well documented elsewhere (Mauss, 1975; Spector and Kitsuse, 1977). Usually, relatively small interest groups (especially business groups, and wealthy or influential persons) get their definitions passed into law, legislation, and regulations. The poor and disadvantaged have limited or little access to the legislative process, and their behaviors are frequently the object of the laws.

But generally, after several years of vigorous enforcement, most citizens come to accept legal definitions as the basis for their personal behavior. Such standards of moral behavior and good health become the "invisible clothing" that the vast majority of people in society "wear" in their personal conduct. Such "invisible clothing" (standards of appropriate behavior) may become reified into absolute right and wrong. The average conventional person can hardly conceive that anyone might engage in or enjoy such wrong behavior, or that such behavior might be defined and treated in a very different way in another society or culture. Most citizens are quite clear about their standards for right and wrong behavior, but are aware that much similar behavior by others might also be in an ambiguous zone.

Behaviors involving the consumption of drugs or nonfood psycho-active substances have always been at the crossroads where health and morality intersect, and where government efforts to promote good health and prevent practices deemed harmful by the majority collide with the rights of the minority, who enjoy and practice such behaviors. In fact, the implicit assumptions about correct behavior made by almost everyone in society consistently confound health and moral considerations, so that policy deliberations, debates, legislation, funding, and enforcement practices regarding drugs frequently contain conflicting purposes.

PARADIGMS OF MORALITY

Paradigms contain all major elements that define a theoretical model being examined. Max Weber (1947) used the term "ideal type" to provide nearly perfect definitions of the phenomena, even though such pure examples are rarely found in reality. But such ideal types or paradigms have heuristic value by making important conceptual distinctions between elements that may be otherwise confounded in reality and policy making. The following five paradigms are defined according to relatively pure ideal types; contrasts with similar paradigms are provided.

Commercial Morality

The commercial paradigm holds that the economic value and returns from a commodity are the most important criteria by which to assess a drug. Thus, if sales of a given drug can earn good profits for the seller, the drug should be made available to those who wish to buy it, and its consumption considered appropriately moral. Most persons consuming the drug are presumed to maintain normal health and to be otherwise moral persons.

Persons with a commercial interest may promote the drug as beneficial to health and as morally correct. Such proponents ignore or refute competing paradigms, which may claim that the drug is harmful or bad for health, or that consuming behavior is immoral or a vice. Proponents can be expected to advertise their product to as many potential customers as possible, and take actions which maximize profits. Historically, commercial interests have sought or used governmental laws or regulations such as patents, taxation policies, restriction of competition, lawsuits, limitations of imports, and even warfare to maximize profits. For example, coffee, tea, and several soft drinks (e.g., Coca-Cola) contain a stimulant (caffeine), but are sold without restrictions as to location, time, place, cost, labeling requirements, or advertising content. Manufacturers and sellers are not required to list the active ingredient, caffeine, nor state the amount of caffeine in a typical dosage unit.

Public Health Morality

The public health paradigm is designed to promote good (normal) health practices and to discourage or restrict practices that might harm health. Public health authorities tend to ignore morality claims and remain very skeptical of claims for product effectiveness issued by those having a commercial interest in a product. Public health practitioners are eager to restore physical health to immoral persons as well as good citizens.

Public health regulations permit purified caffeine to be legally sold in several over-the-counter drugs (e.g., No-Doz). The quantity of caffeine in a dosage unit may be listed on the label, and written directions provided about the number of pills to be taken and the frequency of consumption.

As shown below, opiates were a primary concern as public health practices and regulations were debated and institutionalized during the past two centuries. Authorities issue warnings, teach medical practitioners, and otherwise prevent users from consuming dosages that are too large or that extend for very long periods. Such authorities are also empowered to restrict the actions and profits of manufacturers and sellers of drugs in many ways: requiring labels stating contents and dosages; limiting the number of dosage units in retail packages; regulating pricing practices, advertising content, and targets; and proving that drugs are both safe and effective.

Vice Regulation Morality

The vice regulation morality is quite unfamiliar to most Americans because prohibition-criminalization has dominated in the twentieth century. This paradigm represents an explicit recognition of conflicting moral standards of right and wrong. The vast majority of citizens have clear moral standards that define certain behaviors as immoral and unacceptable; but a sizable minority enjoy and wish to participate and/or pay for that behavior. The vice regulation paradigm provides for laws and regulations that permit the immoral behavior to occur, but generally remain unobserved by publics whose morals would be offended.

In much of Western Europe, for example, prostitution and pornography are legal but highly regulated. In London, prostitutes cannot solicit on the streets or in bars, but may advertise in sex magazines and via discreet announcements in shop windows. Shops selling pornography are permitted no public displays that might offend the average citizen, but can sell any kind of sexually explicit material to adults who enter the premises.

Prohibition-Criminalization Morality

The prohibition-criminalization paradigm represents a collective judgment that a particular behavior is wrong and immoral and should be prohibited by law. Usually, violations of the law are punished by criminal penalties. The prohibition morality may emphasize the "symbolic crusade" (Gusfield, 1963) aspect in which a moral belief of a powerful group is enacted into law, and frequently directed against persons perceived as immoral or disreputable.

While prohibitionist sentiment enacts laws, criminalization occurs when a specific behavior is defined as illegal by criminal law, and specific sentences in jail or prison are provided for convicted violators. Police and various enforcement agencies are created and mobilized to detect and arrest persons committing the illegal act. The types of persons targeted for enforcement of criminal laws, and the severity and certainty of detection, prosecution, and punishment, are critical.

As shown below, laws against heroin in the last half of the twentieth century in America have been based on a strongly held prohibitionist sentiment, and criminal penalties have been vigorously enforced against heroin users and user-dealers by many police and special narcotics units.

Rehabilitation Morality

The rehabilitation paradigm is concerned primarily with restoring to normal social behavior persons who are labeled by authorities or themselves as deviant, criminal, or immoral on some behavioral dimension. The major effort is to eliminate or greatly reduce the undesirable behavior as well as to teach or model appropriate behavior.

During the 1970s and 1980s, therapeutic communities have developed a strong philosophy and treatment regime that attempt to eliminate the use of all illicit drugs and alcohol, stress elimination of any negative behavior including lying and deceit, and impose activities that promote conventional behavior upon participants. In the United States, therapeutic communities have become popular and widespread because the total rehabilitation of addicts is congruent with the strong moral censure against addiction in American society.

Each of these paradigms of morality exerts considerable influence on public policies toward drugs. Each paradigm has had various constituencies promoting their morality interests to government agencies. Moreover, some of these paradigms have become the fundamental operating assumptions of government policies and laws in various historical periods and for different cultures.

Several major themes emerge in the historical record. The commercial morality dominated in the early nineteenth century and reached its zenith in the 1880s. The prohibitionist morality (against opium smoking) and public health morality (to restrict opiates for medical purposes) emerged at the end of the nineteenth century. The prohibitionist and criminalization approach toward opiates (especially heroin) was ascendant in America during the first quarter of the twentieth century and has remained dominant ever since. British policy remained firmly committed to a public health morality for the first two-thirds of the twentieth century, but has shown a shift toward prohibition-criminalization in the 1980s.

Of even greater importance is the fact that drugs, especially opiates (raw opium in various forms, smoking opium, morphine, and heroin), have had a primary role in generating political conflict among competing commercial and morality interests, which has, in turn, forced a clarification of roles among the medical, public health, and pharmaceutical professions.

The public health paradigm ascended after World War I, when the International Opium Conventions were adopted and institutionalized by almost all major nations. Opiates were legally confined to legitimated medical practices, and this worked well through the 1950s. The revival of black markets in heroin after World War II led to further restrictions on medical opiates, and vast expansion of the prohibitionist-criminalization morality (and imprisonment of addicts by the thousands) in America. But the tide of heroin abuse and cocaine/crack addiction in the last half of the 1980s was so great that prisons were not enough. The rehabilitation morality gained proponents, and funding began in the 1960s and has grown steadily ever since.

THE RISE OF COMMERCIAL MORALITY
IN THE NINETEENTH CENTURY

British merchants began to export large quantities of opium from India to China starting in the late eighteenth century. Opium smoking began to be perceived as a major problem in China. The Chinese government was the first major proponent of the prohibition-criminalization morality. About 1800, opium smoking was declared illegal.

> There is a class of evil foreigner that makes opium and brings it for sale, tempting fools to destroy themselves, merely in order to reap a profit. Formerly the number of opium smokers was small; but now the vice has spread far and wide and the poison penetrated deeper and deeper. . . . [The Chinese Empire] regards itself as responsible for the habits and morals of its subjects and cannot rest content to see any of them become victims of this deadly poison. . . . We have decided to inflict very severe penalties on opium dealers and opium smokers, in order to put a stop forever to the propagation of this vice. (Commissioner Lin, 1939, as quoted in Waley, 1958: 29)

Thus, opium importation and sale were criminalized and many smokers/traders were strangled, frequently in front of British merchants whom the Chinese blamed for the problem. Yet Britain and western nations were determined to open China for western-style commercial trade. Britain fought two wars with China, in 1840-1842 and 1856, largely to expand British commercial interest in trading with the Chinese. At the end of the second war, opium was legalized, and British officials collected the import tax for the Chinese government. Between 1860 and 1875 the commercial morality reached its unchallenged zenith with the leading opium export company declaring that "the use of opium is not a curse, but a comfort and benefit to the hard-working Chinese" (Owen, 1934).

But British and foreign missionaries, who were also allowed to enter China, were rapidly confronted with the evil of opium smoking. They began to lobby their supporters in Britain and America to stop the opium trade. A small anti-opium society formed in England advocated the immorality of opium use, and lobbied the government to stop the opium trade during the last quarter of the century, but usually without substantive victory (Johnson, 1975b). In 1982 they forced the appointment of a Royal Commission on Opium. Its 1895 report on the opium situation in the crown colony of India found that the amount of opium eating in India was greatly exaggerated and compared the amount of use to alcohol. The commission also found that opium prohibition would have a serious adverse impact on the revenues of the British government. In addition they found no connection between the use of opium and crime (Berridge and Edwards, 1981).

Public policy regarding drugs in Britain in the nineteenth century was also mainly based on the commercial paradigm and had little concern for individual freedom. The earliest law designed to change the availability of opiates in Great Britain was the 1868 Pharmacy Act, which controlled the sale of 15 substances defined as "poisons" (Berridge and Edwards, 1981). This act required that the seller know the purchaser or an intermediary, and mandated that the purchaser's name be entered in a poisons register. The container had to be labeled as poison and also show the name of the substance plus the name and address of the seller.

Pharmacists protested strongly against the inclusion of opium in the 1868 Pharmacy Act. The Secretary of the Pharmaceutical Society told the Pharmacy Bill Committee of the General Medical Council that: "The promoters of the Bill received such strong representations from chemists residing principally in Cambridgeshire, Lincolnshire, and Norfolk, against interfering with their business—opium as they stated, being one of their chief articles of trade—that the promoters felt compelled to strike opium out of Schedule A" (Berridge and Edwards, 1981). Nevertheless, opium and morphine were included as substances that needed to be listed on the label. Patent medicines, many of which contained opium, were also excluded from the Pharmacy Act entirely.

With the dawning of the twentieth century, a shift away from the commercial morality and toward more formal state controls began. Berridge and Edwards discuss the reasons for this change in policy:

What are the reasons for the shift? One explanation might be attempted by looking at the general disruption of society and culture brought about by the Industrial Revolution in nineteenth-century England. Many aspects of the subtle and informal apparatus which controlled the individual's behavior by expectation and precept must have been smashed or put into disarray. The existence of an apparatus which is otherwise un-noted and taken for granted only becomes apparent when it is overwhelmed by rapid socio-economic change. (Berridge and Edwards, 1981: 260)

Commercial morality was also dominant in the United States. During the nineteenth century the majority of morphine and opium addicts were women, most of whom became addicted through physician prescriptions (Courtwright, 1982). Estimates for the number of opiate addicts in the United States prior to World War I range from 100,000 to 300,000 (King, 1972; Courtwright, 1982). Raw and smoking opium, plus morphine in many forms, were commonly taken in the late nineteenth and early twentieth centuries in the United States for virtually all ailments, including headaches, menstrual pain, rheumatoid arthritis, diarrhea, malaria, and syphilis. Many common patent medicines, such as Mrs. Winslow's Soothing Syrup, Scotch Oats Essence, and White's Head-Ease, contained opium. People also drank cocaine-containing beverages with names such as Coca Cordial, New Ola and Coca-Cola. No import or tax restrictions existed for opiates of cocaine at this time.

Courtwright (1982) maintains that between 1895 and 1914, the character of the opium-using class shifted from a primarily white middle- and upper-class, largely female population to one of largely lower-class urban males. He believes that the former group benefited from the use of other therapies and more widespread knowledge and education about opiate drugs among the medical community. The widespread practice of overprescribing opiate drugs largely ended at this time. Courtwright contends that the transformation of the opium-using class occurred before the anti-maintenance, law enforcement and prohibitionist approach took hold in the United States during the 1920s.

EARLY TWENTIETH CENTURY

In 1898 the United States acquired the Philippines as a result of the Spanish-American War. Opium smoking by Chinese was permitted in the Philippines before the war and the Spanish government operated an opium monopoly; most of its production was exported to China. Bishop Charles Brent, a former missionary to China and the first Episcopal bishop of the Philippines, led the United States to dismantle this monopoly and to impose prohibition of opium in the islands. The regulatory model adopted was essentially borrowed from Japanese practices

(Taylor, 1969). This Japanese and Philippines model was the basis for the public health morality that emerged in the early twentieth century.

In 1906 Brent wrote to President Theodore Roosevelt, asking for an international meeting to deal with the international commerce in opium. Bishop Brent was the chief American delegate to the Shanghai conference in 1909. This conference elicited the support of the convening nations toward restricting international cultivation and commercial sale of opiates, particularly for opium smoking. However no formal agreement was reached nor any action taken. U.S. legislation in 1909 prohibited importation of opium for smoking.

Two more international conferences were held in The Hague, the Netherlands, in 1912 and 1913. Hamilton Wright, who was one of the American delegates at the Shanghai and Hague conferences, believed strongly in the domestic control of narcotics in the United States as a way of taking the moral high ground in U.S. efforts to control the international traffic in opium. He exaggerated consumption of opium in the United States in his *Report on the International Opium Commission* to the U.S. Senate in 1910. He proposed sweeping legislation calling for the registration of all involved in the opium trade and recording all narcotic sales. He also suggested criminal penalties for persons not engaged in medical opium sales. Although the legislation was not enacted, it was the basis for changes to come.

The Hague conferences reached agreements that effectively dismantled the commercial morality toward opium. Conferees agreed to: (1) greatly reduce opium cultivation in all growing countries, (2) stop commercial sales of opium for smoking, and (3) prevent the commercial sale of opiates in patent and other unlabeled medicines.

In addition, these conferences clearly formulated a public health morality that restricted opiates, coca, and their derivatives to legitimate medical purposes. Signatories to the International Opium Convention (1914) were to introduce legislation and regulations which mandated that: (1) manufacturers, importers/exporters, and wholesale distributors must maintain careful records of amounts produced, shipped, and sold; (2) physicians were to be licensed to prescribe (but not sell) such drugs; and (3) pharmacists were licensed to dispense and maintain careful records of all sales of products containing opiates and cocaine.

While the Americans, especially Hamilton Wright, argued for prohibition of opium, rather than mere regulation, and criminal penalties for violation of such regulations, this position was unpopular with delegates from other countries and it was not included in the Hague Convention.

The Hague Opium Convention was formally adopted as part of the Treaty of Versailles in 1919, which ended World War I. Most European and Far Eastern countries ratified it and passed appropriate legislation by the end of the 1930s.

OPIATE PROHIBITION AND CRIMINALIZATION IN THE UNITED STATES

In 1914 the Harrison Narcotic Act was passed by the United States. It enacted the Hague Convention agreements into law in the United States. The Harrison Act was a public health and revenue law, which required that standardized order forms be used by purchasers of narcotics and that copies of all such purchases be filed with the local internal revenue office. All those dealing in narcotics, including manufacturers, importers, distributors, wholesalers, retailers, and physicians, were required to be registered with the federal government. By June 30, 1916, about 221,000 people were registered with the federal government, 124,000 of these were physicians (Musto, 1973).

The Harrison Act, like the Hague Conventions, was silent about whether physicians could prescribe opiates to addicts. This set the stage for much of the legal conflict that was to follow in the years ahead. The medical profession in the United States was divided about this question.

> Numerous editorials and comments criticizing the manner in which the Harrison Act impinged on doctors appeared throughout the country at this time. In a number of instances clinics were sponsored and supported by local medical bodies, which also resisted the government orders closing them. All of this demonstrates beyond any reasonable doubt that the government's program of closing to addicts all avenues of legal access to drugs did not have the undivided support of medical authorities at the time, and that the latter were in fact engaged in a bitter controversy on the question. (Lindesmith, 1965: 147)

The U.S. Supreme Court ruled in the case of *United States v. Jin Fuey Moy* (1916) that the Harrison Act was a revenue measure and could not be used to charge a physician with illegal opiate maintenance of a patient. In addition, regulation of the practice of medicine was a power reserved to the states. Three years later, however, the court reversed itself in *United States v. Doremus* (1919) in which the court held that the Harrison Narcotic Act included federal control over the dispensing of opiate drugs; and in *Webb et al. v. United States* (1919) physician maintenance of opiate addicts was declared to be illegal.

The *Webb* decision was influential in the creation of a brief movement for government-sponsored clinics to dispense opiates (Musto, 1973). Cities with huge numbers of addicts tried to cope with the situation by providing an alternative source for a legal supply of drugs. At its peak in 1920, the New York clinic had 7,500 clients; other cities had no more than 2,500 to 3,000 (Musto, 1973). Most of the clinics closed by 1921, as directed by Levi Nutt, head of the Narcotic Division of the Prohibition Unit within the Bureau of Internal Revenue (Courtwright, 1982). Nutt believed that the Harrison Act prohibited the sale and consumption of opiates and other drugs and that criminal charges should be brought against physicians who prescribed to addicts, and also against black market peddlers of heroin and opiates. The clinics were closed despite the fact that some members of the law enforcement community supported local clinics. In 1920 the Commissioner of Public Safety in Shreveport, Louisiana, wrote to the Louisiana State Board of Health:

> I wish to say that from a police standpoint, the City of Shreveport is greatly benefited by its being here. It has practically eliminated the bootlegger who deals in narcotics, and in this way alone has reduced the number of possible future dope users . . .
>
> Before the establishment of the clinic a greater number of criminals prosecuted through this department were those addicted with the use of opiates. Now however, it is very seldom that we have to prosecute this class, and we are able to keep a direct line upon anyone who might sell morphine, cocaine and other such drugs as are prohibited by law.
>
> The authorities in charge of the Police Department in Shreveport would regard it a calamity should this clinic be removed from this point, and we are as earnestly for it at the present time as we were bitterly opposed to it upon its institution here. We cannot speak in too high terms of Dr. Butler and his methods used at the dispensary. (May, 1971: 64)

The American Medical Association was opposed to the developments that were occurring with respect to the usurpation of the physicians' right to prescribe morphine, heroin, and other opiates where it was deemed medically prudent to do so. In 1921 the AMA's Council on Health and Public Instruction stated:

> In the opinion of your Committee, the only proper and scientific method of treating drug addiction is under such conditions of control of both the

addict and the drug, that any administration of habit-forming narcotic drugs must be by, or under the direct personal authority of the physician, with no chance of any distribution of the drug of addiction to others, or opportunity for the same person to procure any of the drug from any source other than from the physician directly responsible for the addict's treatment. (AMA, 1963; King, 1972)

During the 1920s and 1930s, Richmond P. Hobson, a Spanish-American War hero and an espouser of alcohol prohibition, lectured widely in the United States on the dangers of narcotic drugs, particularly heroin, exaggerating the extent of the problem and depicting all narcotic addicts as dangerous criminals. In 1922 the United States enacted the Narcotic Drugs Import and Export Act, prohibiting the importation of heroin and enacting criminal penalties for violators. A later amendment also prohibited the importation of raw opium (Platt, 1986).

The Supreme Court decided in *United States v. Behrman* (1922) that it was illegal for a physician to prescribe any amount of a narcotic drug. Three years later in *Linder v. United States* (1925) the court overturned itself again, this time ruling that the Harrison Narcotic Act was strictly a revenue measure and had no other purpose. The pattern of law enforcement harassment and prosecution of physicians by the prohibition unit, however, had already been firmly established. Most physicians never attempted to maintain opiate addicts. It was as if the *Linder* case had never been decided in favor of physicians' right to prescribe these drugs to addicts.

During the 1920's there were not one, but two prohibitions: alcohol and narcotics. They were in many respects similar: both were generated by reform efforts concerned with the deleterious effects of these substances on the individual and society; both began with high expectations; and both were failures, in that they generated large and well-publicized black markets on which criminals fattened. Why, then, did the public withdraw its support for the prohibition of alcohol and, if anything, increase its support for the prohibition of narcotics? One factor (in addition to economic and political considerations) must have been that alcohol use was relatively widespread and cut across class lines. It seemed unreasonable for the government to deny a broad spectrum of otherwise normal persons access to drink. By 1930 opiate addiction, by contrast, was perceived to be concentrated in a small criminal subculture; it did not seem unreasonable for that same government to deny the morbid cravings of a deviant group. (Courtwright, 1982: 143-144)

Starting in 1930 and continuing until 1962, Harry J. Anslinger was the head of the law enforcement effort in the United States against narcotics and other illicit drugs. He went to great lengths to accentuate the perceived harmful effects of these drugs and to stress the paramount importance of the law enforcement community in protecting American citizens from the scourge of drugs. He indelibly imprinted the prohibitionist/criminalization paradigm on American policy and in the American psyche (Lindesmith, 1965; King, 1972).

OPIUM AND PUBLIC HEALTH
MORALITY IN BRITAIN IN THE 1920s

The prohibition paradigm and support for the alcohol prohibition movement were never strong in Britain. During World War I, however, the government sharply curtailed alcohol sales and restricted hours for alcohol sales—such steps were guided by the vice regulation paradigm. The absence of alcohol prohibition that provided police powers to bureaucrats committed to a prohibitionist morality helped prevent Britain from following the American lead.

Britain closely followed the language and spirit of the 1912-1913 Hague Opium Conventions. Initially, Britain passed a Dangerous Drugs Act (1920), which outlawed raw opium and opium for smoking, and required the registration of all who were involved in the manufacture, sale, and distribution of heroin, morphine, cocaine, and other drugs. It also licensed and required that pharmacists and physicians dispensing these drugs must keep detailed records. The Home Affairs Secretary issued a set of regulations that dealt with how the law would apply to physicians. The regulations stated that a physician "shall be authorized, so far as may be necessary for the practice or exercise of his said profession, function or employment, and in his capacity as a member of his said class, to be in possession of and to supply drugs" (King, 1972).

The situation in Britain could have easily followed the American course toward strict prohibition, and prosecution of physicians supplying addicts; some law enforcement officials favored this interpretation. Only the diligent efforts of the medical community prevented this outcome and kept the public health paradigm preeminent in British policy (Berridge, 1978).

The disease concept of addiction and all that it entailed was under serious attack. A prohibitionist policy, under which the state would decide treatment and where both doctors and addicts could incur penalties, was, as in America at the same time, in the process of establishment. That this did not happen owed much to intense professional opposition. Many doctors continued to give regular maintenance doses. Grass roots anger, and the parliamentary support it had, secured modification or withdrawal of the more restrictive or unworkable regulations. Leading members of the medical profession came out firmly for medical control and the disease point of view. (Berridge, 1978: 369)

Parliament established a committee to study the problem; the recommendations of the Rolleston Committee, which was composed of nine men from the medical community, were accepted and form the basis for British policy toward opiate drugs. Physicians were allowed to prescribe opiate and other controlled drugs: (1) when an addict is attempting to be cured of addiction through gradual withdrawal; and (2) when the addict could not be withdrawn from the drug completely because of withdrawal symptoms that would require hospitalization, or because a normal life-style would otherwise be interrupted.

Addicted patients were required to visit their physician at least once a week and they were to be given dosages that would be sufficient until the next visit. A set of regulations was adopted that closely followed the Rolleston Report (1926). The British Medical Association was in basic agreement with the Rolleston Report. An editorial in the *British Medical Journal* stated:

> It is of interest to note that no steps are being taken to enforce notification of drug addiction and that no authoritative rules have been issued for guidance in the use of scheduled drugs. The British Medical Association raised strong objections to all these proposals. Its chief contention that drug addiction is a manifestation of a disease frequently associated with nervous instability and frequently requiring treatment and not merely a vice demanding punishments appears now to be definitely recognized. (Bean, 1974: 68)

The British medical community presented a relatively united stand in maintaining control over both defining the meaning of addiction and prescribing the proper course of treatment. Moreover, no prohibition movement or prohibition unit with police powers existed. Police were not eager to interfere in the physician-client relationship in this contentious area. In other spheres of "immoral" behavior, the British government also refused to support the prohibition and criminalization models that were adopted in the United States. In Britain, the 1928 *The Report of the Committee on Homosexual Offenses and Prostitution* defined the moral basis for regulating or prohibiting conduct under the law. Only when a behavior promoted corruption, exploitation, or indecency in public was the government justified in passing laws to prevent these behaviors. Otherwise, the committee concluded:

> Unless a deliberate attempt is to be made by society, acting through the agency of the law, to equate the sphere of crime with that of sin, there must remain a realm of private morality and immorality which is, in brief and crude terms, not the law's business. To say this is not to condone or encourage private immorality. (Wasserstrom, 1971: 26)

This report provided the statutory authority for the vice regulation paradigm that permits persons to legally engage in prostitution, homosexuality, and pornography if they do so discreetly and do not otherwise act indecently in public places. Such vice regulation has been very successful in keeping prostitutes off the streets and "skin magazines" off the newsstands. Yet persons who wish to have sex with a prostitute or purchase pornography can do so by finding the discreet advertisements of prostitutes in shop windows or entering a store that sells sexually explicit materials.

By the mid-1930s, the results of the Hague Convention were quite successful. The commercial morality had been dramatically reduced. Government-sponsored opium monopolies no longer cultivated opium, nor prepared it for smoking purposes, nor exported it to China for sale to opium smokers. Opiates and cocaine had been removed from all medicines that could be purchased without prescriptions. The patent medicine business was eliminated.

The public health morality toward opiates was dominant across the world. Manufacturers, exporters/importers, and wholesalers of opiates maintained careful records and limited production to meet medical needs. Pharmacists dispensed only the amounts of opiates as directed by physicians. Physicians, who could no longer profit from direct sales of opiates to patients, were careful about the amounts of opiates prescribed to patients. The general strategies recommended by the Hague Convention for restricting opiates to legitimate medical practices were followed in almost all countries around the world, although the detailed regulations and enforcement bureaucracies varied widely from country to country.

The nonmedical use and sale of opiates in the 1930s was a fraction of what it had been in 1900—and was to become in the 1970s-1980s.

In Britain, most of Western Europe, Canada, and Australia, the public health paradigm was closely followed and the prohibition-criminalization paradigm was not adopted. These societies had virtually no evidence of a black market or illegal sales of opium, heroin, or morphine prior to World War II.

Only in a few cities in the United States, especially New York City, did a substantial black market in heroin and morphine exist. Users and dealers of black market opiates were mainly involved in other criminal activities, and subjected to penal sanctions (Courtwright et al., 1989). In many small towns in the South, private physicians maintained a few morphine addicts who were otherwise solid citizens (O'Donnell, 1969).

Only in China were opium cultivation and opium smoking widespread, primarily because local warlords needed opium revenues to finance their private armies. The embattled Chinese government in Peking, however, no longer had to contend with foreign opium. Only when the Communists gained control and executed millions as "enemies of the people" (opium cultivators and sellers among them), was opium finally eradicated.

Moreover, the black market in heroin and opium declined even further during World War II as supply routes were disrupted. Scientists in Nazi Germany invented methadone, a synthetic opiate, as a painkiller to replace scarce supplies of morphine available to the Reich.

STRENGTHENING OF THE PROHIBITION-CRIMINALIZATION MORALITY IN POSTWAR UNITED STATES

The first black markets in drugs in the United States started after the passage of the Harrison Narcotic Act in 1914. At first brothels and red-light districts were the primary locations for these black markets. During Prohibition many speakeasies that sold alcohol also sold other illicit drugs. During the postwar period the black market in drugs shifted to the black inner-city ghettos of America's cities (Brecher, 1972).

In the 1950s organized crime began to import large quantities of heroin into the United States, especially into New York City, where it was marketed primarily to low-income youth, especially those from minority backgrounds (Brecher, 1972; Courtwright et al., 1989). In partial response, the United States adopted the Narcotic Control Act (1956), which increased the minimum sentence for all drug offenses, including possession of marijuana, to 2 to 10 years of prison. The year before, the Academy of Medicine in New York had come out in support of opiate maintenance clinics and stated that withdrawal from opiates should be voluntary on the part of the patient. In 1958 the AMA-ABA Committee's *Interim Report* called for more freedom for physicians to prescribe narcotics and it also discussed the possibility of outpatient maintenance clinics. It strongly stated that drug addiction should be treated as a disease, not a crime (King, 1972; Musto, 1973). But these reports did not gain political support and were subsequently ignored.

In 1970 the United States adopted the Comprehensive Drug Abuse Prevention and Control Act, which explicitly stated that federal law has final authority over all aspects of drug abuse prevention and treatment of drug addiction. Despite this legislation, from the late 1950s until the early 1970s, the United States experienced heroin epidemics in its major urban centers (Brecher, 1972; O'Donnell et al., 1975). Concomitant with this upsurge in heroin abuse, a new and greatly expanded emphasis on treatment emerged in the United States, which led to competing moralities and modalities of drug treatment.

In the late 1940s Maxwell Jones developed the concept and philosophy of therapeutic communities to treat drug addicts in Britain. This approach never gained acceptance in Britain, where few heroin addicts existed and the public health morality was firmly in control. In the United States, therapeutic communities started with Synanon in California in 1958, but New York City was the incubator for Phoenix House, Odyssey House, Daytop Village, and other therapeutic communities that have spread to other cities and countries, including England. Therapeutic communities promote a rehabilitation morality that stresses abstinence from illicit drug use. Public confession and participation in rituals and groups are all part of a TC (therapeutic community) treatment regimen. The basic approach is to break down the residents' defenses and justifications and have them see how their use of drugs was maladaptive. Then they are taught good habits and practices and are supported to grow into mature, well-adjusted persons with jobs and useful functions in society. The total rehabilitation morality advocated and practiced by therapeutic communities was also compatible with American forgiveness of "repentant and recovered sinners" after condemnation by the prohibition-criminalization morality.

Since the mid-1960s Americans have developed a unique public health approach, methadone maintenance, for opiate addicts. As recommended by Vincent Dole, heroin addicts should be provided with high doses of methadone (60-100 mg/day) to prevent them from getting high on heroin and to reduce craving for opiates (Dole et al., 1966; Dole and Joseph, 1978; Dole, 1980, 1981). This treatment regime has been greatly constrained by bureaucracies and publics committed to prohibition morality. Nevertheless, methadone maintenance has been the most effective treatment for heroin addiction, because the retention rate is high, abuse of heroin and other drugs is greatly reduced, and drug-related criminality substantially declines (Ball, 1987). This policy has existed simultaneously with the therapeutic community approach for completely rehabilitating addicts. Relative to the number of heroin and cocaine abusers at the end of the 1980s, a severe shortage of slots for any kind of treatment continues in the United States.

SHIFTS IN THE PUBLIC HEALTH MORALITY TOWARD OPIATES AND THE RISE OF THE BLACK MARKET IN HEROIN IN BRITAIN

Until the 1960s the few British addicts were mainly middle-aged professionals, including physicians and nurses (National Clearinghouse, 1973). There were only 68 known heroin addicts and 454 known abusers of all illicit drugs in Britain in 1959 (Johnson, 1975a). The first Brain Committee (1958) reaffirmed the right of British doctors to prescribe heroin, because no evidence showed an increase in the number of heroin users. The British Medical Association, along with the press, was instrumental in 1955 in defeating a U.S.-sponsored proposal to prohibit the manufacture of heroin in Britain.

The second Brain Committee (1964) found that a small number of doctors were overprescribing heroin to patients who were reselling it and creating new addicts. They recommended that maintenance doses of heroin and opiates be available only through government clinics. There were only 753 registered heroin addicts in Britain at this time, but there were stories of abuses by doctors who overprescribed (Judson, 1973; Bean, 1974). The committee's recommendations were implemented in the Dangerous Drugs Act of 1967, which provided for a central registry of all addicts. All doctors were required to report the name, address, dates of treatment, and drugs being prescribed to the Home Office. This law also called for the establishment of government drug treatment clinics and the licensing of doctors to prescribe heroin and other opiates.

The number of registered addicts grew to 1,729 in 1967 (Judson, 1973); 1,299 were heroin addicts. In 1968 there were 2,240 known heroin addicts, plus 542 people known to be addicted to other narcotics (Bean, 1971; Johnson, 1975c).

The Dangerous Drugs Regulations (1968) required doctors to be licensed by the Secretary of State to prescribe heroin and cocaine, and then only for the purpose of alleviating pain caused by injury or disease.

Thus, when a heroin user goes to a general practitioner for treatment: (1) the GP can refuse treatment, (2) the GP can refer the patient to a drug treatment center, (3) a methadone maintenance regimen can be prescribed with declining doses over six months, or (4) regular methadone maintenance can be prescribed. The last possibility is rare; patients normally have to go to drug dependency clinics for this service (Bakx, 1988).

The National Drug Service Drug Dependency Units, or drug clinics, provided a range of services to addicts. The prescription of opiates for addicts was restricted to these clinics, directed by trained consulting psychiatrists. In 1989, 35 drug treatment clinics operated in Great Britain, 15 in London, and 20 throughout the rest of the country. In smaller towns without clinics, one or two physicians may be licensed to prescribe for a few addicts.

British heroin addicts attending the government clinics need a prescription to get their drugs. New applicants are interviewed by social workers and a psychiatrist; their urine is tested to verify opiate use. The patient's prescription is mailed to his neighborhood pharmacist, where he receives the daily dose (Johnson, 1976b; Pearson, 1987).

The rationale for this shift in British policy in the 1960s seems to be a desire to control and contain (Johnson, 1977) the use of heroin, but doing so by staying within the medical and public health approaches to treating addiction and not resorting to a strict law enforcement approach.

The pervasive fear was that the British epidemic would lead to a situation where our cities might, before long, be faced with problems so sadly familiar to America—endemic and intractable illegal narcotic use particularly among young people, a drug sub-culture and a criminal black market. The debates and documents of the time amply chronicle the acute official and public anxiety in this regard, and the determination to avoid any move which by driving the addict into the hands of the criminal dealer would "invite in the Mafie." The nineteenth century had seen addiction treatment as person-directed: the Second Brain Committee report of 1965, the Dangerous Drug Act of 1967 and the system of Drug Treatment Centers which went into operation in 1968 may seemingly still have been about treating the individual, but they marked a shift in emphasis towards official belief in the social function of treatment as preventive strategy. What was to happen to the individual even became in some ways now of secondary importance. (Berridge and Edwards, 1981: 255)

The role of the medical establishment and the drug clinics, however, has been to prescribe drugs, administer methadone maintenance and detoxification programs, and offer individual counseling. Physicians and drug clinics do not emphasize the total rehabilitation of addict life-styles, as in therapeutic communities. The medical/public health approach has played a dominant position in the evolution of British drug policy. Doctors make the final decision concerning the care and treatment of their patients, including opiate addicts, an approach that has never been accepted in the United States.

At the drug clinics in the late 1960s, doctors and consulting psychiatrists made decisions to shift away from prescribing heroin as a maintenance drug. In the first shift, from about 1968 to 1975, heroin prescribing declined, but addicts were maintained on injectable methadone (Johnson, 1975a,c; 1976b). The local chemist would dispense needles, syringes, and small ampules of methadone. Withdrawal symptoms for methadone would occur about every 24 hours, rather than six to eight hours with heroin, so addicts could function better during the day. From about 1975 to the 1980s clinic directors shifted most patients from injectable to oral methadone maintenance. Since the early 1980s many clinics have shifted from oral methadone maintenance to detoxification (gradual withdrawal) over six months. These shifts in prescribing policy have been the result of discussion and cooperation by clinic directors, not dictated by government bureaucrats, as is frequently the case in the United States (Johnson, 1990; Pearson, 1990).

Many heroin addicts encounter difficulties when trying to get methadone prescriptions from local doctors. A 22-year-old man from Merseyside was refused a methadone prescription by his doctor. He was referred to a drug clinic to get it—the purpose of the policy (Pearson, 1987a). Many British heroin addicts today prefer to purchase heroin through illicit means because of this change in prescribing policy.

Americans continue to misunderstand the British public health approach for prescribing heroin and methadone. At the same time there is no willingness to adopt the British model with respect to prescribing heroin. Despite considerable British evidence that legally prescribed heroin and methadone have not done so, Americans claim that many new addicts would be created if the prescribing of heroin were allowed: "This speculation . . . we do believe . . . weighs heavily and tips the balance against heroin maintenance in this country at this time" (U.S. National Commission on Marijuana and Drug Abuse, 1972: 334).

Throughout the 1970s the number of known heroin addicts in Britain hovered around 2,000 (Bewley, 1977; National Clearinghouse, 1978).

The drug clinics switched almost exclusively to oral methadone and detoxification. As a partial result, a heroin black market developed in Britain in the early 1980s as unemployed British working class youth began smoking heroin ("chasing the dragon"—the Oriental form of heroin use and the twentieth-century version of opium smoking) with some injecting it (Pearson, 1987a,b, 1989, 1990; Parker, Bakx, Newcombe, 1988). Heroin consumption in the United Kingdom is estimated to have increased at an annual rate of about 10% for the period 1974 to 1981, and at an annual rate of 21% for the period 1982 to 1984 (Wagstaff and Maynard, 1989). One survey of 845 doctors in 1985 found that 44,000 new users of opiates went to see their doctors concerning their use of drugs (MacGregor and Ettore, 1987). By the mid-1980s the official number of registered heroin addicts in Britain was 12,000. The actual number of heroin users is probably between 50,000 and 80,000 (Pearson, 1987a).

The British have also passed laws that criminalize the illegal sale and possession of heroin and marijuana. As the number of user-dealers of black market heroin has increased, more people are being arrested, convicted, and incarcerated for drug crimes. If a person arrested for heroin or methadone possession or sale can prove that his supplies came from a drug clinic or physician, charges are dropped. But most arrestees for drug crimes have illegal supplies and are now subjected to criminal penalties. Increasingly, many, if not most, offenders serving prison sentences are drug users.

In the 1980s Britain, and other Western European countries, have dual moralities and policies toward opiates. While heroin users can approach drug clinics and request heroin or methadone maintenance, physicians usually provide detoxification. Black marketeers and user-dealers now supply most heroin users. Such user-dealers are subject to criminal penalties and form a growing proportion of the criminals in Britain.

Between 1979 and 1984 the interception of illicit drugs by Customs officials in the United Kingdom tripled, seizures by the police went up by a factor of 10, and the number of drug offenders incarcerated went up fourfold. During the same period of time, however, prices have decreased by 20% and consumption of heroin increased by 350% (Pettyman, 1989).

Recently, British and Dutch researchers and policymakers have begun to promote the public health paradigm under a new slogan, "harm reduction." Harm reduction in the drug field entails these components: (1) information on safer ways to take drugs for those who will continue to take drugs no matter what, (2) alternative nondrug

methods of altering consciousness, (3) how to recognize and respond to drug-related problems (e.g., overdosing), and (4) availability
of injecting equipment and drug treatment with minimal restrictions
(Newcombe, 1987; Parker, Bakx and Newcombe, 1988). This approach
clearly avoids systematically confronting addicts to avoid drugs or
attempting to reform their lifestyles.

Despite the activities of public health authorities, moral condemnation of heroin use and users by the press and public (frequently using
American "war-on-drugs" propaganda) is on the rise. This generates
controversy about the appropriate approaches, for example in a suburb
of Liverpool:

> Wirral's diffidence to harm reduction was not a peculiar local reaction, but
> rather a typical instance of the built-in resistance among many sections of
> society to any "soft" policies which are not geared directly to "stamping
> out drug abuse." This ideological opposition to harm reduction centres
> around particular social institutions, and is based on several deeply held
> and interrelated moral beliefs, including the beliefs that using any prohib-
> ited drug is inherently irresponsible, dangerous and/or sinful; that alcohol,
> tobacco and caffeine are justifiable exceptions because they are relatively
> harmless compared with the prohibited drugs; that heroin is the "hardest
> drug," and inexorably leads to addiction, disorder and death; that drug laws
> prevent drug problems rather than exacerbate them; and, fundamentally,
> that a harm-reduction approach condones drug use, and would, if im-
> plemented, lead to a "Brave New World" society where drugs control
> citizens rather than liberate them. (Parker, Bakx, and Newcombe, 1988:
> 130)

In 1988 two coordinators of drug abuse service programs in Liverpool toured six American cities and were amazed by the virulence of
the American war on drugs:

> We received one early hint of the gulf between the two countries. In
> Washington, drug educators of the "Just Say No" school accused us of
> being "nonbelievers" who would eventually be "converted." While they
> seemed as certain as evangelicals that just saying "no" is the miracle cure,
> to us the very concept of a drug-free society is mildly amusing, if not
> incredible. American drug laws have been in existence since the 1920s,
> and the problem has simply worsened. (Parry and O'Hare, 1988: 10)

The British clinic system, however, does not reach everybody who
might benefit from opiate maintenance; and it is not clear whether

this is the choice of the addict population or the shift in clinic prescribing policy, or both (Stimson, 1988).

> One of the hopes pinned to the British "clinic system" in the late 1960s was that a user who could obtain his or her nostrum from licit sources would not need to enter the illegal market. It became clear however that some users would sell part of their clinic supplies—perhaps because they had been prescribed too much, or because they preferred to obtain some other drugs available in the market, or because they wished to raise income for other purposes, or because such sale and the social contacts around the small-scale illicit market were valued parts of their preferred life-styles. The clinics today have few patients on long-term maintenance, and generally restrict new patients to a short course of decreasing dosage, or offer social casework without drugs. Whether or not "throwing heroin at the problem" would help to reduce today's users' involvements with the irregular economy is a matter of contention in Britain today. (Dorn and South, 1987: 163)

The public health paradigm has assumed even more importance in Britain with the advent of AIDS. Needle exchange programs have been developed in several major British cities in an attempt to prevent the spread of AIDS through contaminated needles, a policy that appears quite successful (Stimson, 1989; Johnson, 1990).

CONCLUSION

This socio-historical review of drug policies in Britain and the United States has shown that both countries in the nineteenth century were dominated by a commercial morality toward opiates. Strong dissatisfaction with opium cultivation, opium smoking in China and the United States, and patent medicines led to international opium conventions, which institutionalized the public health morality regarding legitimate medical uses. Starting with the Harrison Narcotic Act of 1914, the United States rapidly shifted toward a prohibitionist-criminalization paradigm toward opiate and heroin users and prevented opiate maintenance until methadone became available in the 1960s. In the 1920s, Britain rejected the criminalization approach and defined a public health morality, which worked effectively until the 1960s. This approach has remained the core of British policy to the present time. The 1980s, however, have seen the growth of a black market in heroin, a shift away from long-term maintenance of opiate addicts in Britain, and the criminalization of many heroin user-dealers.

While British policy toward opiate addicts allows them to legally obtain opiates from government clinics or their general practitioners, physicians have chosen to greatly restrict opiate maintenance. In the United States the highly moralistic prohibitionist, law enforcement approach to narcotic drugs has become increasingly stronger during three-quarters of a century. This will clearly continue into the 1990s. The National Drug Policy (1989) for fiscal year 1990 allocates a total of $8.8 billion in new spending, of which $1 billion will be spent on the construction of new federal prisons and only $120 million will be spent on drug education.

A new challenge for Britain will come with the removal of trade barriers for the Common Market nations in 1992. Much discussion is occurring among the member nations to develop some uniformity of drug laws and enforcement practices. This could lead to a more liberal atmosphere of tolerance of drug users, as seen in the Netherlands. But Common Market policies toward heroin could be more stringent and punitive, as in Sweden and West Germany.

Frequently overlooked in the heat of the debate in the 1980s about policies to control illicit heroin and cocaine users is the great success of the International Opium Conventions at the beginning of the twentieth century. These conferences and subsequent legislation and public health regulations have institutionalized practices that have dramatically improved health and life expectancy since 1900.

As a major consequence, the general roles of various specialities have clearly defined responsibilities. Scientific researchers, frequently working for commercial laboratories or universities, have invented thousands of drugs that cure specific illnesses, alleviate much physical and mental pain, and must be proven safe and effective before reaching the commercial marketplace. Physicians are authorized to determine, and prescribe (but not dispense or sell), those drugs that can cure or reduce specific illnesses for individual patients. Pharmacists dispense billions of pills that are safely consumed by millions of users for hundreds of illnesses.

The debate about legalization of illicit drugs (especially marijuana, heroin, and cocaine) has reemerged among academics (but not politicians) in the 1980s and among European public health authorities.

"Invisible Clothing" Revisited

The "invisible clothing" of the average British and American citizen of 1890 took for granted that the commercial morality for opiates was appropriate, although heated political debates about morality toward alcohol was raging in that era. They would be astonished to learn that opiate users in 1990 are not only routinely denied very small quantities (by 1890 measures), but routinely arrested and incarcerated for several years for possession or sale of small quantities of these drugs.

In 1990 government agencies, the press, and most people routinely reinforce the beliefs that most Americans take for granted: heroin and crack/cocaine are among the worst evils and greatest vices in the society. Persons who use these drugs become fiends who rob and steal; and society must get tough (and imprison) those who will not volunteer for rehabilitation. Indeed, average Americans in 1990 are so comfortable with prohibition-criminalization that they are surprised and unsettled to discover that not only were such drugs legal and cheap in the past, but also that very different moral standards may exist in other countries. British drug treatment personnel, operating safely within the protective public health morality of the Rolleston Committee (1926), are aware of the power of moral crusades and prohibitionist sentiment in America and its impact on British citizens. They do not want to reproduce America's drug problem.

What will be the moral standards of British and American citizens toward opiates in the future? Prognostications are not possible, but the five paradigms of morality toward opiates suggest possibilities that are not being seriously considered. Perhaps future scientists will invent drugs that are not addictive and do not have other harmful properties and which will be defined as morally correct to consume and sell, so drug users will switch away from heroin and cocaine voluntarily. Perhaps the prohibitionist-criminalization approach will succeed in stopping the growth of opiates and cocaine or their illegal import so addicts cannot get their drugs. But these optimistic scenarios appear improbable in 1990.

It is more likely that the prohibitionist-criminalization sentiment will spread, at least in the near term, thus labeling hundreds of thousands more people as criminals.

Perhaps the current, mainly academic, debate about drug legalization will achieve results as impressive as the British anti-opium movement of the 1890s (Johnson, 1975b) and bring about a willingness to discard prohibitions and criminal penalties against opiate users and sellers, as happened with alcohol in 1935 (Nadelmann, 1989). If this willingness emerges, the precise nature of any legalization will necessitate major changes in international agreements.

Each paradigm of morality offers different possibilities for legal drugs. The commercial paradigm suggests that opiates could be made available at considerably below black market costs to stop the illegal trade; subsequently, taxes could be raised to restrict use. Models borrowed from the nineteenth century and other societies could provide plausible scenarios.

The vice regulation paradigm suggests that opiates and cocaine could be provided commercially to addicts and abusers, but that the sellers would be required to maintain controls over abusers and keep them out of view and concern by straight citizens. Variations of the Dutch willingness to let users purchase and consume marijuana in coffee shops, but repress street sales and consumption in public places, appears possible.

The public health morality suggests that drug dispensing clinics and pharmacies could provide drugs legally to heroin and cocaine abusers, but attempt to constrain and lower dosages, potencies, and frequency of consumption by committed abusers. They could provide other services (counseling, rehabilitation referral, needles, etc.) in continuing efforts to contain the problem and normalize (rather than stigmatize) the user life-style, as part of a harm reduction policy. They could also engage in sustained research to develop safe drug substitutes, rehabilitation therapies, and other ways to both improve the public health and undermine the financial structures of the current black market.

The rehabilitation paradigm suggests that future improvements could be made in creating more programs and placements for drug abusers to enter treatment and attempt to normalize their lives.

In 1990 none of the above scenarios, other than an extension of the prohibitionist-criminalization morality (and many more prisoners), appears even remotely possible in the highly moralized political atmosphere of America. Changes in drug policies are most likely to emerge in Europe, where the public health and vice regulation moralities have been institutionalized for decades. Regardless of the political fate of any particular proposals for changing policies toward opiates and cocaine, policymakers and citizens must become aware of how their personal moral standards affect political life and policy choices toward heroin and cocaine abusers.

REFERENCES

Advisory Council on the Misuse of Drugs. (1988). *AIDS and drugs misuse, part I*. London: Her Majesty's Stationery Office.

AMA-ABA Committee. (1961). *Drug addiction: Crime or disease?* Bloomington: Indiana University Press.

American Medical Association. (1963). *Narcotics addiction: Official actions of the A.M.A.*

Bakx, K. (1988). The heroin users: A suitable case for treatment. *Mersey Drugs Journal, 2* (2), pp. 9-11.

Ball, J. C., Corty, E., Bond, H., Tommasello, A., & Myers, C. P. (1987). The reduction of intravenous heroin use, non-opiate abuse and crime during Methadone maintenance treatment. *Problems of Drug Dependence.*

Ball, J. C., & Tommasello, A. Treatment and demographic characteristics associated with dose satisfaction among Methadone maintenance patients.

Bean, P. (1971). Social aspects of drug abuse: A study of London drug offenders. *The Journal of Criminal Law, Criminology and Police Science, 62* (1), pp. 80-86.

Bean, P. (1974). *The social control of drugs.* New York: John Wiley.

Becker, H. (1963). *Outsiders.* New York: The Free Press.

Bennett, T. (1988, Winter). The British experience with heroin regulation. *Law and Contemporary Problems, 50* (1), p. 299-314.

Berridge, V. (1978). Professionalization and narcotics: The medical and pharmaceutical professions and British narcotic use 1868-1976. *Psychological Medicine, 8,* pp. 361-372.

Berridge, V. (1980, Winter). The making of the Rolleston Report, 1908-1926. *Journal of Drug Issues, 10* (1), pp. 7-28.

Berridge, V., & Edwards, G. (1981). *Opium and the people: Opiate use in nineteenth-century England.* London: Allen Lane.

Bewley, T. H. (1977). Drug abuse in the United Kingdom. *Addictive Diseases: An International Journal, 3* (1), pp. 27-32.

Blumberg, H., et al. (1975, June 16). Opiate use in London. *Journal of the American Medical Association, 232* (11), pp. 1131-1132.

Brecher, E. (1972). *Licit and illicit drugs.* Mount Vernon, NY: Consumer Reports.

Brunn, K., Pan, L., & Rexed, I. (1975). *The gentlemen's club: International control of drugs and alcohol.* Chicago: University of Chicago Press.

Busch, C., & Edwards, G. (Eds.). (1981). *Drug problems in Britain.* London: Academic Press.

Carr, J., & Dalton, S. (1988). Syringe exchange: The Liverpool experience. *Druglink, 3* (3), pp. 12-14.

Chadwick, C., & Parker, H. (1988). Wirral's enduring heroin problem. *Mersey Drugs Journal, 2* (2), p. 8.

Courtwright, D. (1982). *Dark paradise.* Cambridge, MA: Harvard University Press.

Courtwright, D., Joseph, H., & DesJarlais, D. (1989). *Addicts who survived.* University of Tennessee Press.

DeMott, B. (1962). The great narcotics muddle. *Harper's, 224,* pp. 46-54.

Dole, V. P. (1980, December) Addictive behavior. *Scientific American, 243* (6), pp. 138-154.

Dole, V. P., et al. (1966). Narcotic blockade. *Archives of Internal Medicine, 118,* pp. 304-309.

Dole, V. P., & Joseph, H. (1978). Long-term outcome of patients treated with Methadone maintenance. *Annals of the New York Academy of Science, 331,* pp. 181-189.

Dole, V. P., et al. (1981). *Costs and benefits of treating chronic users of heroin with Methadone maintenance.* Internal report of the New York State Division of Substance Abuse Services, Bureau of Research.

Donoghoe, M., Dorn, N., James, C., Jones, S., Ribbens, J., & South, N. (1987). How families and communities respond to heroin. In N. Dorn & N. South (Eds.). *A land fit for heroin?* (pp. 95-124). London: Macmillan Education.

Dorn, N., & South, N. (Eds.). (1987). *A land fit for heroin?* London: Macmillan Education.

Duster, Troy. (1970). *The legislation of morality.* New York: The Free Press.

Edwards, G. (1989). What drives British drug policies? *British Journal of Addiction, 84,* pp. 291-226.

Fazey, C. *The evaluation of Liverpool drug dependency clinic: The first two years, 1985 to 1987.* A report to Mersey Regional Health Authority.

Feinberg, J., & Gross, H. (Eds.). (1975). *Philosophy of law.* Encino, CA: Dickenson.

General medical council-pharmacy. (1868). *Medical Times and Gazette, 2,* pp. 51-52.

Gusfield, J. (1963). *Symbolic crusade: State politics and the American temperance movement.* Urbana, IL: University of Illinois Press.

Home Office. (1984a). *Prevention.* London: Her Majesty's Stationery Office.

Home Office. (1984b). *Statistics of the misuse of drugs, United Kingdom, 1983.* (Home Office Statistical Bulletin, 18/84). London: Home Office.

Home Office. (1987). *Statistics of the misuse of drugs, United Kingdom, 1986.* (Home Office Statistical Bulletin, 28/87). London: Home Office.

ISDD Research and Development Unit. (1987). Heroin today: Commodity, consumption, control and care. In N. Dorn & N. South (Eds.). *A land fit for heroin?* (chap. 6, pp. 11-34). London: Macmillan Education.

Johnson, B. D. (1974, July). Similarities and differences between New York City Methadone maintenance centres and London drug maintenance centres. *Proceedings of the Fifth International Institute on the Prevention and Treatment of Drug Dependence,* Copenhagen, Denmark.

Johnson, B. D. (1975a). Understanding British addiction statistics. *Bulletin on Narcotics, XXVII* (1), pp. 49-66.

Johnson, B. D. (1975b, Fall). Righteousness before revenue: The forgotten moral crusade against the Indo-Chinese opium trade. *Journal of Drug Issues,* pp. 304-326.

Johnson, B. D. (1975c). Interpreting official British statistics on addiction. *The International Journal of the Addictions, 10* (4), pp. 557-587.

Johnson, B. D. (1976a, August 29). *Social movements in the origin of a social problem: The moral passage of commercial opium trading in the nineteenth century.* Paper presented to the Society for the Study of Social Problems, New York City.

Johnson, B. D. (1976b). The social functioning of opiate maintenance clinics in London and New York City. *The British Journal of Addiction, 71,* pp. 175-182.

Johnson, B. D. (1977). How much heroin maintenance (containment) in Britain? *The International Journal of the Addictions, 12* (2 & 3), pp. 361-398.

Johnson, B. D., Williams, T., Dei, K., & Sanabria, H. (1990). Drug abuse and the inner city: Impact on hard drug users and the community. In J. Q. Wilson & M. Tonry (Eds.). *Crime and justice series: Vol. 13. Drugs and crime.* Chicago: University of Chicago Press.

Judson, H. F. (1973). *Heroin addiction in Britain.* New York: Harcourt Brace Jovanovich.

Kagan, D. (1989, November 20). How America lost its first drug war. *Insight, 5* (47), pp. 8-17.

King, R. (1972). *The drug hang-up.* Springfield, IL: Charles C Thomas.

Lindesmith, A. R. (1965). *The addict and the law.* Bloomington: Indiana University Press.

MacGregor, S., & Ettore, B. (1987). From treatment to rehabilitation—aspects of the evolution of British policy on the care of drug-takers. In N. Dorn & N. South (Eds.). *A land fit for heroin?* (chap. 5, pp. 125-145). London: Macmillan Education.

Mahon, T. A. (1971, December). The British system, past and present. *The International Journal of the Addictions, 6* (4), pp. 627-634.

Mauss, A. L. (1975). *Social problems as social movements*. Philadelphia: J. B. Lippincott Company.

May, E. (1971, July). Drugs without crime. *Harper's, 243* (1454), pp. 60-65.

McDermott, P. (1988, June). *A survey of drug injectors in the Chester District*. The Mersey AIDS Prevention Unit.

Media drug campaigns may be worse than a waste of money. (1985). *British Medical Journal, 290*, p. 416.

Musto, D. F. (1973). *The American disease*. New York: Oxford University Press.

Nadelmann, E. A. (1988, Spring). U.S. drug policy: A bad report. *Foreign Policy, 70*, pp. 83-108.

Nadelmann, E. A. (1988, Summer). The case for legalization. *The Public Interest, 92*, pp. 3-31.

Nadelmann, E. A. (1989, September 1). Drug prohibition in the United States: Costs, consequences, and alternatives. *Science, 245*, pp. 939-947.

National Clearinghouse for Drug Abuse Information. (1973, April). *The British narcotics system*. U.S. Department of Health, Education and Welfare, Series 13, No. 1.

National Clearinghouse for Drug Abuse Information. (1978, April). *The British narcotics system*. U.S. Department of Health, Education and Welfare, Series 13, No. 2.

Newcombe, R. (1987). High times for harm reduction. *Druglink, 2*, pp. 10-11.

Newcombe, R. (1988a, March/April). Drugs and AIDS: Radical proposals shelved. *Mersey Drugs Journal, 1* (6), pp. 10-13.

Newcombe, R. (1988b, March/April). The Liverpool syringe exchange scheme for drug injectors: Initial evidence of effectiveness in HIV prevention. *Mersey Drugs Journal, 1* (6), pp. 4-5.

Newcombe, R., & O'Hare, P. (1988a, May). *A survey of drug use among young people in South Sefton in 1987*. South Sefton (Merseyside) District Health Authority.

Newcombe, R., & O'Hare, P. (1988b, July/August). A survey of drug use among young people in South Sefton in 1987. *Mersey Drugs Journal, 2* (2), pp. 6-7.

Newcombe, R., & Parry, A. (1988, October 22). *The Mersey harm-reduction model: A strategy for dealing with drug users*. Presented at the International Conference on Drug Policy Reform, Bethesda, Maryland.

O'Donnell, J. A. (1969). *Narcotic addicts in Kentucky*. Washington, DC: Government Printing Office.

O'Hare, P., et al. (1988, October 22). *Drug education: A basis for reform*. Presented at the International Conference on Drug Policy Reform, Bethesda, Maryland.

Owen, D. (1934). *British opium policy in China and India*. New Haven, CT: Yale University Press.

Parker, H., Bakx, K., & Newcombe, R. (1988). *Living with heroin: The impact of a drugs "epidemic" on an English community*. Milton Keynes, England: Open University Press.

Parry, A., & O'Hare, P. (1988, May/June). This means war! *Mersey Drugs Journal, 2* (1), p. 10.

Pearson, G. (1987a). Social deprivation, unemployment and patterns of heroin use. In N. Dorn & N. South (Eds.). *A land fit for heroin?* (chap. 3, pp. 62-94). London: Macmillan Education.

Pearson, G. (1987b) *The new heroin users*. Oxford: Basil Blackwell.

Pearson, G. (1989, September 15). The street connection. *New Statesman and Society*, pp. 10-11.

Pearson, G. (1990). Drug problems and policies in Britain. In J. Q. Wilson & M. Tonry (Eds.). *Crime and justice series: Vol. 13. Drugs and crime.* Chicago: University of Chicago Press.

Pettyman, S. (1989). Commentary: The failure of enforcement (pp. 469-470). In A. Wagstaff & A. Maynard (1989). Economic aspects of the illicit drug market and drug enforcement policies in the United Kingdom: Summary of the report. *British Journal of Addiction, 84,* pp. 461-475.

Plant, M. (1988, March/April). Drug policy? No thanks, we're British. *Mersey Drugs Journal, 1* (6), pp. 8-9.

Platt, J. J. (1986). *Heroin addiction: Theory, research and treatment.* Vol. 1 (2nd ed.). Malabar, FL: Robert E. Kriege.

Report of the Pharmacy Bill Committee to the General Medical Council. (1868). *British Medical Journal, 2,* p. 39.

Rumbarger, J. J. (1989). *Profits, power, and Prohibition.* Albany, NY: State University of New York Press.

Schur, E. M. (1960, September). Drug addiction in America and England. *Commentary,* pp. 241-248.

Schur, E. M. (1962). *Narcotic addiction in Britain and America.* Bloomington: Indiana University Press.

Spector, M., & Kitsuse, J. I. (1977). *Constructing social problems.* Menlo Park, CA: Cummings.

Stimson, G. (1987). The war on heroin: British policy and the international trade in illicit drugs. In N. Dorn & N. South (Eds.). *A land fit for heroin?* (chap. 2, pp. 35-61). London: Macmillan Education.

Stimson, G., et al. (1988, November). *Injecting equipment exchange schemes final report.* London: Monitoring Research Group, University of London, Goldsmiths' College.

Taylor, A. H. (1969). *American diplomacy and the narcotics traffic, 1900-1939.* Durham, NC: Duke University Press.

U.S. National Commission on Marijuana and Drug Abuse. (1972). *Drug use in America.*

U.S. Senate Judiciary Committee, Subcommittee on Improvements in the Federal Criminal Code. (1955). *Illicit narcotics traffic.* (Hearings, parts 1-10, June 2 through November 25). Washington, DC: Government Printing Office.

Wagstaff, A., & Maynard, A. (1988). *Economic aspects of the illicit drug market and drug enforcement policies in the United Kingdom.* A Home Office Research and Planning Unit Report. London: Her Majesty's Stationery Office.

Wagstaff, A., & Maynard, A. (1989). Economic aspects of the illicit drug market and drug enforcement policies in the United Kingdom: Summary of the report. *British Journal of Addiction, 84,* pp. 461-475.

Waley, A. (1958). *The opium war through Chinese eyes.* London: Allen and Unwin.

Walker, W. O., III. (1981). *Drug control in the Americas.* Albuquerque: University of New Mexico Press.

Wasserstrom, R. A. (Ed.). (1971). *Morality and the law.* Belmont, CA: Wadsworth Publishing Company.

Weber, M. (1947). *The theory of social and economic organization.* New York: Oxford University Press.

Willis, J. (1971). Delinquency and drug dependence in the United Kingdom and the United States. *British Journal of Addiction, 66,* pp. 235-248.

Name Index

Subject Index

About the Contributors

Karst J. Besteman, Ph.D., is a former Deputy Director of the National Institute on Drug Abuse and Assistant Surgeon General, PHS (Ret.). He participated in the implementation of federal drug abuse prevention, treatment, and research programs from 1957 through 1980. Currently, he serves as the Executive Director of the Alcohol and Drug Problems Association, an advocacy organization interested in the development of effective public policy that contributes to solutions of the problems of alcohol and drug abuse.

Rick Doblin coordinates the efforts of psychologists and psychiatrists interested in developing MDMA into a legal medicine. He graduated in 1990 from the Kennedy School of Government at Harvard with a master's degree in Public Policy; founded a nonprofit research and educational organization, Multidisciplinary Association of Psychedelic Studies (MAPS) in 1986, which has opened a Drug Master File for MDMA at the Food and Drug Administration; and co-founded Earth Metabolic Design (EMD) in 1984, the organization that coordinated the defense of MDMA in the DEA administrative hearings.

James A. Inciardi, Ph.D., is Professor and Director of the Division of Criminal Justice at the University of Delaware. He received his doctorate in sociology at New York University, and has extensive research, field, teaching, and clinical experience in the areas of drug abuse, criminal justice, and criminology. He has been director of the National Center for the Study of Acute Drug Reactions at the University of Miami School of Medicine, Vice-President of the Washington, DC-based Resource Planning Corporation, and associate director of research for both the New York State Narcotic Addiction Control Commission and the Metropolitan Dade County (Florida) Comprehensive Drug Program. Inciardi has done extensive consulting work both nationally and internationally, and has published more than 100 articles, chapters, and books in the areas of substance abuse, history, folklore, criminology, criminal justice, medicine, law, public policy, and AIDS. He is also a member of the South Florida AIDS Research Consortium.

Bruce D. Johnson, Ph.D., is a Principal Investigator at Narcotic and Drug Research, Inc. He received his doctorate from Columbia University in 1971. Johnson's career in drug abuse research spans two decades. He initiated and completed several major multiyear federal grants, among them the Economic Behavior of Opiate Users (NIDA), and Interdisciplinary Research Center for Study of Drugs and Alcohol to Crime (NIJ). He has published numerous articles in the drugs/crime area; the most recent of his four books is *Kids, Drugs, and Crime* (1988). He directs the nation's largest pre- and postdoctoral program in any field (Behavioral Sciences Training in Drug Abuse Research-NIDA). He currently directs other major grants: "Natural History of Crack Distribution" (a study of crack distributors and their careers), "Changing Patterns of Drug Abuse and Criminality Among Crack Cocaine Abusers," and "Careers in Crack, Drug Use, Drug Distribution, and Nondrug Criminality" (quantitative studies of the careers of crack and noncrack drug abusers).

Steven Jonas, M.D., is Professor of Community and Preventive Medicine, School of Medicine, State University of New York at Stony Brook. Born and educated in New York City, he received his M.D. from Harvard Medical School in 1962, and his M.P.H. from the Yale School of Medicine in 1967. He is a Fellow of the American College of Preventive Medicine, the American Public Health Association, and the New York Academy of Medicine. He has authored three books, co-authored five others, and published more than 100 articles and book reviews in professional journals and books, and has delivered more than 50 papers at conferences and seminars.

Richard B. Karel is a Washington-area journalist who has written and lectured on drug policy. In August 1988 he participated in a drug policy workshop under the auspices of Mayor Kurt Schmoke of Baltimore, Maryland. He was subsequently asked to testify before the U.S. House Select Committee on Narcotics Abuse and Control in September 1988 during a nationally televised series of hearings on drug legalization. He has spoken on local and national radio programs on the topic of drug legalization and alternative drug policy.

Duane C. McBride, Ph.D., is Professor in the Department of Behavioral Sciences and School of Business at Andrews University in Berrien Springs, Michigan; Chairman of his university's Institute of Alcoholism and Drug Dependency Research Center; and a member of the South Florida AIDS Research Consortium. He received his doctorate in sociology from the University of Kentucky, and has published widely in the areas of criminology, criminal justice, substance abuse, and AIDS.

Douglas McVay is a researcher, writer, and public relations consultant living in Washington, D.C. He was the projects coordinator for the National Organization for the Reform of Marijuana Laws from 1987 until 1989. Prior to that, he worked on the campaign staff for the Oregon Marijuana Initiative/Ballot Measure '5' campaign from 1985 through the general election in November 1986. He attended the University of Iowa, where he studied political science.

Ethan A. Nadelmann, Ph.D., is Assistant Professor of Politics and Public Affairs, Woodrow Wilson School of Public and International Affairs, Princeton University. He earned his J.D. at Harvard Law School in 1984, and his doctorate in political science at Harvard University in 1987. Nadelmann has published extensively on American drug policy, with recent articles in *Science, Foreign Policy,* and *The Public Interest.*

Marsha Rosenbaum, Ph.D., is the Director of the Center for Drug Studies and Principal Investigator at the Institute for Scientific Analysis in San Francisco. She is the recipient of numerous grants from the National Institute on Drug Abuse and has completed studies of heroin, methadone maintenance, MDMA (ecstasy) and drug abuse treatment policy. She is currently involved in drug policy and is working on studies of women and cocaine as well as methadone maintenance and AIDS. Rosenbaum is the author of *Women on Heroin, Just Say What?: An Alternative View on Solving America's Drug Problem,* and numerous scholarly articles about drug use and abuse, treatment, and policy.

John Jay Rouse, Ph.D., received his doctorate in criminal justice from City University of New York in 1988. His interests focus on citizen crime patrols and the social history of corrections and drug use. While a postdoctoral fellow at NDRI, he read widely in drug policy and the British approach to opiate drugs. He currently works as a Research Associate for the New York City Department of Probation. His publications appear in criminal justice and drug journals.

Steven Wisotsky has been a member of the Nova Law Center faculty since 1975, and has taught and published extensively on drug law enforcement issues. Wisotsky's major work, *Breaking the Impasse in the War on Drugs,* was published in 1986. Drawing upon his experiences as an appellate practitioner in federal and state courts, he documented the attack on civil liberties—both of the accused and of the citizenry in general— in "Crackdown: The Emerging 'Drug Exception' to the Bill of Rights," *38 Hastings L. J. 889* (1987). Other critiques of government drug law and policy appear in "The Ideology of Drug Testing," *11 Nova L. J. 763* (1987); a symposium issue of the Nova Law Journal "The War on Drugs: In Search of a Breakthrough," *11 Nova L. J. #3;* and a presentation in June 1989 at the ACLU biennial conference in Madison, Wisconsin. In 1990 *Beyond the War on Drugs* was published. The book contains his latest assessment of the social, political, and economic harms wrought around the world by the U.S. war on drugs.

NOTES

NOTES